Facilities Planning Handbook

W9-AGB-329

Facilities Planning Handbook

Third Edition

■

Edited by

Lee Ingalls
Barbara V. Bruxvoort
Jason Mihos

Facilities Planning Handbook
Third Edition

Published by Facilities Planning News
A Division of Tradeline, Inc.
ISSN 1049-2925
ISBN 09627204-2-9

Copyright © 1995 by Tradeline, Inc.
All rights reserved.

No part of this publication may be reproduced, stored in any
information storage or retrieval system or transmitted in any form or
by any means, electronic or mechanical, photocopying, recording or
otherwise, without the prior written permission of Tradeline, Inc.
Printed in the United States of America.

Tradeline, Inc.
115 Orinda Way
Orinda, CA 94563

Cover design by Camille Sobalvarro

FOREWORD

This third edition of The *Facilities Planning Handbook* represents a radical expansion of the first two editions, published in 1988 and 1990. In this edition you will find planning ideas covering everything from office space, research labs and training facilities, to facilities management, interstitial space, flexibility features and project management.

All "Facilities Planning Concepts" pages have been completely revised. "100 Recent Project Profiles" features 100 all-new project summaries of significant facilities projects showing square footages, building efficiencies, designers, consultants and project costs. In addition, "Key Terms and Issues," our glossary of facility planning terminology now contains over 800 words.

This edition also contains two valuable new reference sections: "101 Representative Floor Plans: What Works and Why" and "Facilities Organization and Management Profiles."

It has been said that there are only three kinds of mistakes you can make in facilities projects: 1) failing to learn from others' mistakes, 2) failing to learn about the good ideas others have discovered and 3) failing to implement what you know on time and on budget.

It is my hope, as it is the hope of the all contributors listed on the following pages, that this extensive and useful body of information will help you build better projects and save you from reinventing the wheel.

Steven L. Westfall
President
Tradeline, Inc.

CONTRIBUTORS

3M Austin Center
ACENTECH, Inc.
Affiliated Engineers, Inc.
Amdahl Corporation
A.M. Kinney Associates, Architects, Engineers
Anderson De Bartolo Pan, Inc.
Anshen + Allen
The Austin Company
Ayers/Saint/Gross Architects and Planners
Ballinger
Baltimore Gas & Electric Company
Baxter Hodell Donnelly Preston, Inc.
Bechtel Corporation
The Blurock Partnership
Bottom Duvivier
Briggs Associates
CANNON
Charles Schwab & Co., Inc.
The Christner Partnership, Inc.
Compaq Computer Corporation
Cooper, Carry and Associates, Architects
CRSS Architects
CUH2A
Dewberry & Davis
DPR Construction Inc.
Ellenzweig Associates, Inc.
Ellerbe Becket
Engberg Anderson
Ewing Cole Cherry Brott
F & S Partners Incorporated
Flad & Associates
Freeman-White Architects, Inc.
Steve Frei, Affiliated Engineers, Inc.
Geddes Brecher Qualls Cunningham
GEZ Architects/Engineers
Gilbane Building Company
Goody, Clancy & Associates
Gordon H Chong + Associates Architects/Engineers
Gresham, Smith and Partners

H2L2 Architects/Planners
Haines Lundberg Waehler (HLW)
Hammel Green & Abrahamson, Inc.
Hansen Lind Meyer Inc.
Harley Ellington Pierce Yee Associates, Inc.
Hayes Large Architects
Hellmuth, Obata and Kassabaum
The Henderson Design Group, Inc.
Henningson, Durham & Richardson, Inc.
Hewlett-Packard Company
The Hillier Group
Hixson Architecture/Engineering/Interiors
Holabird & Root
Holmes & Narver
Hoover Berg Desmond
Hoskins, Scott & Partners, Inc.
Hospital Designers, Inc.
JBA Architects, P.C.
Kaplan/McLaughlin/Diaz Architects
Kell Muñoz Wigodsky
The Kling-Lindquist Partnership, Inc.
Kornberg Associates
Lawrence Livermore National Laboratories
Lehrer McGovern Bovis
Lemay & Associates
Leslie Saul & Associates, Inc.
Lockwood Greene Engineers
Loebl, Schlossman and Hackl
Lord, Aeck & Sargent, Inc.
LPA Inc.
MBT Associates
McCarthy Bros. Co.
McGraw/Baldwin Architects
McLellan & Copenhagen
Mitchell/Giurgola Architects
MPB Architects
The National Institutes of Health
NBBJ
The Neenan Company
Payette Associates, Inc.
The Ratcliff Architects
Research Facilities Design
RTKL Associates
Satulah Group
Shepley Bulfinch Richardson and Abbott
Skidmore Owings Merrill

Smith, Hinchman & Grylls
SRG Partnership, P.C.
The Stichler Design Group
Stone Marraccini Patterson
Sundt Corp.
SWBR Architects, P.C.
Symmes Maini & McKee Associates, Inc.
TRA
TRO/The Ritchie Organization
Tsoi/Kobus & Associates Inc.
Turner Construction Company
Vitetta Group Incorporated
Webb Zerafa Menkes Housden Architects
Xerox Corporation
The Zimmerman Design Group

TABLE OF CONTENTS

Foreword .... *v*

Contributors .... *vii*

101 Representative Floor Plans **1**
  Animal Facilities
  Corporate Office Facilities
  Healthcare Facilities
  Pharmaceutical/Biotechnology Production Facilities
  R&D Facilities
  Training and Conference Facilities
  University Science Facilities

Facilities Planning Concepts **133**
  Acoustics
  Conceptual Project Planning
  Healthcare Facilities
  HVAC Systems
  Programming
  R&D Facilities

100 Recent Project Profiles **185**
  Animal Facilities
  Corporate Office/Mixed Use
  Healthcare Facilities
    Inpatient
    Outpatient
    Inpatient/Outpatient
    Medical Office/Patient Education
  R&D Facilities
    Biomedical Research
    Biotechnology
    Pharmaceutical

Miscellaneous
University Facilities
Biomedical
Healthcare
Science
Miscellaneous
Miscellaneous Facilities

Facilities Organization and Management Profiles 273

Key Facilities Terms and Issues 297

101
Representative
Floor Plans:
What works and Why

TABLE OF CONTENTS

Animal Facilities 7
  Amgen, Thousand Oaks, Calif., Animal Facility & Research Lab 9
  Boston University Medical Center Boston Center for Biomedical Research 10
  Brookfield Zoo, Brookfield, Ill., Veterinary Care Facility 11
  Fred Hutchinson Cancer Research Center, Seattle 12
  Hazleton's Laboratories, Madison, Wis., Animal Facility 13
  University of California—San Francisco, Mt. Zion Research Building 14
  University of Maryland at Baltimore, Health Sciences Facility 15
  University Of Missouri—Columbia, Lefevre Hall 16
  Washington University, St. Louis, Clinical Sciences Research Building 17
  Washington University, St. Louis, East McDonnell Specialized Research Facility . 18
      Barrier Suite and Corridor 19

Corporate Office Facilities 21
  American Home Products, Madison, N.J., Corporate Headquarters 23
  Baltimore Life Corporate Headquarters, Baltimore 24
  Bancroft Whitney, Co., San Francisco, Corporate Office 25
  Comerica Incorporated, Auburn Hills, Mich., Operations Center 26
  CUH2A, Inc., Princeton, N.J., Corporate Office 27
  ENRON Gas Services Group, Columbus, Ohio, Corporate Office 28
  Loctite Corporation, Rocky Hill, Conn., North American Headquarters Facility ... 29
  Modern Woodmen of America, Rock Island, Ill., Home Office Expansion 30
  Northern Illinois Gas Company, Naperville, Ill., Corporate Headquarters and
      Operations Facility 31
  Scariano, Kula, Ellch & Himes, Chicago, Office Building 32
  State Auto Insurance Companies, Columbus, Ohio, Corporate Pavilion 33
  USAA Federal Savings Bank, San Antonio, Bank Services Building 34

Healthcare Facilities 37
  AMI Palmetto Hospital, Hialeah, Fla., Cancer Treatment Center 39
  Battle Creek Health System, Battle Creek, Mich., Radiation Oncology Center 40
  Bay Area Medical Center, Corpus Christi, Texas, Surgical Center 41
  Brigham and Women's Hospital, Boston, Emergency Suite 42
  County of Merced Medical Center, Merced, Calif., Marie Green
      Psychiatric Center 43
  Grand View Hospital, Sellersville, Pa., Department of Emergency Medicine 44
  Kaiser Permanente, North Hollywood, Calif., Regional Reference Laboratory 45

Mary Birch Hospital For Women, San Diego 46
Maryview Medical Center, Portsmouth, Va., Surgery Suite 47
Mayo Clinic Scottsdale, Ariz., Family Medicine Clinic............................. 48
Metropolitan Hospital, New York, Neonatal/Labor & Delivery Suite Renovation . 49
Mid Coast Hospital, Brunswick, Maine, Med-Surg Nursing Unit............... 50
Morristown Memorial Hospital, Morristown, N.J., Emergency Department
    Renovation 51
Plastic Surgery Associates, Grand Rapids, Mich., Ambulatory Surgery Facility 52
Rockdale Hospital, Conyers, Ga., Surgery Suite 53
Rush North Shore Medical Center, Skokie, Ill., Gross Point Addition 54
South Shore Hospital, South Weymouth, Mass., Emergency Center 55
Taylor Hospital, Ridley Park, Pa., Department of Emergency Medicine 56
University of California—Davis Medical Center, Tower II 57
University of California—San Francisco, Mt. Zion Cancer Center............... 58
Veterans Administration, Brooklyn, N.Y., Ambulatory Care Addition 59
Waukesha Memorial Hospital, Waukesha, Wis., Intensive Care Unit 60
Del E. Webb Memorial Hospital, Sun City West, Ariz., Emergency & Ambulatory
    Services Expansion 61
West Allis Memorial Hospital, West Allis, Wis., Emergency Department
    Renovation 62

Pharmaceutical/Biotechnology Production Facilities 65
Bausch & Lomb Pharmaceuticals, Inc., Tampa, Fla., Production Facility.............. 66
Hybridon, Inc., Milford, Mass., cGMP Pilot Production Plant 67
Miles Biotechnology, Berkeley, Calif., Media Production Facility 5A 68

R&D Facilities 71
Allergan, Inc., Irvine, Calif., Research & Development Facility II 73
BASF Bioresearch Corporation, Worcester, Mass., Biomedical Research Center ... 75
Biogen, Inc., Cambridge, Mass., Biology and Chemistry Labs 76
    Chemistry Research Laboratory—8 person module 76
    Biology Research Laboratory—12 person module 77
Brigham and Women's Hospital, Boston, Longwood Medical Research Center ... 78
The Cancer Therapy & Research Center, San Antonio, The Alice McDermott
    Building 79
Children's Hospital Of Philadelphia, Research Building............................. 80
David Axelrod Institute For Public Health, Albany, N.Y. 81
DowElanco World Headquarters, Indianapolis, Research and Development
    Building—Lab modules... 82
Eli Lilly and Company, Indianapolis, New Research Building 83
Ford Motor Company, Dearborn, Mich., Scientific Research Laboratory 84
Hewlett-Packard Company, Wilmington, Del., Analytical Products Facility
    Lab Modules 85

Hoechst-Roussel Pharmaceuticals Inc., Bridgewater, N.J., Molecular Neurobiology Building Lab Modules 86
IDEC Pharmaceuticals Inc., San Diego, R&D Facility 87
Immulogic Pharmaceutical Corporation, Waltham, Mass., Headquarters R&D Center 88
James River Corporation, Cincinnati, Technology and Business Center 89
Lederle-Praxis Biologicals, Rochester, N.Y., Vaccine Research Facility 90
Metropolitan Water District Of Southern California, La Verne, Calif., Water Quality Laboratory Expansion 91
Parke-Davis/Warner Lambert, Ann Arbor, Mich., Pre-Clinical Pharmaceutical Research Laboratory 92
Pharmakon USA, Waverly, Pa., Toxicology Research Facility 93
Physikalisch-Technische Bundesanstalt, Braunschweig, Germany Reinraumzentrum (Cleanroom Center) 94
Promega Corporation, Fitchburg, Wis., Biopharmaceutical Technology Center ... 95
The Upjohn Company, Kalamazoo, Mich. 96
    Central Core Support Functions 96
    Public Access Security Issues 97

Training and Conference Facilities 99
Eagleville Hospital, Eagleville, Pa., Center for Drug and Alcohol Rehabilitation 101
Household International, Prospect Heights, Ill., Edwin P. Hoffman Career Development Center 102
Howard Hughes Medical Institute, Chevy Chase, Md., Conference Center 103
Illinois Institute of Technology, Chicago, Chicago-Kent College of Law 104
Palmetto International Exposition Center, Greenville, S.C., James H. Woodside Conference Center 105
Plymouth Rock Assurance Company, Boston, Computer Training Rooms 106

University Science Facilities 109
Emory University, Atlanta, Chemistry Building Addition 111
Emory University, Atlanta, Physics Building 112
Harvard Medical School, Boston, Medical Education Center 113
Indiana University, Bloomington, Ind., Chemistry Building 114
Massachusetts of Technology, Cambridge, Mass., Biology Building No. 68 115
Medical College of Pennsylvania, Philadelphia, Queen Lane Campus Building 116
Northern Illinois University, De Kalb, Ill., Faraday Hall West 117
Rutgers University, New Brunswick, N.J., Foram Hall, Cook & Douglas Colleges 118
Stanford University, Stanford, Calif., Medical School Lab Surge Building 119
Texas A&M University, Corpus Christi, Texas, Classroom/Laboratory Building .. 120
University of California—Berkeley, Chemistry Unit III 121
University of California—San Francisco, Mt. Zion Research Building 122
University of Chicago, The Biological Sciences Learning Center and The Jules F.

Knapp Medical Research Building Complex 123
    Second Level 123-124
    Lower Level 125
University of Florida, Gainesville, Fla., Chemistry Building 126
University of Maryland at Baltimore, Medical Research Building 127
University of Massachusetts, Amherst, Mass., Polymer Research Center 128
University of Wisconsin—Madison, Grainger Hall of Business Administration .. 129
Virginia Commonwealth University, Richmond, Va., Medical Sciences Building 130
Washington University Medical Center, St. Louis, Biochemistry And Molecular
    Biophysics Laboratories 131

ANIMAL FACILITIES

Amgen, Thousand Oaks, Calif.
Animal Facility & Research Lab

Architect: McLellan & Copenhagen Inc., Cupertino, Calif.

This new animal facility connects to an existing building that houses both animal facilities and research labs. In the new building, facilities include transgenic research, surgery, necropsy, toxicology and histology as well as animal holding. Animal rooms for small and medium-sized animals use a standard 14′ planning module. A typical holding suite includes an anteroom, one procedure room and three holding rooms. The procedure and holding rooms are designed to be interchangeable for flexibility. Isolation cubicles in a number of holding rooms allow researchers the option of having several different research populations housed in one room. This three-story, 72,000-gsf building incorporates interstitial space which allows for change, facility repairs and modifications without interrupting research activity. The third floor houses animal research labs.

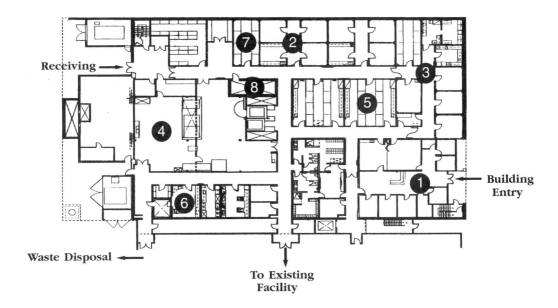

(Floor plan courtesy of McLellan & Copenhagen, Inc.)

LEGEND—

1 Administrative
2 Holding suite
3 Transgenic suite
4 Cage wash
5 Holding/Procedure
6 Necropsy/Histology
7 Quarantine
8 Cold room

Boston University Medical Center
Boston Center for Biomedical Research

Architect: CANNON, Boston

These cage rooms were designed as part of a facility housing many species of lab animals within a new biomedical-research laboratory building. The Boston University Medical Center has been developing higher standards of housing, as well as a psychological enrichment program, for its resident baboon population.

Cage and room design were integrated to provide improved maintenance and a improved conditions for the animals. A two-section cage connects adjacent cage rooms through the dividing wall. This design not only provides for greater social interaction among the animals, but also allows animals to be easily moved to an adjacent room while each room is thoroughly cleaned. Drainage trenches with flushable drains add to the ease of maintenance.

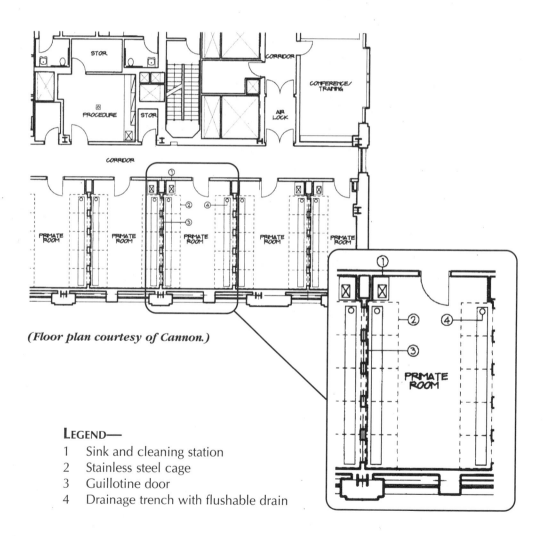

(Floor plan courtesy of Cannon.)

LEGEND—
1 Sink and cleaning station
2 Stainless steel cage
3 Guillotine door
4 Drainage trench with flushable drain

Brookfield Zoo, Brookfield, Ill.
Veterinary Care Facility

Architect: Flad & Associates, Madison, Wis.

Examination rooms, operating rooms, an ICU, quarantine facilities and individual holding facilities make up 15,000 sf of the new 20,000-sf Brookfield Zoo Veterinary Care Facility. The corridor system in the animal-holding area is arranged so that large, hoofed animals can be moved to various pens without endangering keepers. Quarantine and necropsy areas have separate outside entrances with foot baths to keep the rest of the hospital from being contaminated.

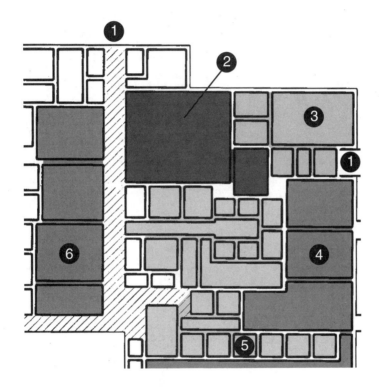

(Floor plan courtesy of Flad & Associates.)

LEGEND—

1 Entry
2 Mechanical
3 Necropsy
4 Quarantine/Isolation
5 Hoofed animal holding
6 Treatment

Fred Hutchinson Cancer Research Center, Seattle

Lab/Animal Facilities Planner: McLellan & Copenhagen, Inc., Cupertino, Calif.

The 305,000-gsf, phase-I facility consists of research laboratories and support space. The 24,000-sf small-animal facility is located to provide access to all researchers in the three buildings above, yet be an inconspicuous and secure facility. A single access point, with connections to both the office area and vivarium, provides a controlled entry. The corridor system connects all areas of the small-animal facility: quarantine/isolation, animal holding rooms, procedure rooms, animal support, barrier colony, biohazard suite, and irradiation suite. The rooms are designed to be convertible from holding to procedure rooms. There is full interstitial above throughout. The facility is designed to be expandable into the second phase of development on the new campus, currently in design.

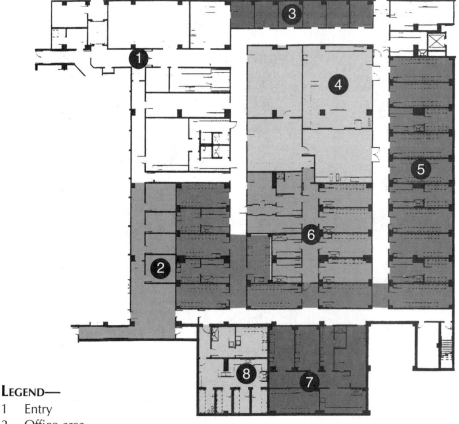

(Floor plan courtesy of McLellan & Copenhagen, Inc.)

LEGEND—
1   Entry
2   Office area
3   Quarantine and isolation
4   Animal support
5   Animal holding and procedure
6   Barrier colony
7   Biohazard suite
8   Radiation suite

Hazleton's Laboratories, Madison, Wis.
Animal Facility

Architect: Strang, Inc., Madison, Wis.

This addition was constructed adjacent to an existing animal facility. The original rodent rooms use a dual corridor system while the addition uses a single corridor. The two animal facilities are linked by a shared central-support core including necropsy, locker rooms and a new cage/tunnel wash area. Open office areas are provided for animal-care technicians and scientists.

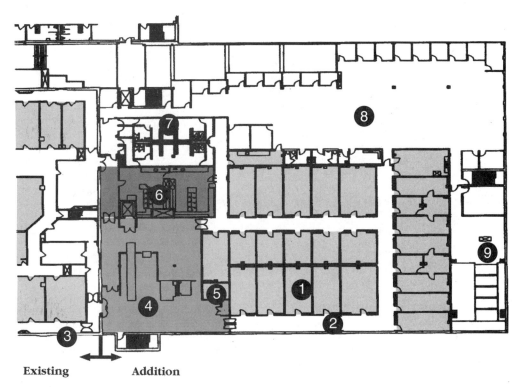

Existing   Addition

(Floor plan courtesy of Strang, Inc.)

LEGEND—
1   Rodent room
2   Single corridor
3   Dual corridor
4   Cage/Tunnel wash
5   Prewash
6   Necropsy
7   Locker/Shower
8   Office
9   Mechanical/Electrical

University of California—San Francisco
Mt. Zion Research Building

Architect: Stone Marraccini Patterson, San Francisco

Located in the basement of the building, the animal care facility is organized into three barrier zones/suites, around a loop corridor. The cage-wash facility is designed to provide a clean work flow from dirty to clean sides. The animal holding and procedure rooms are planned to allow maximum flexibility for current and future use.

Animal Care Facility

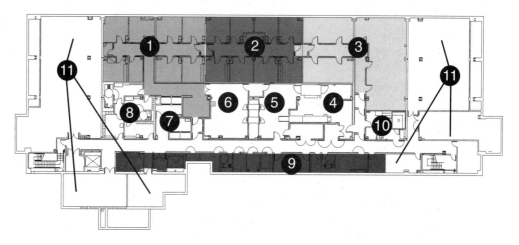

(Floor plan courtesy of Stone Marraccini Patterson.)

LEGEND—
1 Typical suite/Barrier zone
2 Typical suite/Barrier zone
3 Typical suite/Barrier zone
4 Dirty cage wash
5 Clean cage wash
6 Autoclave
7 Animal receiving
8 Staff lockers
9 Support spaces
10 Necropsy room
11 Mechanical/building spaces

University of Maryland at Baltimore Health Sciences Facility

Architect/Engineer: CUH2A & Ayers/Saint/Gross (A Joint Venture), Princeton, N.J.

This building has three types of bacteria colonies located on one floor, located so as to expand and connect to existing animal facilities in adjoining buildings. The standard animal housing area comprises holding rooms with anterooms. The barrier facility houses immunodeficient and transgenic animals which must be protected from outside influences; therefore, all materials entering this area pass through an autoclave. Protection must be provided to everything located outside of the biohazard containment facility, so all materials must also pass through an autoclave before exiting this area. A single, centrally-located cage wash serves all three types of animal-housing facilities. A dedicated service elevator at one end of the building provides vertical transportation of animals and the associated bedding and feed. An elevator at the other end serves research personnel.

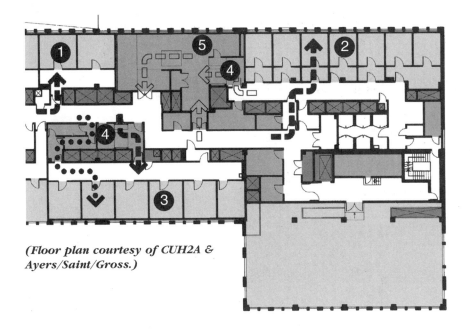

(Floor plan courtesy of CUH2A & Ayers/Saint/Gross.)

LEGEND—

1   Standard animal holding rooms
2   Biohazard containment suite
3   Barrier suite
4   Autoclave
5   Cage wash

University Of Missouri—Columbia
Lefevre Hall

Architect: The Christner Partnership, Inc., St. Louis

This animal suite balances efficiency with flexibility, containing a preparation area with four animal cubicles each designed to hold two animal cages (small mammals/ rodents) or two aquaria (fish or crustaceans). Within a compact space, this layout allows separation of species and research projects to avoid cross-contamination or other interference to the research outcomes.

Animal Suite

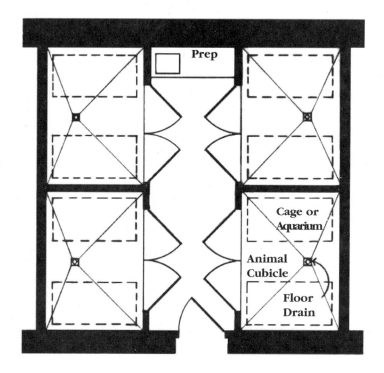

(Floor plan courtesy of The Christner Partnership, Inc.)

Washington University, St. Louis
Clinical Sciences Research Building

Architect/Engineer: CUH2A, Inc., Princeton, N.J.

Clearly organized circulation is one of the most important factors in the design of safe barrier and biohazard containment facilities. This facility houses animals that must be protected from outside influences, with protection also provided to personnel outside of the facility. It is a Biohazard Level 3 facility, and all materials entering and leaving pass through an autoclave. The holding rooms (for large animals in the center of the plan and for rodents at the perimeter) are arranged with a clean/soiled supply traffic system, and a procedure room is directly adjacent to the holding room with access to the soiled corridor. Vertical transportation of animals is separate from that of personnel, as is that of clean from soiled animals.

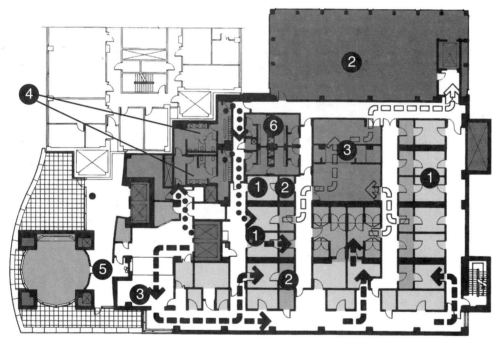

(Floor plan courtesy of CUH2A, Inc.)

LEGEND—
1 Animal holding rooms
2 Animal procedure rooms
3 Autoclave/Support
4 Lockers
5 Common area
6 Showers

Washington University, St. Louis
East McDonnell Specialized Research Facility

Architect/Engineer: CUH2A, Inc., Princeton, NJ

The protection of animals is the primary concern in a transgenic animal facility and therefore all materials that enter the facility pass though an autoclave. Vertical transport of clean animals and personnel is separate and the vertical transport of soiled materials and personnel is combined. All of the animal-holding rooms are designed as a suite which allows for the segregation of animals for various studies. The arrangement of these suites does not compromise the flow of clean and soiled materials.

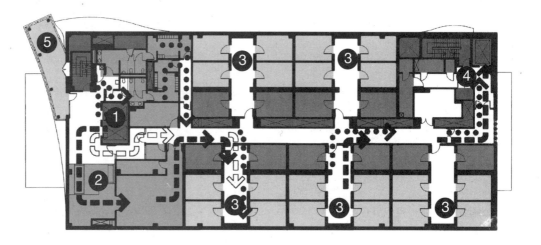

(Floor plan courtesy of CUH2A, Inc.)

LEGEND—

1 Clean elevator
2 Autoclave
3 Barrier suite
4 Soiled elevator
5 Work room

Corridor

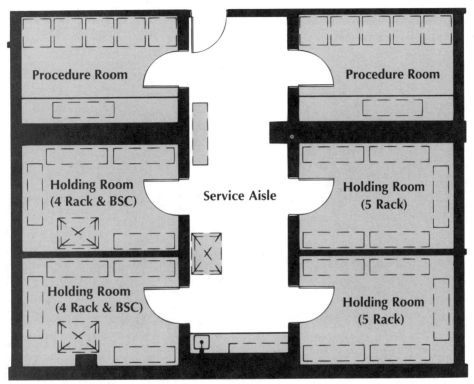

Procedure Room

Procedure Room

**Holding Room
(4 Rack & BSC)**

Service Aisle

**Holding Room
(5 Rack)**

**Holding Room
(4 Rack & BSC)**

**Holding Room
(5 Rack)**

(Floor plan courtesy of CUH2A, Inc.)

Barrier Suite

This barrier suite provides desirable isolation of different studies from one another. The suite's service aisle allows the maintaining of proper air flow and provides an enclosed space for rack changes. Designing flexibility into the suite by creating rooms of equal size allows rooms to be used either as holding rooms or as procedure rooms. The holding-room and procedure-room air pressurization is positive to the service aisle and the service aisle is positive to the main corridor outside of the suite. Animal holding rooms are designed with flexibility either for five racks, or for four racks and a biosafety cabinet. The procedure room requires a bench on one side with a microinjection station and the opposite side of the room has ample space for instrumentation and equipment.

CORPORATE OFFICE FACILITIES

American Home Products, Madison, N.J. Corporate Headquarters

Architect: The Hillier Group, Princeton, N.J.

The first-floor plan breaks down the floor plates into small manageable areas with perimeter exposure for enclosed office areas. A three-story, central pedestrian spine runs the entire length of the building, serving as a "main street." The reception area, common support spaces such as the employee cafeteria, company store, conference center, personnel/health services and credit union are located on the first floor along with general office areas.

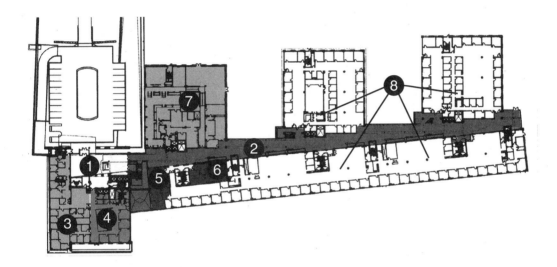

(Floor plan courtesy of The Hillier Group.)

Legend—

1 Lobby/Reception
2 Pedestrian circulation
3 Personnel/Health services
4 Conference
5 Credit union
6 Company store
7 Employee cafeteria
8 General office

Baltimore Life Corporate Headquarters, Baltimore

Architect: Ayers/Saint/Gross Architects and Planners, Baltimore

The 103,000-sf Baltimore Life corporate headquarters building consolidates all corporate functions into one facility. The curved wall in the entrance area on the second floor is repeated on every floor above. This, along with the central connecting stairway, unifies the building vertically. All major functional areas are linked into this center area— the dining room on the first floor, the training room on the second floor and the executive offices and boardroom on the third floor. This arrangement provides nearly every employee with a view of the outside. Open-plan offices are situated with a view of the pond behind the building. Closed-plan offices are located on the other three sides.

Second Floor

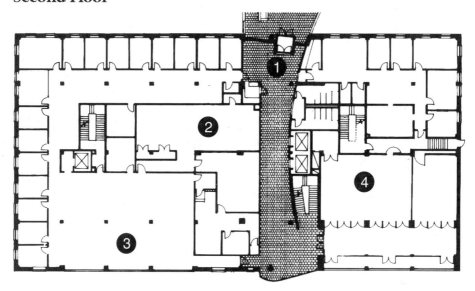

(Floor plan courtesy of Ayers/Saint/Gross Architects and Planners.)

LEGEND—

1　Main entry with curved wall
2　Computer room
3　Open-plan offices
4　Training room

Bancroft Whitney, Co., San Francisco
Corporate Office

Architect: Gordon H Chong + Associates Architects/Engineers, San Francisco

This renovation of a three-story, 135,000-sf warehouse into corporate offices for a law book publishing company required the creation of a high percentage of closed offices and the organization of the second floor (editorial offices) into distinct "teams." Office clusters are arranged using a pyramid configuration, affording all offices equal views and privacy. The administrative staff is housed in open systems, located between the closed office clusters. A primary circulation spine and formal entry for each team ensures privacy for team members.

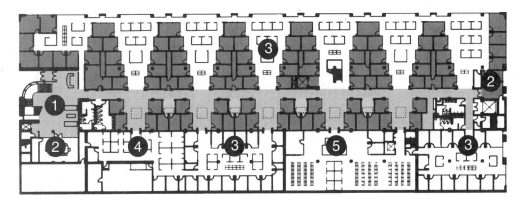

(Floor plan courtesy of Gordon H Chong + Associates Architects/Engineers.)

LEGEND—
1 Lobby
2 Conference
3 Editorial department
4 Computer department
5 Library

Comerica Incorporated, Auburn Hills, Mich. Operations Center

Architect: Harley Ellington Pierce Yee Associates, Inc., Southfield, Mich.

This 400,000 gsf office/operations center, designed for maximum flexibility, is structured to adapt to changing office and operations needs. Located on a sloping site overlooking a river, the four-story building steps back, providing larger floor plates on the upper levels. To provide maximum open office areas, all mechanical, toilet and lobby areas are located at the ends of the building. The central atrium space allows natural light into the center of the building. The office space utilizes a 30' x 30' column grid and features raised-access flooring throughout.

First Floor

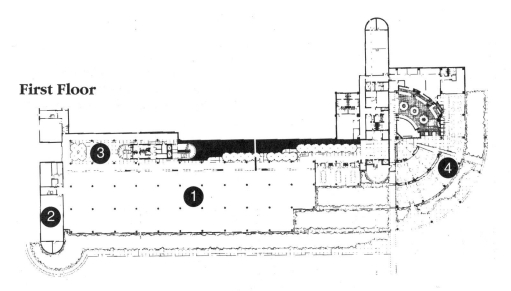

(Floor plan courtesy of Harley Ellington Pierce Yee Associates, Inc.)

LEGEND—
1   Office area
2   Mechanical cores
3   Atrium
4   Cafeteria

CUH2A, Inc., Princeton, N.J.
Corporate Office

Architect/Engineer: CUH2A, Inc., Princeton, N.J.

This office plan demonstrates an open arrangement of a vertical hierarchy organization that fosters interaction among groups. Directors' offices flank the perimeter on two sides and those of team leaders line the other perimeter. Open office workstations are amassed in between, allowing for visibility and communication between employees and project directors. The open office areas are designed as open loft areas in which project teams can be reconfigured as required for the duration of a project. Communication between the two major office areas is facilitated in a common open library area located between them.

LEGEND—
1 Directors enclosed offices
2 Team leaders open offices
3 Employee open office workstations
4 Library
5 Conference rooms
6 Huddle rooms
7 Support spaces

(Floor plan courtesy of CUH2A, Inc.)

ENRON Gas Services Group, Columbus, Ohio
Corporate Office

Architect: Wandel and Schnell, Architects Inc., Columbus, Ohio

The ENRON Gas corporate office was designed to promote and sustain an established teamwork concept among employees. The plan organizes employees by department into a series of individual work pods which encourage team gathering about a state-of-the-art activity center. Fax and copy machines, computer printers and office supplies are all contained within the activity center. Centralized file and work rooms store information that can be utilized by all employees. In addition, each pod is adjacent to several conference rooms that have varying degrees of privacy. This enables users to continue team meetings and impromptu gatherings to discuss work-related issues.

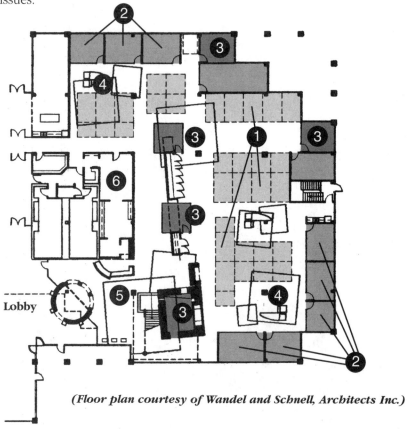

(Floor plan courtesy of Wandel and Schnell, Architects Inc.)

LEGEND—

1   Open office
2   Private office
3   Conference room
4   Team activity center
5   Reception
6   Files, mail, storage

Loctite Corporation, Rocky Hill, Conn.
North American Headquarters Facility

Architect: Flad & Associates, Madison, Wis.

The new 198,000-sf North American Headquarters Facility places administrative offices and research laboratories on either side of a central core area that provides shared amenities including a lobby, training room, fitness facilities, library, conference area and cafeteria. This central interaction zone enhances communication between previously separated administrative and research groups. The central service corridor in the laboratory wing provides accessibility for lab services; people corridors provide a circulation, work and interaction zone separate from research materials and equipment. The facility also features upgraded R&D laboratory work areas and employee workstations in both administrative and research areas.

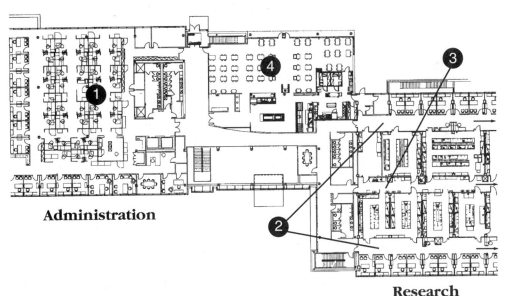

Administration

Research

(Floor plan courtesy of Flad & Associates.)

LEGEND—
1   Logistics
2   Tech corridor
3   Service corridor
4   Kitchen/Cafeteria

Modern Woodmen of America, Rock Island, Ill. Home Office Expansion

Architect: Flad and Associates, Madison, Wis.

Modern Woodmen's new five-story, freestanding addition is built on a simple plan that maximizes the quality of the workspace through the strategic arrangement of its components. Open office space dominates the north side of the plan where the building's transparent, multi-layered skin reveals pleasant views to the Mississippi River and riverfront. Indirect northern light fills the offices because the perimeter is kept free of enclosed rooms. The building's south side takes on a more solid approach with the horizontal floor plates locking into three granite-clad walls, which block the direct light and less enticing views to the south. Vertically stacked along this closed face lie the facility's training center, data center and mechanical support. A curved wall provides direction into the office space from the public lobby area and separates the two primary functions of the floor.

Level 1

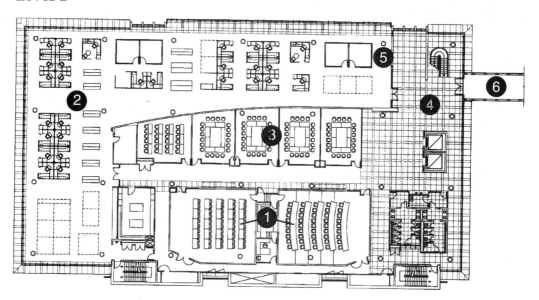

(Floor plan courtesy of Flad & Associates.)

LEGEND—
1 Training room
2 Open office
3 Breakout room
4 Lobby
5 Lounge
6 Bridge

Northern Illinois Gas Company, Naperville, Ill.
Corporate Headquarters And Operations Facility

Architect/Engineer/Interiors: Holabird & Root, Chicago

The floor plan for this new corporate headquarters is laid out to provide the optimal column spacing for the furniture. The north column bay is smaller than the south column bay and is dimensioned to accommodate the corporate standard office size, the secretarial support and the main circulation path without interrupting columns. The only internal column is then incorporated into a freestanding file bank that sets up the pattern for the open office plan. Secondary "streets" lead to the systems furniture centered on the file banks and create small neighborhoods within the large floor plan area. All floors have a service cluster which has conference rooms, copiers and other support centrally located in the hinge of the two wings.

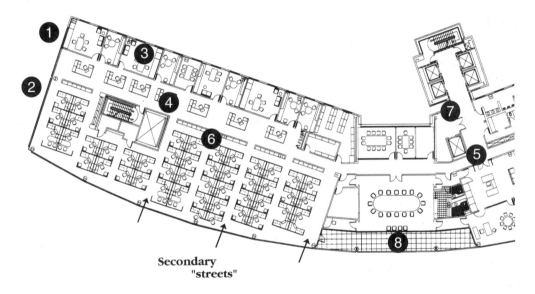

Secondary "streets"

(Floor plan courtesy of Holabird & Root.)

LEGEND—
1 North bay column spacing
2 South bay column spacing
3 Standard office
4 Secretarial support
5 Main circulation
6 Freestanding file bank
7 Service cluster
8 Building setback

Scariano, Kula, Ellch & Himes, Chicago Office Building

Interior Architects: LSH/Hague-Richards Associates (a division of Loebl Schlossman and Hackl), Chicago

Relocating these law offices involved an expansion of existing space, millwork retrofit and appropriate planning for existing furniture and an extensive artwork collection. The firm upholds the ideology that personal interaction and teamwork are central to their successful business. With this in mind, the office's design, including open-plan workstations, private offices and support areas makes these goals easily achievable. Basic geometric shapes are arranged in non-traditional modes to create a sensible progression through public spaces. Corridors are translated into a functional library where existing, full-height mahogany bookcases were retrofitted with clerestory windows allowing natural light into interior spaces.

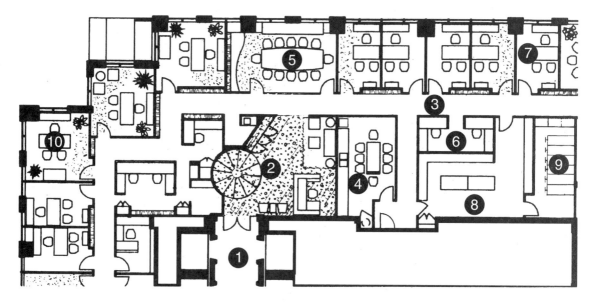

(Floor plan courtesy of LSH/Hague-Richards Associates.)

LEGEND—

1 Entry
2 Rotunda
3 Corridor library
4 Pantry
5 Conference room
6 Support staff
7 Associates office
8 Training
9 General filing
10 Partner's office

State Auto Insurance Companies, Columbus, Ohio
Corporate Pavilion
Architect: NBBJ, Columbus, Ohio

The first level of this four-story addition forms the corporate "main street." All interactive functions are grouped around the central atrium: arrival/entry; reception; vertical circulation; dining; conference and continuing education center. The interaction is continued vertically through the atrium on all upper levels with support areas clustered around the atrium.

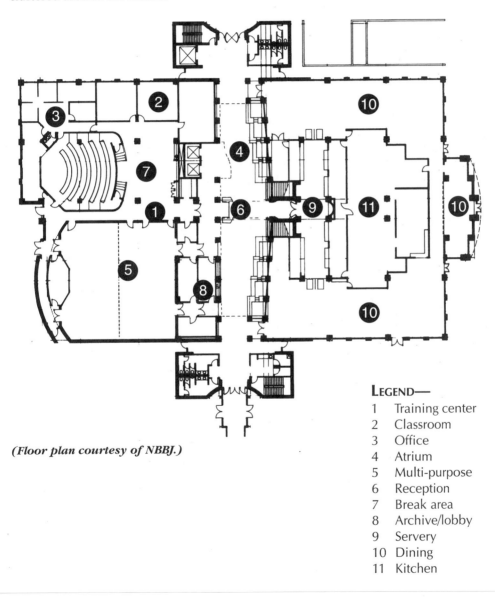

(Floor plan courtesy of NBBJ.)

LEGEND—
1 Training center
2 Classroom
3 Office
4 Atrium
5 Multi-purpose
6 Reception
7 Break area
8 Archive/lobby
9 Servery
10 Dining
11 Kitchen

USAA Federal Savings Bank, San Antonio
Bank Services Building

Architects: Marmon Mok/JonesKell* - A Joint Venture, San Antonio

A bank services building intended for "back of the house" functions to complement an adjacent, existing bank building. The new building utilizes flexible, open office spaces designed for systems furniture on raised-access floor. Open spaces are arranged around core spaces and oriented to create circulation paths between a curving glass wall to the north and a segmented wall to the south.

name changed to Kell Muñoz Wigodsky

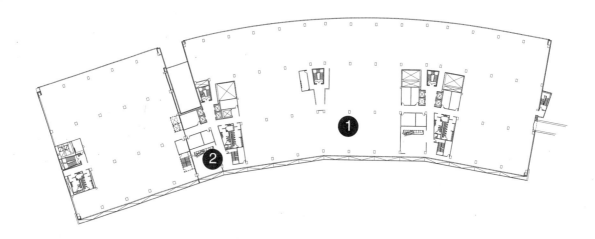

(Floor plan courtesy of Kell Muñoz Wigodsky Architects.)

LEGEND—
1   Open office
2   Break area

HEALTHCARE FACILITIES

AMI Palmetto Hospital, Hialeah, Fla.
Cancer Treatment Center

Architect: Flad & Associates, Gainesville, Fla.

This new satellite cancer-treatment center located on the hospital campus offers both radiation and chemotherapy for outpatients. The reception desk at the main entry allows staff to separate patients, based on the treatment modality. An education center offers counseling and support group space, as well as future expansion capability.

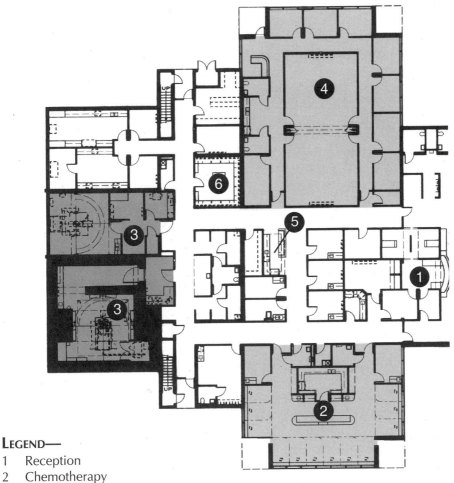

(Floor plan courtesy of Flad & Associates.)

LEGEND—
1   Reception
2   Chemotherapy
3   Radiation therapy
4   Education center
5   Nurses station
6   Treatment planning

Battle Creek Health System, Battle Creek, Mich.
Radiation Oncology Center

Architect: Harley Ellington Pierce Yee Associates, Inc., Southfield, Mich.

Prior to renovation, the radiology department was located in a dimly-lit basement area. Due to the nature of the treatment provided, the hospital hoped to make the experience as pleasant as possible for its patients. This was accomplished by creating an aesthetically pleasing, serene environment with easy access for both inpatients and outpatients. The oncology expansion was placed adjacent to the existing radiology department to allow direct access by the hospital staff and inpatients. On the exterior, a new grade-level entrance was created for use by outpatients. Inside the oncology unit, the waiting room has two glass walls to add natural light. A single-loaded corridor provides access to both simulator and linear accelerator rooms. In addition, this corridor features floor-to-ceiling glass on one wall for its entire length.

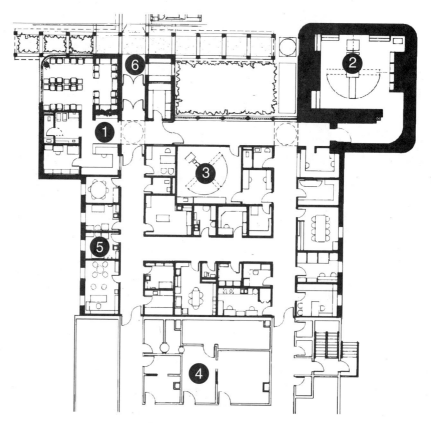

(Floor plan courtesy of Harley Ellington Pierce Yee Associates, Inc.)

LEGEND—

1	Reception/Waiting	4	Existing radiology
2	Treatment	5	Examining/Consultation
3	Simulator	6	Outpatient entrance

Bay Area Medical Center, Corpus Christi, Texas
Surgical Center

Architect: The Stichler Design Group, Inc., San Diego

This new surgery center is located within the recently completed Bay Area Medical Center. In a unique arrangement, the South Texas Surgery Center has teamed up with the Bay Area Medical Center—while retaining separate identities—to form the South Texas Bay Area Surgery Center. The surgery center and hospital share the nine operating rooms and related support facilities including central sterilization. Both organizations have their own Stage I and Stage II recovery areas as well as individual entrances and waiting.

LEGEND—

1   Bay Area surgical suites
2   Bay Area doctor's lounge
3   Mechanical
4   Anatomical lab
5   Lab
6   South Texas surgical suites
7   South Texas storage
8   South Texas pre-op
9   South Texas admin./wait
10 South Texas stage II recovery
11 South Texas stage I recovery
12 Bay Area stage I recovery
13 Bay Area endo prep
14 Bay Area stage II recovery
15 Bay Area waiting
16 Courtyard

(Floor plan courtesy of The Stichler Design Group, Inc.)

Brigham and Women's Hospital, Boston
Emergency Suite

Architect: Tsoi/Kobus & Associates, Cambridge, Mass.

After arriving at the main reception desk in this renovated suite, both walk-in and wheelchair patients are triaged and registered in one of three booths where level of acuity is determined. Non-ambulatory patients arrive through a separate entry and are triaged proximate to the acute area. The patient is then transferred to one of three care units, each with its own nurses station: acute/trauma, urgent and STAT (short term assessment and treatment). Two main interior corridors facilitate easy movement throughout the suite. A "fast track" section just off the reception area has four cubicles. Family support provisions include two family rooms, a volunteer desk, a social-services office and convenient access to food-service facilities. Radiology and CT-scan facilities are shared with and connected to the radiology department in an adjacent building.

(Floor plan courtesy of Tsoi/Kobus & Associates.)

LEGEND—

1 Reception/Triage
2 Waiting
3 Acute care unit
4 STAT care unit
5 Urgent care unit
and fast track
6 Radiology
7 Staff support
8 Toilets

County of Merced Medical Center, Merced, Calif.
Marie Green Psychiatric Center

Architect: Gordon H Chong + Associates Architects/Engineers, San Francisco

This 32-bed mental health facility was designed to provide a secured locked environment which minimizes the need for staff resources and encourages patient interaction. Key elements of the plan include:

- Centralized nurses station which maximizes visibility to patient and public areas.
- Patient rooms accessible to public dayrooms encourage interaction.
- Dayrooms are large vaulted spaces with well balanced natural daylight and indirect illumination.
- Exterior spaces are designed for a variety of activity levels.
- Phasing from adult daycare to acute psychiatric care.

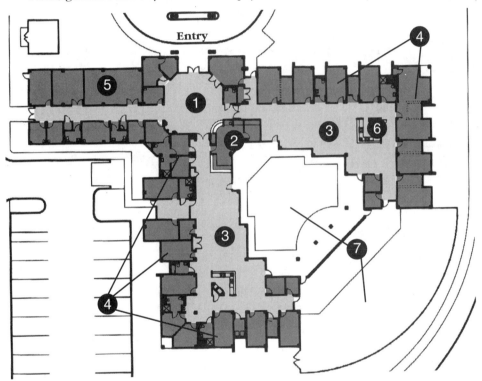

(Floor plan courtesy of Gordon H Chong + Associates Architects/Engineers.)

LEGEND—

1 Lobby
2 Nurse station
3 Dayroom
4 Patient bedrooms
5 Administration & support
6 Kitchen
7 Courtyard

Grand View Hospital, Sellersville, Pa.
Department of Emergency Medicine

Architect: MPB Architects, Philadelphia

This department is organized around one nurses station serving all major care, minor care and trauma rooms. This set-up allows for interchangeable assignments of all nursing staff. There are two separate entrances and drop offs: one for ambulances and the other for walk-ins. The entrances reduce the traffic congestion. The X-ray room is located in the center of the department, equally accessible to all levels of care. Registration and triage are interconnected and can be staffed by one person during off-peak hours.

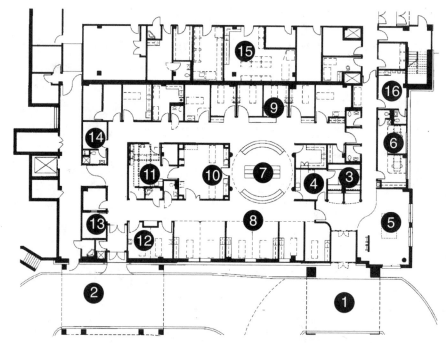

(Floor plan courtesy of MPB Architects.)

LEGEND—

1 Walk-in entrance	9 Minor care treatment rooms
2 Ambulance entrance	10 Trauma
3 Registration	11 X-Ray
4 Triage	12 Observation
5 Waiting	13 Psychiatric hold & consultation
6 Industrial medicine	14 On-call
7 Nurses station	15 Laboratory
8 Major care treatment rooms	16 Staff lounge

Kaiser Permanente, North Hollywood, Calif.
Regional Reference Laboratory

Architect: Stone Marraccini Patterson, San Francisco

This clinical lab facility services Kaiser's Southern California facilities. Major departments have been grouped three to a floor with each department occupying a block of lab modules. Each block is six 11′ x 11′ modules wide and seven modules deep, separated by a support zone two modules wide. Within each block most lab functions are grouped into an open studio adjacent to the personnel gallery. Large, continuous windows between the lab and the gallery allow natural light into most work areas. A service gallery provides a separate circulation path for materials and samples and allows access to all building utilities.

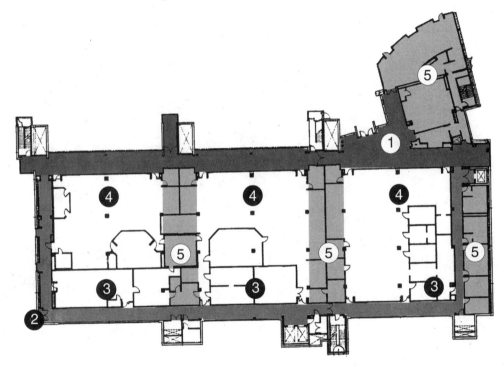

(Floor plan courtesy of Stone Marraccini Patterson.)

LEGEND—
1. Personnel gallery
2. Service gallery
3. "Closed" labs
4. "Open" labs
5. Support spaces

Mary Birch Hospital For Women, San Diego

Architect: The Stichler Design Group, San Diego

This six-story, freestanding, 197,000-sf facility is completely dedicated to serving the inpatient and outpatient needs of women. The third floor of the women's hospital features 22 labor/delivery/recovery (LDR) beds, 9 operating rooms, 16 recovery beds, an in vitro fertilization laboratory and prenatal testing. The LDR features the "cluster concept." Four LDR rooms are clustered around a mini nurse station accessible through an entrance from the corridor. Medical equipment and warming cabinets are available in each cluster. Physicians can access this floor through a dedicated corridor containing a computer station which provides details on each LDR patient.

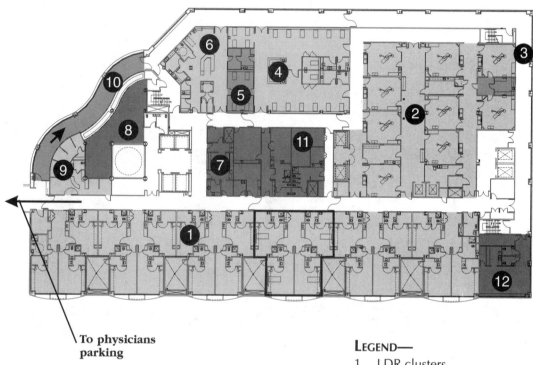

To physicians
parking

(Floor plan courtesy of The Stichler Design Group.)

LEGEND—

1   LDR clusters
2   Cesarean surgery
3   In vitro fertilization lab
4   OB/GYN recovery
5   Pre/Post-op
6   Outpatient prep
7   Nurses station
8   Waiting
9   Antenatal testing
10 Physicians corridor
11 Staff support
12 Nurses conference

Maryview Medical Center, Portsmouth, Va.
Surgery Suite

Architect: Gresham, Smith and Partners, Nashville, Tenn.

This plan illustrates an OR suite that incorporates the "sterile core" concept in its layout. The OR rooms are wrapped around a central sterile core from which the rooms are serviced. The OR suite and central sterile supply were designed together with the "clean" and "dirty" sides in alignment with one another to allow clean materials and dirty materials to follow a circular flow, thus eliminating common paths of travel. Prep holding/recovery have been placed side by side so that each space may serve as a "swing space" for the other during peak demand times in each respective unit. Located around the periphery of the OR suite are surgical ICU, prep holding/recovery, anesthesia workroom, staff lounge, lockers and surgery waiting.

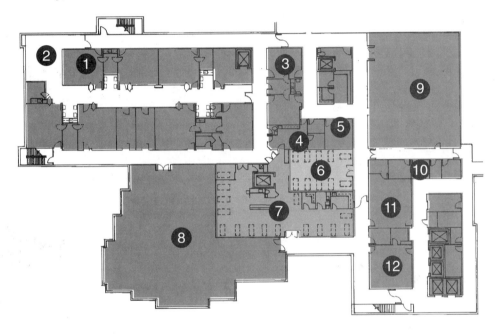

(Floor plan courtesy of Gresham, Smith and Partners.)

LEGEND—

1	Operating room	7	Recovery
2	Equipment storage	8	Surgical ICU suite
3	Endoscopy	9	Staff lounge/Lockers/Toilets
4	Anesthesia workroom	10	Office
5	General procedure	11	Surgery waiting
6	Holding	12	ICU waiting

Mayo Clinic, Scottsdale, Ariz.
Family Medicine Clinic

Architect: Smith, Hinchman & Grylls, Phoenix/Mahlum & Nordfors McKinley Gordon, Manhattan Beach, Calif.

This 16,400-sf primary care clinic utilizes the "Mayo planning concept," in which staff can view the full length of exam room corridors from a central patient-service desk. It has also been designed to minimize paperwork and storage requirements through an electronic medical records system, connected to other Mayo facilities. Voice and data communication outlets are provided in every exam room.

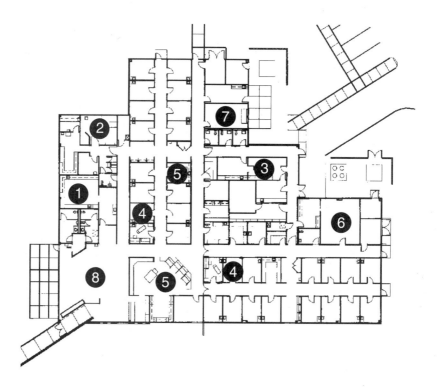

(Floor plan courtesy of Smith, Hinchman & Grylls.)

LEGEND—
1   Laboratory
2   X-ray
3   Procedure room
4   Exam room
5   Control station
6   Administrative
7   Conference room
8   Waiting

Metropolitan Hospital, New York
Neonatal/Labor & Delivery Suite Renovation

Architect: Urbahn Associates, Inc., New York

The departments are located side by side and are linked electronically; the neonatal staff is therefore prepared by the time a patient arrives. This renovation encompasses 20,000 sf on the hospital's fourth floor. The planning optimizes circulation of patients, staff and family members. A centrally located nursing station controls the entire area, thus freeing the staff to attend to the provision of care. The labor and delivery suite has four fully-equipped LDR rooms and two labor rooms, as well as two delivery rooms for invasive procedures. The neonatal unit has a capacity of 26 bassinets and is self-contained with both patient-care areas and support facilities located within the suite.

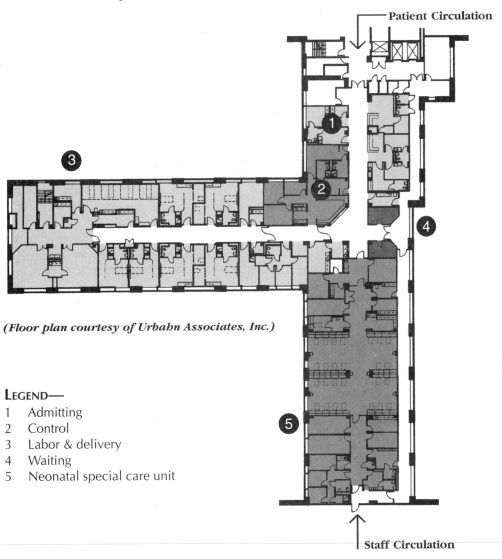

Patient Circulation

Staff Circulation

(Floor plan courtesy of Urbahn Associates, Inc.)

LEGEND—
1 Admitting
2 Control
3 Labor & delivery
4 Waiting
5 Neonatal special care unit

Mid Coast Hospital, Brunswick, Maine
Med-Surg Nursing Unit

Architect: Payette Associates Inc., Boston

The Med-Surg Nursing Unit is designed to provide each patient room with a toilet/ shower room along the exterior wall, which offers adaptability to a changing future— more sick and elderly inpatients. By relieving all functional aspects from the corridor wall, the plan can convert to a telemetry or intensive care unit with minimal disruption. Staff-to-patient adjacencies have largely reduced the distance factor common in conventional hospitals. The nursing station and support services form a triangle with good exposure and sight lines toward patient rooms on two sides of the pod. Four nursing units are combined on each floor allowing for cross-staffing between units. Exposure to outdoor spaces and natural lighting has been considered for the patient and the visitor. While the nursing-unit pods view the natural exterior landscape, an inner corridor for the general public surrounds an exterior courtyard. Public circulation is separate from patient areas to accommodate access to nursing-unit pods without disturbing patient privacy.

Typical Med-Surg Nursing Unit

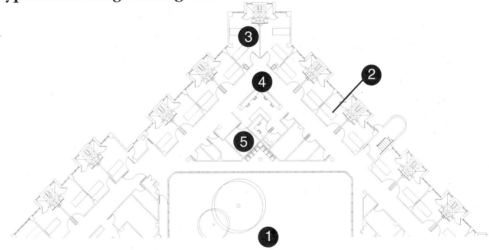

(Floor plan courtesy of Payette Associates Inc.)

LEGEND—
1 Courtyard
2 Private patient room
3 Semi-private patient room
4 Nursing station
5 Nursing support

Morristown Memorial Hospital, Morristown, N.J.
Emergency Department Renovation

Architect: The Hillier Group, Princeton, N.J.

The interior is designed to enhance the patients' sense of well-being while providing an improved workplace. Curved walls with colored accent finishes clearly define administrative locations and a separation between public and patient care spaces. New skylights located at the center core of acute care provide natural light.

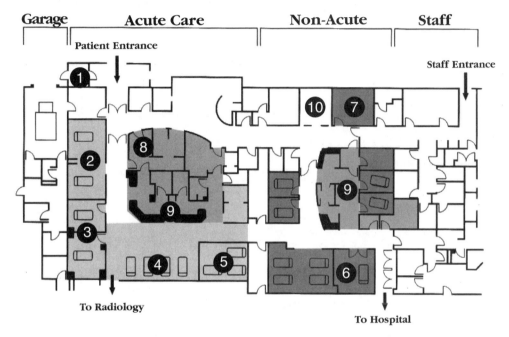

(Floor plan courtesy of The Hillier Group.)

LEGEND—
1 Decontamination shower
2 Trauma room
3 Cardiac exam
4 Open treatment
5 Pediatrics
6 Orthopedic
7 Eye/ENT exam
8 Triage/Registration
9 Nurse station/Patient support
10 Waiting room

Plastic Surgery Associates, Grand Rapids, Mich. Ambulatory Surgery Facility

Architect: Harley Ellington Pierce Yee Associates, Inc., Southfield, Mich.

Plastic Surgery Associates (PSA), a group of five plastic surgeons, requested a dual-function facility be designed within the Grand Plaza Place Building, an eight-story historic building adjacent to the Amway Grand Plaza Hotel. One function of PSA's program was to develop an office suite occupying one floor of the facility. The second function was a private, outpatient surgical suite with three operating rooms, which is located on the floor below the office suite. The surgical suite was designed primarily to serve as an area where elective cosmetic surgery could be performed.

(Floor plan courtesy of Harley Ellington Pierce Yee Associates, Inc.)

LEGEND—

1 Lobby
2 Reception
3 Recovery
4 OR's
5 Existing building

Rockdale Hospital, Conyers, Ga.
Surgery Suite

Architect: Lord, Aeck & Sargent, Atlanta

Rockdale Hospital's new surgery suite is organized for optimal patient and materials flow to maximize aseptic conditions. Ambulatory surgery patients enter through a new "greeting facility" which leads to the surgery suite from one side through pre-op. Leaving surgery, patients are led through the same side of the surgery suite to recovery areas. Inpatients are led to the surgery suite in elevators and then join the patient flow in pre-op. Materials are brought up on elevators from central sterilization and enter the surgery suite from the opposite side, never "encountering" the patient paths. Operating rooms are arranged in clusters of four around a surgical support "core."

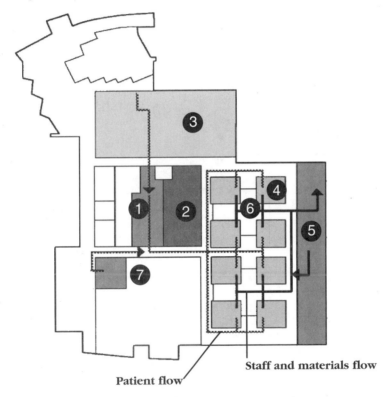

Staff and materials flow

Patient flow

(Floor plan courtesy of Lord, Aeck & Sargent.)

LEGEND—

1 Pre-operative procedures
2 Primary anaesthetic recovery
3 Outpatient first stage pre-op/
   Second-stage recovery
4 Operating room
5 Material support space
6 Surgical support core
7 Elevator from inpatient rooms

Rush North Shore Medical Center, Skokie, Ill. Gross Point Addition

Architect: Hansen Lind Meyer Inc., Chicago

The $17-million Gross Point Addition creates a new entrance and image for the hospital and updates medical services. The 100,000-sf project reorganizes the first floor as an "ambulatory mall" that includes such outpatient services as cardiology, radiology and endoscopy. The ambulatory surgery and presurgical services entrance is located directly off the lobby, offering patients the convenience of a freestanding surgery center with the benefits of a full-service hospital.

Adjacent to the surgery center are special diagnostic and treatment areas for minor outpatient surgery and endoscopic testing. The lobby entry corridor continues past an orientating courtyard directly to the major diagnostic centers of the hospital, including a post/anesthesia recovery/holding unit, sterile processing center, 12-bed medical ICU, and an eight-bed surgical ICU.

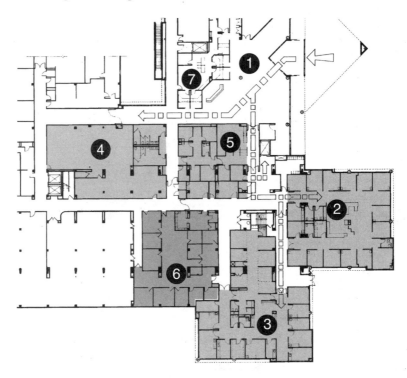

(Floor plan courtesy of Hansen Lind Meyer Inc.)

LEGEND—
1 Lobby
2 Ambulatory surgery
3 Special diagnostics/treatment
4 Breast imaging
5 Pre-surgical services
6 Administrative
7 Admitting

South Shore Hospital, South Weymouth, Mass.
Emergency Center

Architect: TRO/The Ritchie Organization, Newton, Mass.

The Center is designed with two primary zones: an acute-care unit for the more seriously ill or injured and an urgent care unit to accommodate and treat patients quickly. A triage/registration area and radiology suite serve both zones from a central location. Patients arrive either by ambulance, accessing the acute care unit directly, or as walk-ins through the ambulatory entrance. Upon arrival, walk-ins are greeted at reception and then seen by a triage nurse. After the degree of the emergency is ascertained, patients are directed to the appropriate unit.

The overall acute care unit is designed with 27 treatment areas clustered around a central nurses' station, which serves as a focal point, allowing the nurses continual visibility of a maximum number of patients.

Flexible general exam rooms convert to psychiatric treatment rooms through the use of pull-down walls that shield casework and equipment. Thus, the general exam room becomes an isolation room for the acute psychiatric patient. Also, the two trauma rooms can convert to one large critical care area in response to a crisis.

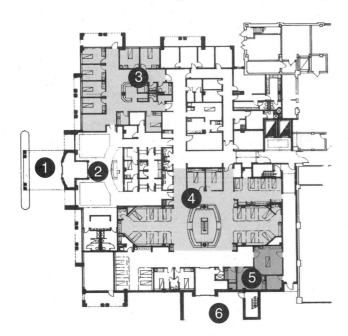

(Floor plan courtesy of TRO/The Ritchie Organization.)

LEGEND—
1   Main entrance
2   Lobby
3   Urgent care
4   Acute care
5   Critical care/Trauma
6   Ambulance entrance

Taylor Hospital, Ridley Park, Pa.
Department of Emergency Medicine

Architect: MPB Architects, Philadelphia

This emergency department is part of a new addition which includes a "short procedure unit" and an elevator tower. The nurses station is centrally located to afford full supervision of all treatment rooms as well as the ambulance entrance. A triage room is adjacent to the walk-in entrance allowing immediate screening of patients. An X-ray unit, a stat lab and a "chest-pain" suite were incorporated into the department for quick response time.

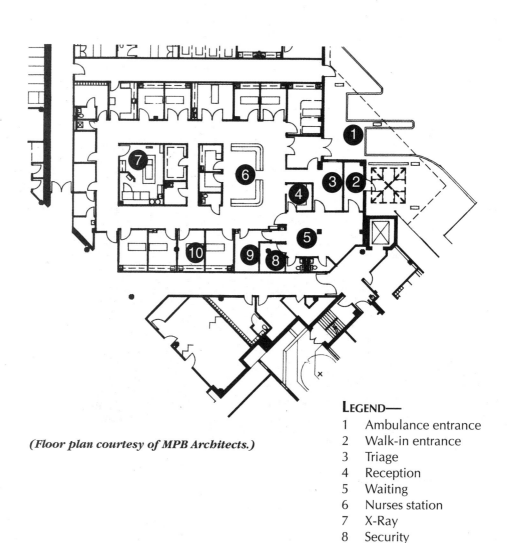

(Floor plan courtesy of MPB Architects.)

LEGEND—

1   Ambulance entrance
2   Walk-in entrance
3   Triage
4   Reception
5   Waiting
6   Nurses station
7   X-Ray
8   Security
9   Conference
10 Minor care treatment room

University of California—Davis Medical Center Tower II

Architect: Hammel Green and Abrahamson, Minneapolis

The typical nursing unit's floor plan is composed of three components: patient room, support core and caregiver station. All patient rooms (private, semi-private and isolation) are based on a consistent module, which provides planning flexibility through the facility's lifetime. Each room has corridor exposure along its full width. As a result, caregivers have a maximized view of patients, and patients have the greatest possible exposure to the exterior. Patient rooms surround the support core, a central zone for staff, supplies and other clean/soil functions. The logistics elevators are located here, so that supplies can be delivered or removed without mixing with patients, visitors and caregiver staff. The support core is bounded by four caregiver stations. Each station serves as a visual and physical portal, a connection between the support core and the seven to ten patients each station serves. These stations meet the needs of the nursing staff, physicians and residents, and a range of support staff (dietary, pharmacy, administration, etc.).

Typical Nursing Unit

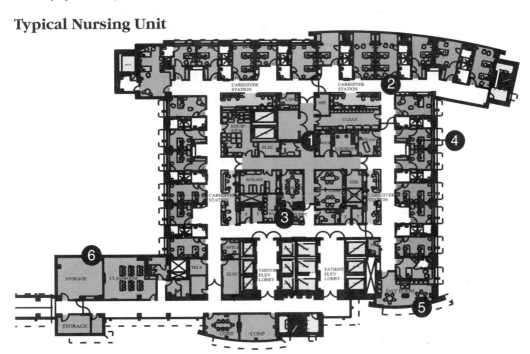

(Floor plan courtesy of Hammel Green and Abrahamson.)

LEGEND—

1   Support core
2   Care-giver station
3   Family reception
4   Typical patient wing
5   Day room
6   Conferencing/Classrooms/Decentralized support

University of California—San Francisco
Mt. Zion Cancer Center

Architect: Hammel Green and Abrahamson, Minneapolis

To achieve an intimate, human scale within the Cancer Center, the team designed a conceptual clinical module. Each clinical module located on the first, second and fourth floors features two small, distinct physician practice areas, which share common staff and support facilities. Each practice has its own waiting area, five exam/consulting rooms and one larger treatment/procedure room. Thus, patients experience a small waiting area and a single cluster of rooms, rather than anonymous, complex corridors.

First Floor with Typical Clinic Module

(Floor plan courtesy of Hammel Green and Abrahamson.)

Veterans Administration, Brooklyn, N.Y.
Ambulatory Care Addition

Architect: Urbahn Associates, New York

This 130,000-sf addition to the existing Brooklyn VA Medical Center consolidates all outpatient services in one newly organized building. The ground floor is planned around four clinic modules, each with approximately 25 exam rooms and a number of consultation rooms. Satellite radiology, specimen lab and patient benefits/social services are centrally located. The second level contains specialty clinics including ambulatory surgery, ENT, genitourinary, eye, podiatry, dermatology, ADTC and mental hygiene.

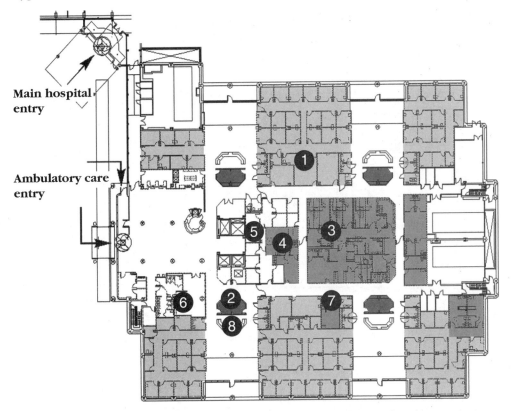

Main hospital entry

Ambulatory care entry

(Floor plan courtesy of Urbahn Associates, Inc.)

LEGEND—
1 Exam/Treatment/Consultation
2 Pharmacy consultation
3 Satellite radiology
4 Specimen lab
5 Benefits/Social service
6 Operations/Support
7 Orthopedics
8 Clinics control/Reception

Waukesha Memorial Hospital, Waukesha, Wis.
Intensive Care Unit

Architect: Engberg Anderson, Inc., Milwaukee

This 24-bed ICU was designed to be staffed by day in four separate nursing centers overseeing six beds each. At night, the central arena is divided into two nurse centers with responsibility for 12 beds each. In case of emergency, nurses from one side can assist those on the other. This design allows extremely flexible staffing and coverage for the unit. The articulated corners provide the hexagonal interior arrangement for superior visibility into all rooms from the nurses centers.

The location of the addition was chosen for direct access to the surgery wing and cath labs with closest beds designated for heart surgery pre-op and post-op care. Head walls in patient rooms were custom-designed to ease nursing staff movement and to accommodate current heart surgery post-op equipment.

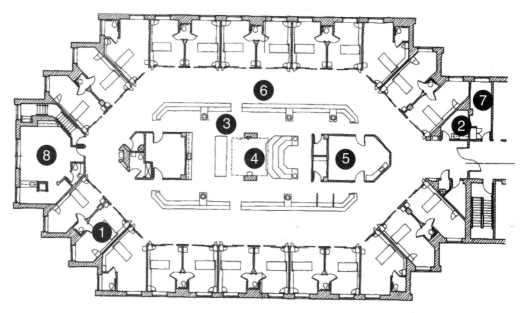

(Floor plan courtesy of Engberg Anderson, Inc.)

LEGEND—
1   ICU
2   Soiled holding
3   Nurse center
4   ICU pharmacy
5   Clean supply
6   Corridor
7   Head nurse
8   Lounge/report

Del E. Webb Memorial Hospital, Sun City West, Ariz. Emergency & Ambulatory Services Expansion

Architect: Smith, Hinchman & Grylls, Phoenix

A new front door guides patients to a central registration area, used for all hospital services. A new emergency department, registration area and waiting areas were provided in the expansion and the existing emergency department was renovated to crate a new endoscopy suite for a total project of 15,000 sf.

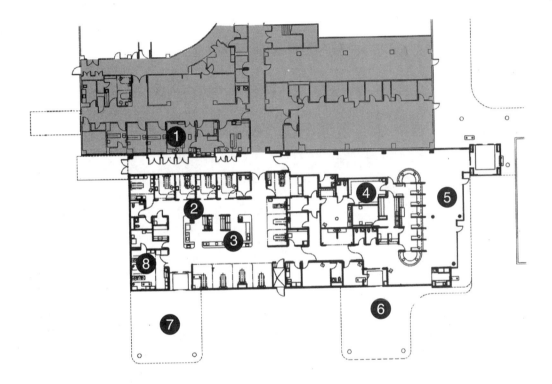

(Floor plan courtesy of Smith, Hinchman & Grylls.)

LEGEND—
1. Endoscopy
2. Treatment
3. Nurse station
4. Conference room
5. Waiting
6. Drop-off
7. Ambulance
8. Trauma

West Allis Memorial Hospital, West Allis, Wis.
Emergency Department Renovation

Architect: Flad & Associates, Madison, Wis.

This renovated emergency department is located directly adjacent to outpatient treatment areas. A triage desk, located near the walk-in entry, allows the staff to determine which patients are in need of the most urgent care. Patients with less urgent health problems are sent to a separate "Fast Track" treatment area within the department. This area has its own staff and waiting areas, as well as smaller, less extensively equipped treatment rooms.

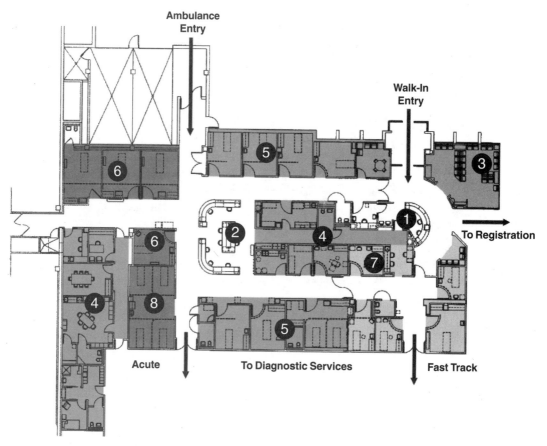

(Floor plan courtesy of Flad & Associates.)

LEGEND—

1	Triage	5	Acute treatment
2	Staff workstation	6	Trauma
3	Waiting	7	"Fast-track" area
4	Support	8	Observation

Pharmaceutical/Biotechnology Production Facilities

Bausch & Lomb Pharmaceuticals, Inc., Tampa, Fla.
Production Facility

Architect: Flad & Associates, Madison, Wis. and Gainesville, Fla.

The interior arrangement of Bausch & Lomb Pharmaceuticals' production facility supports the required aseptic environment and equipment that facilitates the flow of people and materials. Upon entering the complex, a long, light-filled space greets and directs incoming visitors and employees while functioning as the unifying link between the primary elements of the facility. Strategically placed along this skylit vestibule lie the people-driven spaces of the offices and research labs, while the process and equipment-driven areas are more internalized and recessed into the suites. With the potential need for expansion, the design of flexible laboratory and office modules became a key objective for the project. The logical organization of these spaces facilitates vertical expansion, while removable precast concrete panels along the north facade foster horizontal expansion for production and warehousing.

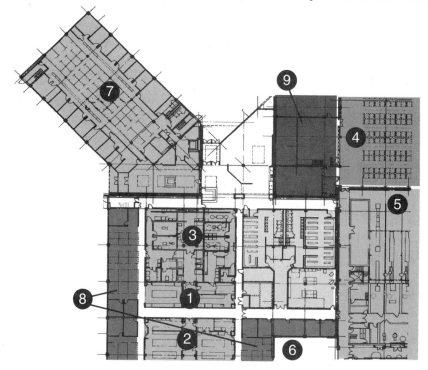

(Floor plan courtesy of Flad & Associates.)

LEGEND—

1 R&D labs
2 Quality control labs
3 Development pilot plant
4 Warehousing
5 Packaging
6 Process Waste Systems
7 Administrative
8 Office
9 Support

Hybridon, Inc., Milford, Mass.
cGMP Pilot Production Plant

Architect: Raytheon Engineers & Constructors, Cambridge, Mass.

The pilot plant layout shown below was designed on the basis of 25′ x 30′ modules, which are all interchangeable as process suites or laboratories. The space comprises class 100,000 clean rooms, entry/exit air locks and four process suites, two of which will be used initially as analytical labs—to be fit out for process in the future.

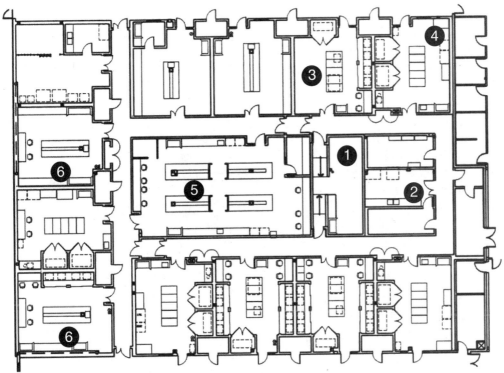

(Floor plan courtesy of Raytheon Engineers & Constructors.)

GROUND FLOOR PLAN—

1   Solution prep
2   Glass wash
3   Synthesis suites
4   Purification suites
5   QC labs
6   Process-development labs

Miles Biotechnology, Berkeley, Calif.
Media Production Facility 5A

Architect and Engineer: GEZ Architects Engineers, San Francisco

The open floor plan with wide door entry is optimal for movement of large portable drums. The centralized staging area (1) is shared between the cold room for in-building fermentation use (2) and the storage cold room for fermenters in remote buildings (3). Incoming materials enter through a staging area (4) and empty drums enter through an automated drum washer (5). Media ingredients are transferred into batch size volumes within the chem weigh area (6), reducing the idle time for the mix tanks (7). The floor plan enables the sterilizing filters to move in an efficient manner from cleaning (8) through assembly and sterilization (9) and into media preparation and filtration (10). Gowning space is conserved because the same gown room (11) is used for entry to the media area and the cleaning room, which is at a lower bioclean classification.

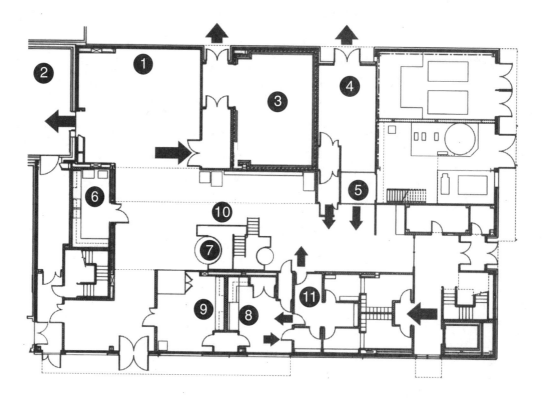

(Floor plan courtesy of GEZ Architects Engineers.)

R&D FACILITIES

Allergan, Inc., Irvine, Calif.
Research & Development Facility II

Architect: The Blurock Partnership, Newport Beach, Calif.
Lab Planner: Earl Walls Associates, San Diego

Laboratories in Allergan's new three-story facility occupy a middle ground between "generic" and "customized" in that they are designed to accommodate specific scientific disciplines rather than individual investigators. For flexibility, all utilities, HVAC systems and ceiling and lighting layouts in the 10'6" x 27' modules are configured to allow easy partitioning of each lab along the module lines. Service corridors (12' wide, 16' high) run parallel to the labs, doing dual duty as utility distribution routes and lab support zones. The areas provide space for noisy, bulky, hazardous or heat-producing devices that typically clutter the labs.

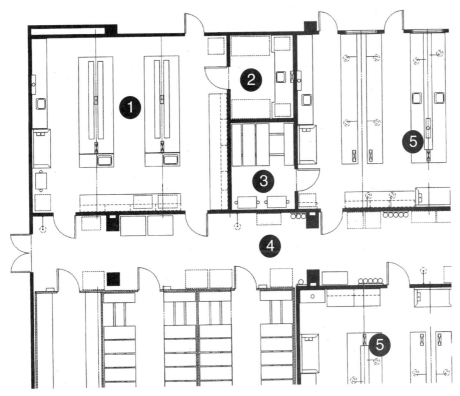

(Floor plan courtesy of The Blurock Partnership.)

LEGEND—
1   Double module biology lab
2   Procedure room with biosafety cabinets and incubators
3   Storage room
4   Service equipment corridor
5   Pharmaceutical labs

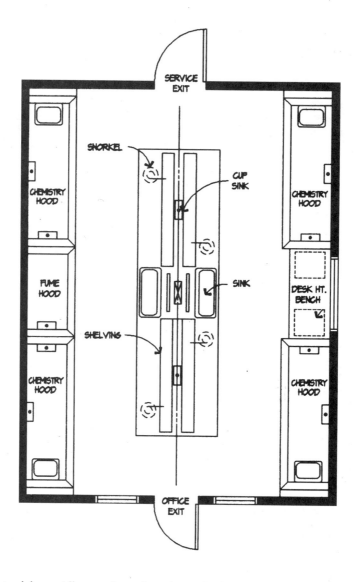

Chemistry labs at Allergan (see above) are double-module, four-person rooms with a fume hood for each scientist and a small island bench in the middle of the room. To enhance safety, scientists are provided with large, flush-sill, horizontal-sash fume hoods.

Biology labs (see previous page) consist of two to six modules, with two to four small procedure rooms right off the lab. Most of these labs contain one fume hood, as scientists here tend to use more biosafety cabinets in their work.

The two blocks of pharmaceutical labs on the third floor (see previous page) are the largest—one more than 100 feet long. Pharmaceutical researchers require only a few fume hoods but a lot of bench space for instruments. Split benches with an 18" aisle between them provide convenient access to all utility connections for instruments.

BASF Bioresearch Corporation, Worcester, Mass. Biomedical Research Center

Architect/Engineer: Smith, Hinchman & Grylls, Detroit

The research center was planned to maximize functional efficiency, direct daylighting (a legal requirement in Germany) and proximity to labs and offices. Overall functional interrelationships are intended to optimize adjacencies of pharmaceutical/biotechnology research with central technical services and administrative support, and at the same time, segregate animal care from GMP pilot plant operations.

The typical laboratory suite has been developed with four double module laboratories and eight, 144-sf Ph.D. scientist offices. Each suite has clerical support, storage, gathering space, a unit kitchen and interconnecting stair. Each 700 sf of laboratory module accommodates two Ph.D. scientists and four to six associates. Generic labs are fitted out to accommodate either cell culture/cell biology, molecular biology/biochemistry, protein chemistry or wet chemistry configurations. Each suite has corridor-accessible utility distribution shafts with gas cylinder storage. The lab modules also provide flexibility for incremental fit-out of partitions and utility systems of shelled space.

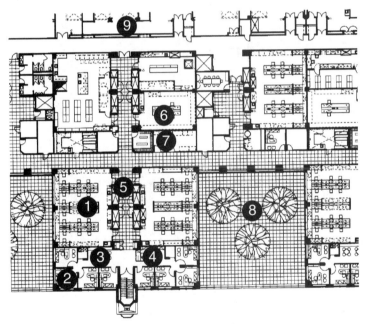

(Floor plan courtesy of Smith, Hinchman & Grylls.)

LEGEND—		
1	Double-lab module	5 Utility shaft
2	Research office	6 Process development lab
3	Gathering space	7 Scientific support
4	Clerical/Files	8 Courtyard
		9 Pilot plant

Biogen, Inc., Cambridge, Mass.
Biology and Chemistry Labs

Architect: Payette Associates Inc., Boston

The biology laboratories and offices for Biogen's new research facility accommodate 12 researchers in one open lab space with four private offices and eight tech desk areas at the perimeter. The chemistry laboratories accommodate eight researchers in one lab space with four private offices and four tech desk areas at the perimeter. Strict size requirements for offices forced the boundaries to stretch beyond the length of the lab. This has created an extension which is a major architectural component on the building exterior.

The ceilings step up from the corridor and equipment spaces through the lab and the office zone in order to maximize the penetration of natural light.

The benches are not centered on the structural grid, which allows for an easy coordination with the mechanical trades. A shared equipment room between two labs, and atypical laboratories at the edges complete the "rhythm."

Chemistry Research Laboratory—8 person module

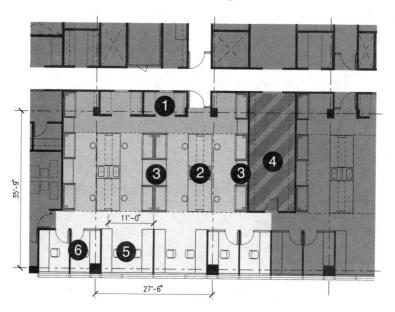

(Floor plans courtesy of Payette Associates Inc.)

Biology Research Laboratory—12 person module

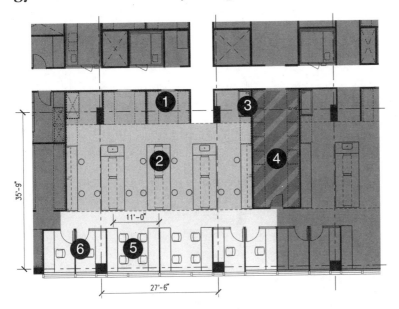

LEGEND—

1. Equipment alcove
2. Bench
3. Fume hood
4. Shared equipment
5. Tech desk area
6. Principal investigator's office

Brigham and Women's Hospital, Boston
Longwood Medical Research Center

Architect: Tsoi/Kobus & Associates, Cambridge, Mass.

This biomedical research facility replaced a demolished wing of the historical Boston Lying In Hospital for Women; zoning laws, close abutters on three sides and the building complex defined the new wing's floor plate and low floor-to-floor heights. An efficient, flexible and economical floor zoning system was necessary to accommodate various types of medical research. Consequently, spaces with similar functions are stacked vertically and building systems are run through vertical chases, minimizing horizontal distribution. At opposite corners of this typical floor are office suites and generous conference and lounge/kitchen areas. The area between is left open for laboratories along the perimeter and shared lab support facilities in the core.

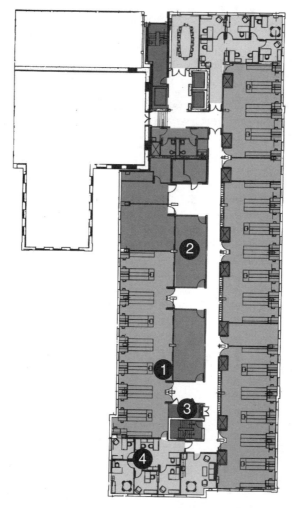

LEGEND—
1 Laboratory
2 Lab support
3 Vertical circulation
4 Administrative

(Floor plan courtesy of Tsoi/Kobus & Associates.)

The Cancer Therapy & Research Center, San Antonio
The Alice McDermott Building

Architect: Kell Muñoz Wigodsky Architects, San Antonio

A classical plan for a bio-sciences research facility with public access at one end, private circulation at the other, and a "block" of laboratories and support spaces located in between. Laboratories and the adjacent offices are located along the exterior walls sharing common support areas in the central core. The building is two stories; level two is shown below. Level one is organized in similar fashion with the lobby located on the left side.

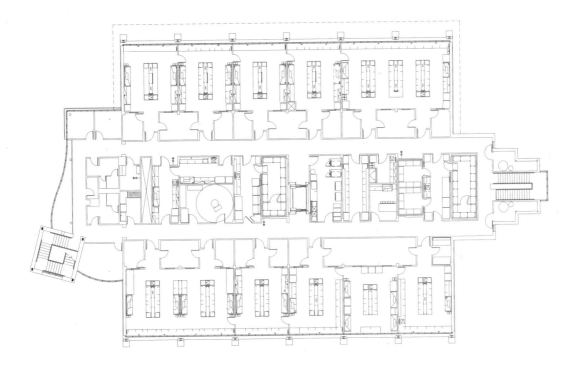

(Floor plan courtesy of Kell Muñoz Wigodsky Architects.)

Children's Hospital Of Philadelphia Research Building

Architect: Ellenzweig Associates, Inc., Cambridge, Mass.

This new pediatric research building is designed with 63 generic laboratory modules, arranged to ensure the most functional, versatile floor layout and configured to accommodate larger or smaller research groups. Each module is designed to accommodate two or three researchers at each 15-foot bench, for a total of 12 to 18 researchers per module. Flexibility is thus achieved for the possible future expansion of the research staff by up to 50 percent. The typical module provides half of the researchers' desks in the laboratory itself, and half in separately enclosed adjacent write-up areas, promoting flexibility as well as safety.

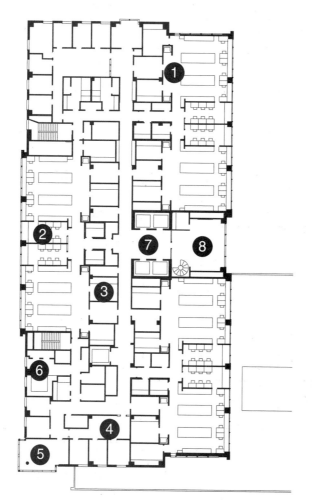

LEGEND—

1   Research laboratory
2   Desk room
3   Lab support
4   Office suite
5   Conference room
6   Glass wash
7   Elevator lobby
8   Lounge

(Floor plan courtesy of Ellenzweig Associates, Inc.)

David Axelrod Institute For Public Health, Albany, N.Y.

Architect: Urbahn Associates, Inc., New York

This new research facility replaces an accumulation of aging, obsolete buildings dating back to 1917. The planning of the three laboratory floors implements a concept of generic labs adjacent to utility corridors. Modular casework and equipment, combined with ease of access to utility corridors, enables each investigator to customize labs to specific work requirements. Modular lab components are warehoused and inventoried within the building, thereby eliminating lead time for installation. Each cluster of generic labs is provided with ample support space which consists of environmental rooms, equipment rooms, darkrooms and offices. Animal services and Biosafety Level 3 Containment labs are included.

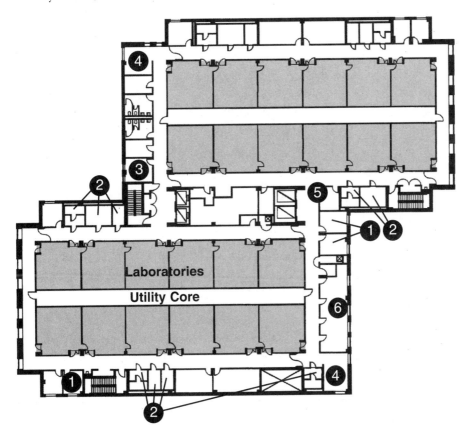

(Floor plan courtesy of Urbahn Associates, Inc.)

LEGEND—
1 Office
2 Controlled temperature room
3 Conference room
4 Employee lounge
5 Darkroom
6 Storage

DowElanco World Headquarters, Indianapolis
Research and Development Building—Lab modules

Architect: JBA Architects, Newark, Ohio

DowElanco's Research and Development facility includes both semi-enclosed and open-plan laboratories based on a 10′ x 30′ planning module. The majority of semi-enclosed spaces are three modules in width with open access to adjacent labs, as well as cross access through the service corridor to labs. Open-plan spaces have no walls between labs and service corridors, making it easier to accommodate changes in bench layouts and restructuring of research teams. Workstations are directly adjacent to labs and employ both open- and closed-plan configurations; offices are placed near "people" corridors and receive natural light through the atrium spaces.

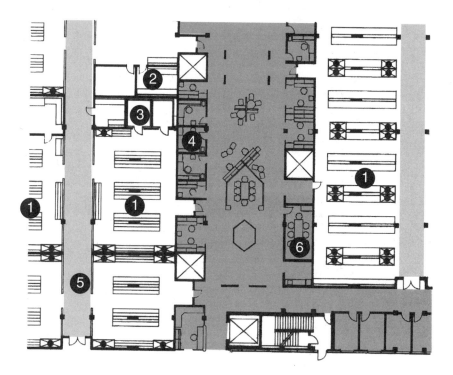

(Floor plan courtesy of JBA Architects.)

LEGEND—

1   Laboratory
2   Hot lab
3   Cold room
4   Office
5   Conference room
6   Service corridor

Eli Lilly and Company, Indianapolis, Ind.
New Research Building

Architect/Engineer: CUH2A, Inc., Princeton, N.J.

Interaction among researchers of different disciplines can foster the advancement of science, as demonstrated in this pharmaceutical research facility. Shared areas within each wing provide an opportunity for scientists to interact with members of like disciplines, while a central atrium with common functions allows interaction among various disciplines within the same therapeutic areas. The two different specialties of chemistry and biology are linked together through this common area, which includes functions at various floors such as an auditorium, a project team room, a periodical reading room, conference rooms, and informal lounge/break areas.

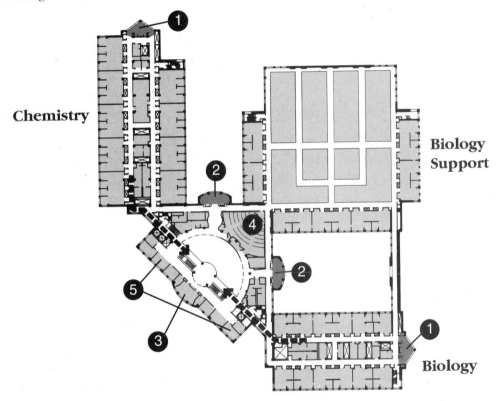

(Floor plan courtesy of CUH2A, Inc.)

INTERACTION SPACES—

1 Break - Informal within discipline
2 Lounge - Informal between disciplines
3 Reading - Informal between disciplines
4 Auditorium - Formal between disciplines
5 Administration areas - Managers, offices, meeting rooms, mail distribution, vending rooms

Ford Motor Company, Dearborn, Mich.
Scientific Research Laboratory

Architect: Harley Ellington Pierce Yee Associates, Inc., Southfield, Mich.

This three-story, 185,000-gsf addition to Ford's existing research complex houses new flexible research laboratories for chemistry and physics. L-shaped in plan, the addition parallels two existing research wings and is separated by a new three-story atrium space. Modular labs are located along a central 12'-wide service corridor. Office areas are located along the exterior building and atrium perimeters. Access to the existing building runs through the atrium via pedestrian bridges.

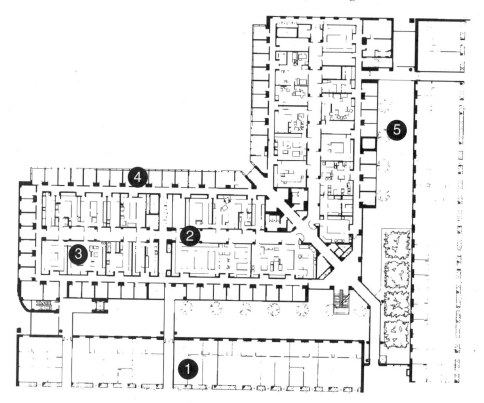

(Floor plan courtesy of Harley Ellington Pierce Yee Associates, Inc.)

LEGEND—
1   Existing building
2   Service corridor
3   Laboratory
4   Office
5   Atrium

Hewlett-Packard Company, Wilmington, Del.
Analytical Products Facility Lab Modules

Architect: Ellerbe Becket, Washington, D.C. and Minneapolis
Lab Planner: GPR Planners Collaborative, White Plains, N.Y.

Versatility is a key issue in this facility because the labs house a variety of users with different requirements including prototyping, chemical tests and specialized research projects. Lab benches are 14' by 30" deep to allow additional space for equipment and provide a seven foot workstation for each researcher. Two rows of benches, separated by a 6'-wide ghost corridor, stretch across the 36'-wide labs. Always perpendicular to the outside walls, the benches can be arranged in any combination of configurations—single-sided, back-to-back, split or traditional back to back— thanks to the flexible perimeter utility distribution scheme.

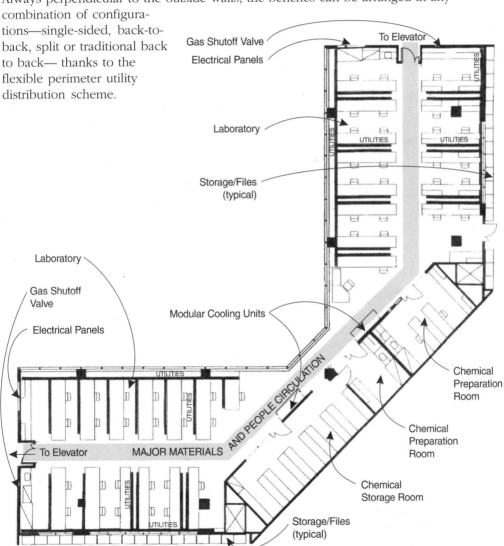

(Floor plan courtesy of Ellerbe Becket.)

Hoechst-Roussel Pharmaceuticals Inc., Bridgewater, N.J. Molecular Neurobiology Building Lab Modules

Architect/Engineer: CUH2A, Inc., Princeton, N.J.

This molecular neurobiology laboratory addition features an open lab to encourage sharing of resources, team interaction, and group involvement in research activities. The primary open lab has a zone of benches and fume hoods at the center with shared equipment rooms on one side and open office workstations on the other. This strengthens the relationship between lab, lab office and lab support spaces and allows natural light into both the lab and office spaces. The open lab "concept" enhances flexibility, since research team space can easily expand and contract as needed without major renovations or functional compromises. Dedicated specialized labs requiring physical separation from other activities are located on the opposite side of the corridor.

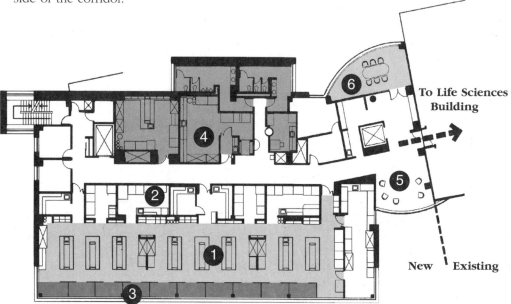

(Floor plan courtesy of CUH2A, Inc.)

LEGEND—
1 Laboratory
2 Shared lab support
3 Lab office
4 Specialized lab
5 Break/Interaction space
6 Conference room

IDEC Pharmaceuticals Inc., San Diego
R&D Facility

Architect: McGraw/Baldwin Architects, San Diego

An existing two-story office building was modified to house a vivarium, pilot production plant, research laboratories and administrative offices for IDEC Pharmaceuticals Inc. Each of these functions was located based on adjacency, site access, security and FDA requirements. The vivarium has a receiving area and is separated from other functions to eliminate the risk of contamination. The pilot plant uses an isolated shipping/receiving area with a loading dock to control the flow of raw materials and finished product. Pilot plant rooms are arranged in a product-flow sequence and are connected to the research labs via a "soiled" corridor. Laboratories and offices are located to take advantage of the internal courtyard and exterior views. The entry bridge, which leads to the lobby, library and conference rooms also serves to shield the vivarium loading dock located beneath the entry.

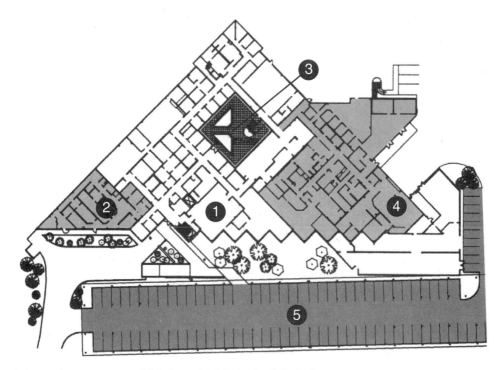

(Floor plan courtesy of McGraw/Baldwin Architects.)

LEGEND—
1 Laboratory/Office
2 Vivarium
3 Courtyard
4 Pilot plant
5 Parking deck

Immulogic Pharmaceutical Corporation, Waltham, Mass. Headquarters R&D Center

Architect: Raytheon Engineers & Constructors, Cambridge, Mass.

Shown below is the second-floor plan of a renovated, three-story, 80,000-sf integrated R&D facility. The laboratories were designed on an open, modular basis at the interior, with windows on the corridor. The perimeter offices have interior windows to allow light penetration to the labs. Common personnel spaces such as conference rooms, library, break areas and lobby are located in the center of each floor. Central glass wash, animal facility and materials support areas are on the ground floor. Pilot plant and development labs are located on the third floor.

Second Floor

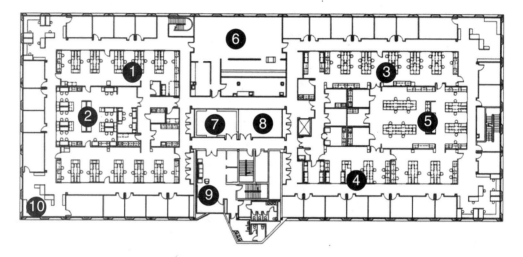

(Floor plan courtesy of Raytheon Engineers & Constructors.)

LEGEND—

1   Immunology lab
2   Tissue culture
3   Molecular biology lab
4   Peptide synthesis lab
5   Protein chemistry lab
6   Break room & kitchen
7   Library
8   Conference room
9   Lobby/Core
10   Perimeter office

James River Corporation, Cincinnati Technology and Business Center

Architect: Baxter Hodell Donnelly Preston, Inc., Cincinnati

This section of the technology center includes research and development laboratories and sensory testing areas, all of which are located directly adjacent to a pilot plant and a warehouse. The lab area in the technical center is the focal point of all new product development. It consists of open lab modules with split benches, an adjacent bank of constant temperature/constant humidity rooms and a sensory and evaluation test center.

Lab Neighborhoods

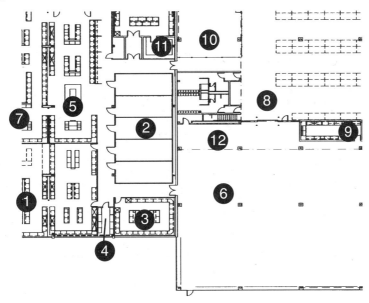

(Floor plan courtesy of Baxter Hodell Donnelly Preston, Inc.)

LEGEND—

1. Product development lab area
2. Constant temperature/Constant humidity room
3. TAPPI condition laboratory
4. Chemical dispensing room
5. Expandable lab module
6. Pilot plant
7. Analytical lab
8. Warehouse
9. Quality-control lab
10. Machine shop
11. Pre-conditioning room
12. Engineering department

Lederle-Praxis Biologicals, Rochester, N.Y.
Vaccine Research Facility

Architect: Flad & Associates, Madison, Wis.

The functional service systems of LPB's new facility were envisioned and designed as essential components making up the entire building. The plan provides a service corridor, or "spine," which successfully brings together many functions. Stemming from this spine is a second-floor clerestoried library. The structure also features a cantilevered entrance canopy and administrative wing.

Known as "Main Street," the spine integrates circulation and service systems within the building. Main Street cleanly bisects the building, with modular labs and lab offices to either side, which are in turn supported by the mechanical and electrical services stemming from the spine. The glass-lined corridor also facilitates interaction among researchers, administration and office support staff by providing an interface between the labs and researcher workstations.

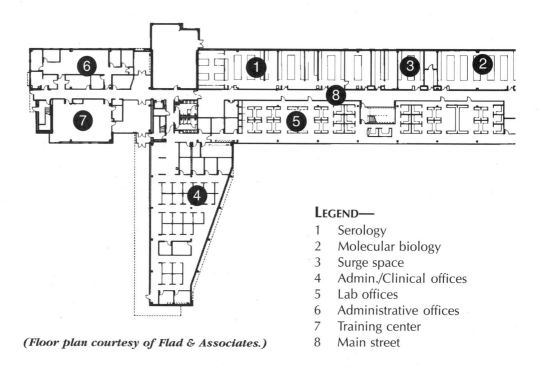

(Floor plan courtesy of Flad & Associates.)

LEGEND—

1 Serology
2 Molecular biology
3 Surge space
4 Admin./Clinical offices
5 Lab offices
6 Administrative offices
7 Training center
8 Main street

Metropolitan Water District Of Southern California, La Verne, Calif.
Water Quality Laboratory Expansion

Architect: Stone Marraccini Patterson, Santa Monica, Calif.

This addition to the Metropolitan Water District Water Quality Lab adds 31,000 sf and approximately doubles the size of the existing facility. The building is zoned into three distinct parts: (1) research laboratories for chemistry and microbiology, (2) new administrative and conference facilities and (3) a demonstration and testing greenspace for 'xeriscape' water-conservation landscaping. The landscape between these zones provides appropriate sun orientation; the laboratories have access to north light, administration and open offices to south light. The connection of these wings is through glazed corridors and the entry lobby/exhibition space. This blurs the boundaries of outside and inside making the landscape fully accessible for staff and tour groups. These corridors which continue from the existing circulation run north and south and terminate at the main conference room. The building is frequented by tour groups from around the world examining water-quality research.

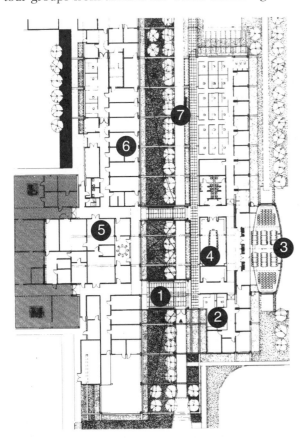

LEGEND—

1 Lobby/Waiting
2 Administrative
3 Conference room
4 Library
5 Instrument room
6 Microbiology laboratory
7 Xeriscape display garden

(Floor plan courtesy of Stone Marraccini Patterson.)

Parke-Davis/Warner Lambert, Ann Arbor, Mich.
Pre-Clinical Pharmaceutical Research Laboratory

Architect: Harley Ellington Pierce Yee Associates, Inc., Southfield, Mich.

This four-story, 131,000-gsf research facility features a highly efficient and flexible rectangular floor plate. Generic eight-person laboratories are located on each side of a central shared equipment zone. Laboratory offices (7' x 14') are located on the building perimeter separated from the labs by a "ghost corridor." Administrative offices are located on each level at opposite corners. The central equipment zone is capable of transforming to an animal holding area in the future. The lobby is located in an-adjacent one-story component.

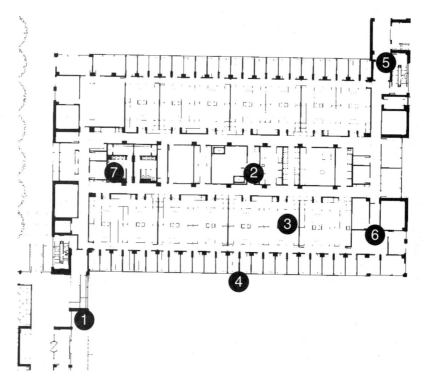

(Floor plan courtesy of Harley Ellington Pierce Yee Associates, Inc.)

LEGEND—

1 Lobby
2 Shared equipment
3 Laboratory
4 Laboratory offices
5 Receiving
6 Administrative
7 Interaction

Pharmakon USA, Waverly, Pa.
Toxicology Research Facility

Architect: The Henderson Design Group, Inc., Raritan, N.J.

This new, stand-alone, 22,000-sf toxicology research facility has been designed to allow for future expansion. The design centralizes the facility's support functions within a single limited-access corridor that can be lengthened to accommodate a future wing.

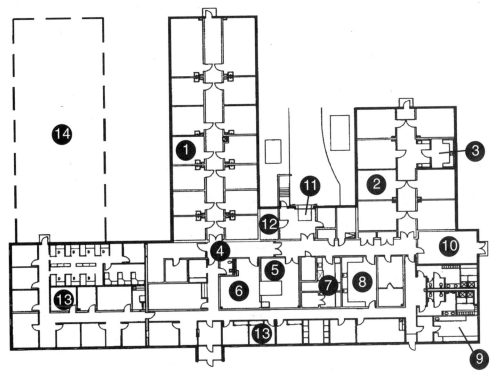

(Floor plan courtesy of The Henderson Design Group, Inc.)

LEGEND—

1	Small animal rooms	8	Necropsy
2	Dog rooms	9	Clinical pathology lab
3	ECG room	10	Mechanical room
4	Limited access corridor	11	Receiving
5	Cage wash (dirty)	12	Quarantine
6	Cage wash (clean)	13	Administration
7	Pharmacy/diet prep	14	Future small animal wing

Physikalisch-Technische Bundesanstalt, Braunschweig, Germany Reinraumzentrum (Cleanroom Center)

Architect/Builder: Siemens

The 810-m² (net) cleanroom space is designed as ten modules, 8.400 m x 9.600 m each. Each module has its own temperature control. Modules can be joined together by removing partitions, connecting ductwork and opening dampers in the basement air-return space.

Large tanks for liquid and gaseous nitrogen are housed in a screened enclosure behind the building. This area also contains a duplex air compressor with twin-cell driers.

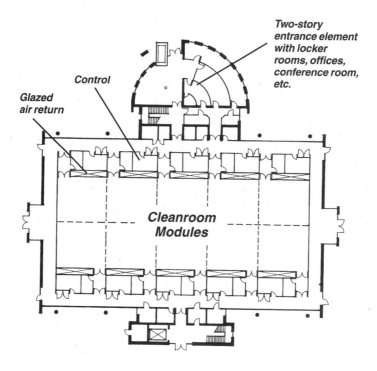

(Floor plan by Physikalisch-Technische Bundesanstalt, courtesy of HDR, Inc.)

Promega Corporation, Fitchburg, Wis.
Biopharmaceutical Technology Center

Architect: Strang, Inc., Madison, Wis.

The new Biopharmaceutical Technology Center provides specialized training and education rooms for public and private use. Labs meet FDA Good Manufacturing Practices and accommodate a variety of production methods including protein refolding, resin manufacturing, large-scale cell biology, organic synthesis, electromagnetic separations, dialysis and precipitation, lyophilization, ultrafiltration and large-scale buffer manufacturing.

(Floor plan courtesy of Strang, Inc.)

LEGEND—

1 Research office/ Conference area
2 Laboratory
3 Lab support
4 Service corridor
5 Crossroad

The Upjohn Company, Kalamazoo, Mich.

Architect/Engineer: The Austin Company, Des Plaines, Ill.

In this plan Upjohn laboratories and an associated administrative area are served by a central core of shared laboratory support facilities. These shared-core facilities will ultimately serve thirteen lab modules and include those areas listed below as well as miscellaneous equipment and storage rooms. By grouping and sharing these common support functions and equipment, facility costs are reduced and laboratory space can be utilized more efficiently. Grouping of laboratories and support functions also creates a concentration of staff members which in turn helps foster communication, interaction and teamwork. Glass is used in the corridor walls to help promote this cooperation.

Central Core Support Functions

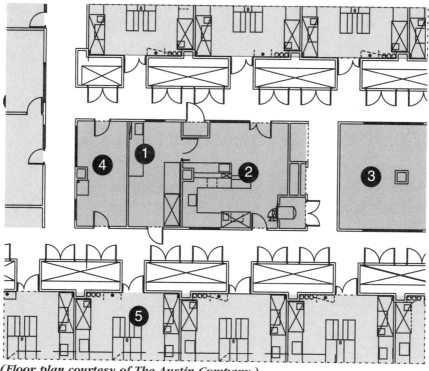

(Floor plan courtesy of The Austin Company.)

LEGEND—

Central Core Facilities
1 Tissue culture lab
2 Tissue prep room
3 Central instrument room
4 Scintillation counting rooms

Perimeter Facilities
5 Laboratory modules w/scientists offices
6 Administrative

The Upjohn Company, Kalamazoo, Mich.

Architect/Engineer: The Austin Company, Des Plaines, Ill.

The public lobby serves to separate and control visitor access to the facility. The lobby is a non-secured public space containing a waiting area, conference rooms, toilet and telephone facilities as well as the security control desk. Placement of these functions in the lobby allows for interaction between Upjohn staff and non-security-cleared visitors without penetrating the secured areas of the facility. Security-cleared visitors can be escorted by Upjohn staff through the facility. From the control desk the receptionist/security guard can electronically control door locks, loading dock doors, parking lot and perimeter security devices. Electronic card control systems and closed circuit television provide efficient and effective security.

Public Access Security Issues

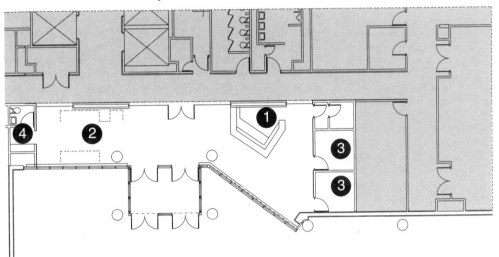

(Floor plan courtesy of The Austin Company.)

LEGEND—

Public Areas
1 Control desk
2 Waiting area
3 Visitor conference rooms
4 Toilet and telephone area

Secured Areas
5 Central core elevators and toilets
6 Seminar room and associated amenities

Training and Conference Facilities

Eagleville Hospital, Eagleville, Pa.
Center for Drug and Alcohol Rehabilitation

Architect: MPB Architects, Philadelphia

The flexible layout of the training center allows for conferences ranging in size from 12 to 300 people. The facility will be used for patient activities, community outreach and regional drug and alcohol conferences. The facility is organized along a skylit gallery tied to parking by way of a pedestrian bridge. The building also houses the hospital's admissions, detox and physical medicine departments.

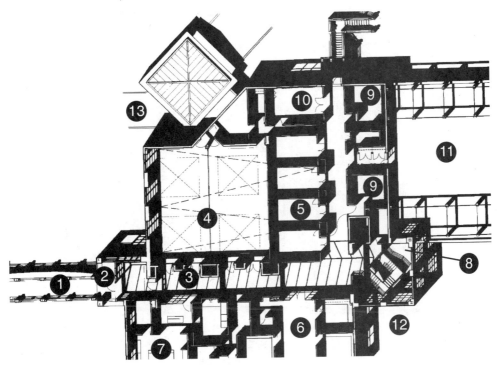

(Floor plan courtesy of MPB Architects.)

LEGEND—

1   Bridge to drop-off for visitors & conference attendees
2   Entrance for visitors, conference & training attendees
3   Skylit gallery
4   Large "subdivisible" meeting rooms (200 capacity total)
5   Small "subdivisible" meeting rooms (20 capacity each)
6   Library
7   Records administration
8   Two-story atrium
9   Toilets
10 Conference room
11 Trellis deck (future expansion)
12 Campus entrance (lower level)
13 Admissions entrance (lower level)

Household International, Prospect Heights, Ill.
Edwin P. Hoffman Career Development Center

Architect: Loebl Schlossman and Hackl, Inc., Chicago

Lacking adequate training space in their headquarters, this company built a new facility on their corporate campus to meet their needs for additional training space more efficiently. Located 300 feet from the main facility, the Career Development Center provides training areas near the headquarters. The first level contains a training room, five breakout rooms, a lounge, dining room and full kitchen. A monumental stair ascends to the second level where additional training rooms, adjacent breakout rooms and office space are provided. Corporate intern programs take place in the lower level, where trainees observe senior executive meetings and have access to private study carousels with computers.

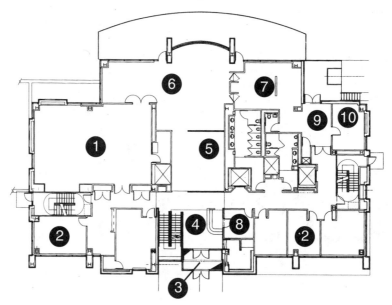

(Floor plan courtesy of Loebl Schlossman and Hackl, Inc.)

LEGEND—

1 Training room
2 Breakout rooms
3 Vestibule
4 Entry
5 Lounge
6 Dining room
7 Kitchen
8 Work room
9 Receiving
10 Storage

Howard Hughes Medical Institute, Chevy Chase, Md.
Conference Center

Architect: The Hillier Group, Princeton, N.J.

Located at HHMI's headquarters, the conference center is organized around a central foyer with a beamed ceiling, couches and chairs. Off this main entrance area are the auditorium, group meeting rooms and an enclosed garden. Small groups—of 10 to 20—meet in one of two 200-sf rooms, with a break-out area furnished like a living room nearby. Another small room can hold up to 16 people, each at a computer, for training on the Institute's business systems. Two 800-sf rooms, outfitted with audio-visual and computer projection equipment, hold groups of 20 to 40, depending on the way furniture is configured.

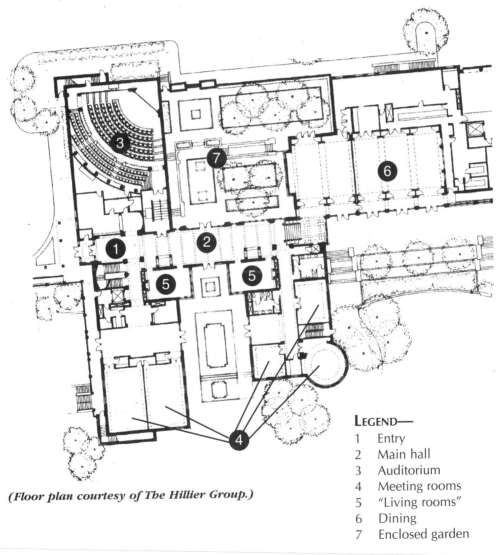

(Floor plan courtesy of The Hillier Group.)

LEGEND—
1   Entry
2   Main hall
3   Auditorium
4   Meeting rooms
5   "Living rooms"
6   Dining
7   Enclosed garden

Illinois Institute of Technology, Chicago
Chicago-Kent College of Law

Architect: Holabird & Root, Chicago
Interiors: Powell/Kleinschmidt, Chicago

The plan for this new ten-story law school is designed for the efficient movement of students and faculty between the lower, populated classroom floors while accounting for the privacy required for the upper, library and faculty-office floors.

An ornamental staircase unites the lower level through third floors, supplementing elevator usage at peak times between classes and offering an expansive open area in which students and faculty can mingle. The elevator core is located on the exterior wall which abuts an adjoining building, allowing maximum daylight exposure for the faculty offices and library on the upper floors.

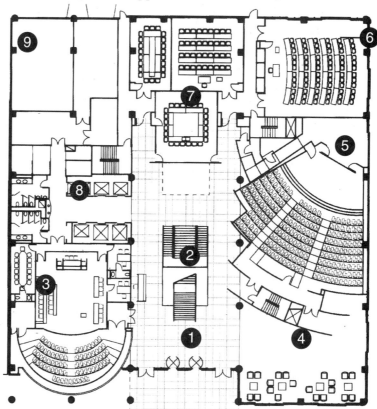

(Floor plan courtesy of Holabird & Root.)

LEGEND—

1 Main entrance	5 Auditorium
2 Ornamental staircase	6 Classroom
3 Moot courtroom	7 Seminar room
4 Lounge/Preconvene	8 Elevator core
	9 Loading dock/Support

Palmetto International Exposition Center, Greenville, S.C.
James H. Woodside Conference Center

Architect: HOK (formerly CRSS) Architects, Inc., Greenville, S.C.

This addition to Palmetto International Exposition Center provides a new "front door" and improves circulation for the entire facility. The massing of the building pulls the structure away from the existing loading dock, creating an exterior courtyard. A sky-lit monumental wall separates the new facility from the existing facility.

First Floor

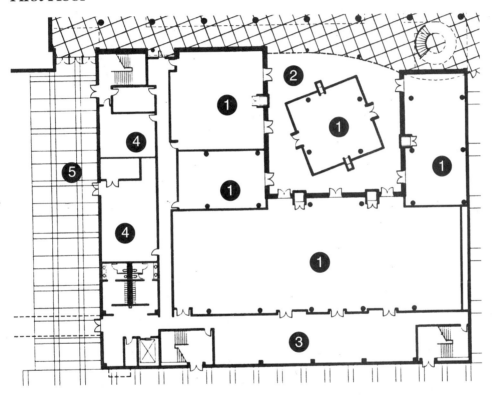

(Floor plan courtesy of HOK Architects, Inc.)

LEGEND—
1 Meeting room
2 Prefunction
3 Service area
4 Mechanical
5 Courtyard

Plymouth Rock Assurance Company, Boston
Computer Training Rooms

Architect: Leslie Saul & Associates, Boston

This corporate training center features training rooms, library, a model office and a PC training room. Wherever possible, the building's existing column coffers have been kept as a design element. In the PC training room, plexiglass panels at the top of the wall allow more light into the room. To maximize available space, the furniture carries and conceals electrical and computer cabling. Ergononmic seating with narrow dimensions was selected.

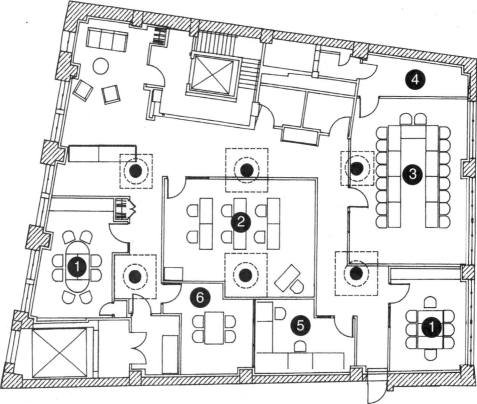

(Floor plan courtesy of Leslie Saul & Associates.)

LEGEND—

1 Breakout room
2 PC training room
3 Training room
4 Storage
5 Model office
6 Library

UNIVERSITY SCIENCE FACILITIES

Emory University, Atlanta
Chemistry Building Addition

Architect: Cooper Carry and Associates, Inc., Atlanta

Designed to house two new research initiatives in biomolecular and materials chemistry, this project reflects current laboratory-planning concerns in the zoning of its program components. To provide a safe environment for graduate students and other lab occupants (traditionally housed in the lab) the project incorporates segregated office suites adjacent to the laboratories. Lab processes are monitored from these offices through windows or electronically. Flexible, shared-support spaces are housed centrally along the main corridor.

Total net area for the project is 27,000 sf. Total gross area is 50,100 sf.

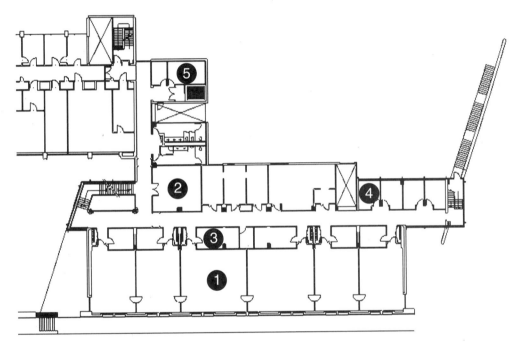

(Floor plan courtesy of Cooper Carry and Associates, Inc.)

LEGEND—
1   Research laboratory
2   Research laboratory support
3   Lab tech/Grad student office
4   Faculty office
5   Core support

Emory University, Atlanta
Physics Building

Architect: Cooper Carry and Associates, Inc., Atlanta

The plan for the physics facility was developed to accomplish a three-fold range of educational goals. Research laboratories and related support space, balanced for a mixture of experimental and theoretical work, will allow the development of a medium-sized, highly competitive graduate program in physics. Classroom and laboratory instructional space will allow the department to maintain its excellent undergraduate major programs in physics and applied physics. The astronomy facilities will allow the department to offer a program of laboratory-based physical science instruction for non-science majors.

Total net area for the project is 53,100 sf, with 21,450 nsf occupied by research laboratories and 8,580 nsf occupied by teaching laboratories. Total gross area for the facility is 87,947 sf.

LEGEND—
1   Administration
2   Lecture
3   Classroom
4   Auditorium/Planetarium
5   Faculty/Researcher office
6   Laboratory research
7   Laboratory support
8   Quadrangle terrace

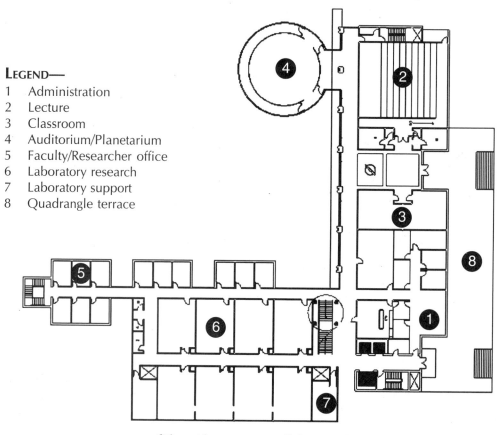

(Floor plan courtesy of Cooper Carry and Associates, Inc.)

Harvard Medical School, Boston
Medical Education Center

Architect: Ellenzweig Associates, Inc., Cambridge, Mass.

This medical teaching facility was designed in response to Harvard's innovative curriculum which emphasizes small-group, hands-on, problem-based learning over the traditional lecture-based approach. A three-story skylit commons encourages student-student and student-faculty interaction, essential to this new curriculum. For formal instruction, the building contains a deep-U, tiered floor, case-study method classroom, as well as five "skills areas." These clusters of small group meeting rooms and spontaneous discussion areas, each grouped around a 40-seat classroom, replace the traditional laboratory in Harvard's curriculum. The skills areas are laid out so that classes can break into small groups and recombine into larger sessions. These spaces are flexible enough to accommodate both the case-study approach and traditional lecture-based teaching.

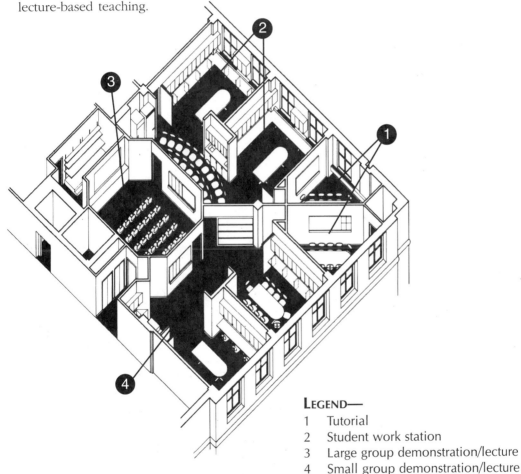

LEGEND—

1   Tutorial
2   Student work station
3   Large group demonstration/lecture
4   Small group demonstration/lecture

(Floor plan courtesy of Ellenzweig Associates, Inc.)

Indiana University, Bloomington, Ind.
Chemistry Building

Architect: Harley Ellington Pierce Yee Associates, Inc., Southfield, Mich.

This 85,000-gsf chemistry building addition was designed to create a new entry to the chemistry complex while occupying minimal ground area. The addition is comprised of two four-level wings wrapped around the existing building. A new entry is formed at the intersection of the two wings allowing access to each, and creating a small exterior courtyard. Teaching labs are housed in one wing, research labs in the other. All labs are modular in design.

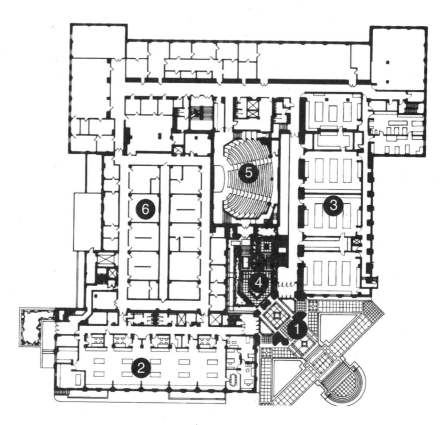

(Floor plan courtesy of Harley Ellington Pierce Yee Associates, Inc.)

LEGEND—
1   New entry
2   Research laboratories
3   Teaching laboratories
4   Courtyard
5   Remodeled auditorium
6   Existing building

Massachusetts of Technology, Cambridge, Mass.
Biology Building No. 68

Architect: Goody, Clancy & Associates, Boston

This 250,000-sf, six-story building contains research laboratories and associated support spaces and offices on the five lab floors (levels two through six); administrative headquarters and meeting spaces on the first floor; teaching lab in the basement; and an animal care facility on the sub-basement level.

A critical design determinant was to facilitate informal communication among the researchers. This typical laboratory grouping (part of a larger floor plan) focuses on a central point of arrival and gathering for the researchers who work in the surrounding labs and share the tea and conference rooms.

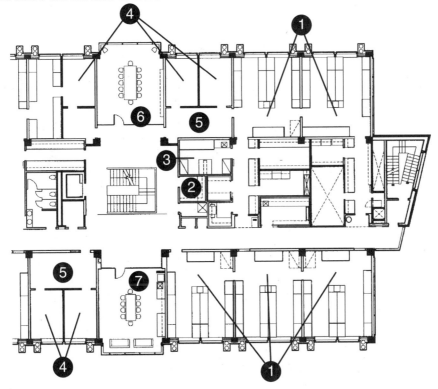

(Floor plan courtesy of Goody, Clancy & Associates.)

LEGEND—

1   Laboratory
2   Hot lab
3   Tissue culture
4   Faculty office
5   Administrative office
6   Conference room
7   Tea room

Medical College of Pennsylvania, Philadelphia
Queen Lane Campus Building

Architect: Ewing Cole Cherry Brott, Philadelphia

Formerly a publishing facility, this building houses administration, academic and research areas. The three-story structure also has two new 150-seat auditoriums and a library. Administrative functions are grouped around the main entrance. Student and classroom functions—including flexible-use classrooms, teaching labs, a book store and cafeteria—are clustered on one side of the semi-circular structure. Research activities—including microbiology/immunology, pathology, biochemistry and physiology labs, offices, technical support spaces and a vivarium—are on the other side. Both student and research areas have separate entrances from the main entrance, allowing users direct, secure access to their wings of the building.

LEGEND—

1   Student services (lounge, book store, etc.)
2   Administration
3   Cafeteria
4   Lecture halls
5   Library
6   Main entrance
7   Laboratories

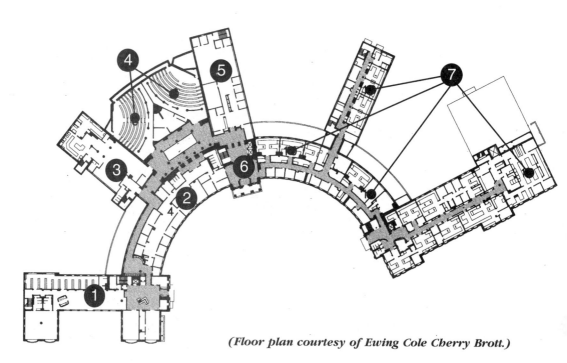

(Floor plan courtesy of Ewing Cole Cherry Brott.)

Northern Illinois University, De Kalb, Ill.
Faraday Hall West

Architect/Engineer/Interiors: Holabird & Root, Chicago

This new building provides additional space for Northern Illinois University's science facilities. The west facade of the building faces the main street, while the second-floor bridge to the east provides a connection between the new Faraday Hall West and the existing Faraday Hall East. The new building houses physics, biology and chemistry departments. Spaces which contain heavy equipment or generate noise such as shops, storage rooms and mechanical areas are located at the lower level. Frequently used general-purpose spaces such as classrooms, lecture halls and teaching laboratories are located on the entry level. This arrangement provides easier access from the main entrance for the general student population and concentrates the most populated spaces near the lobby and three-story stair, which visually connects the new and the existing Faraday Halls.

The majority of the special-use functions such as faculty offices and research laboratories are located on the second, third and fourth floors. This layout allows faculty to be adjacent to their research and teaching laboratories, and away from general classroom space. The office spaces interface between the existing and new buildings. The skylit "street" on the fourth floor visually links the corridor spaces from floor to floor with light that filters down between articulated mechanical services.

Second Level

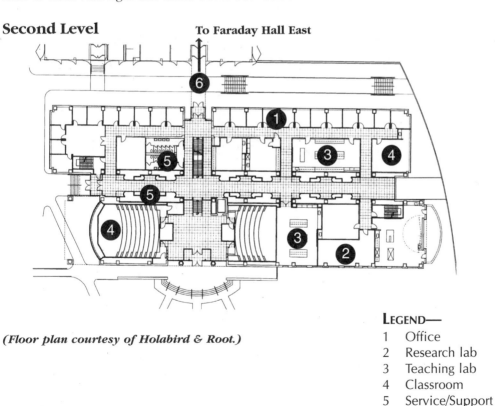

(Floor plan courtesy of Holabird & Root.)

LEGEND—
1 Office
2 Research lab
3 Teaching lab
4 Classroom
5 Service/Support
6 Bridge

Rutgers University, New Brunswick, N.J.
Foram Hall, Cook & Douglas Colleges

Architect: Haines Lundberg Waehler, New York

This facility, designed to accommodate plant sciences research, houses a dedicated research institute (A); faculty and graduate research labs and support for an academic department (B); a teaching laboratory (C); and shared academic and research support functions (D). The difference in the layout of lab wings reflects differences in organization style between collaborative industry — academic research and departmental academic research functions. The organization of the ground floor is intended to promote communication between faculty, students and the larger campus community.

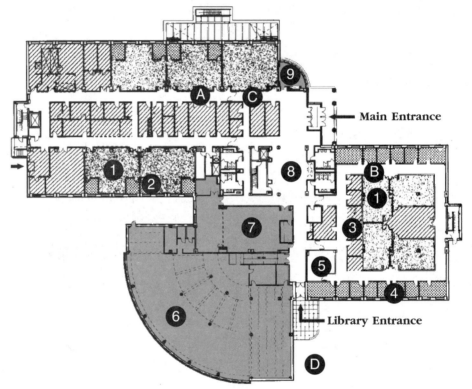

(Floor plan courtesy of Haines Lundberg Waehler.)

LEGEND—

1	Laboratory	5	Conference room
2	Lab office	6	Library
3	Support	7	Seminar room
4	Faculty/Graduate student offices	8	Lobby
		9	Break area

Stanford University, Stanford, Calif.
Medical School Lab Surge Building

Architect: Stone Marraccini Patterson, San Francisco

The typical lab floor plan features two banks of four- or six-person labs flanking a central core of support spaces. Circulation is achieved via use of a perimeter personnel corridor complemented by two service galley areas adjacent to the lab support core. The service galleys provide non-fire-rated circulation space within the core and serve a lab support function. The main administrative offices are located at one end of the plan which allows an office-occupancy classification to complement the hazardous-occupancy classification of the labs. The atrium space enhances the environment and provides a unifying entry space for the building.

Typical lab floor

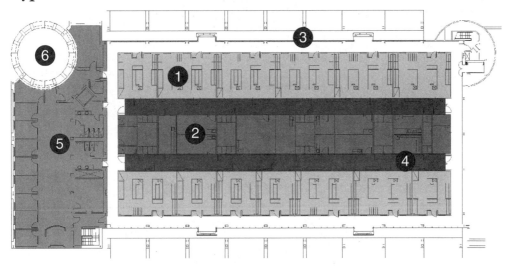

(Floor plan courtesy of Stone Marraccini Patterson.)

LEGEND—
1 Laboratories
2 Lab support
3 Personnel corridor
4 Service gallery
5 Office area
6 Atrium

Texas A&M University, Corpus Christi, Texas
Classroom/Laboratory Building

Architect: Kell Muñoz Wigodsky Architects, Houston

A new academic building built in a conventional "L"-shaped plan, the large lecture halls and stairways provide geometric interest at the intersecting corner. Repetitive classrooms lie along both legs of the "L". The building is three stories with similar organization on level two and faculty offices on level three.

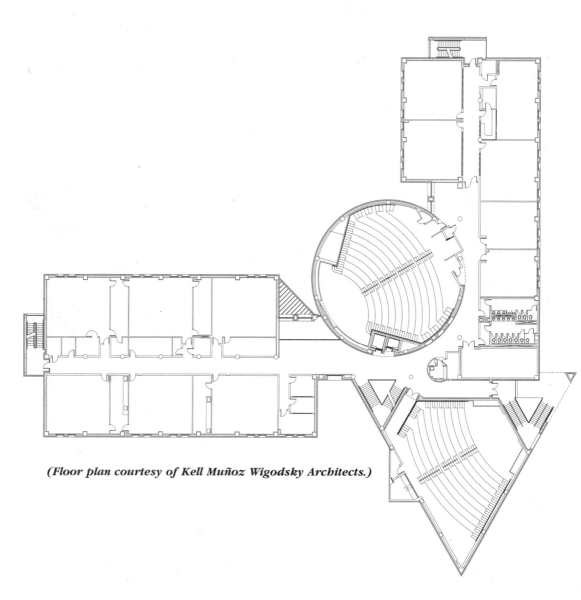

(Floor plan courtesy of Kell Muñoz Wigodsky Architects.)

University of California-Berkeley
Chemistry Unit III

Architect: Stone Marraccini Patterson, San Francisco

Chemistry Unit III contains research and teaching laboratories, a lecture hall, and offices on seven above-ground floors and two below-ground floors. On the typical lab floor, seven lab modules are located on either side of a central corridor system. Student work spaces are located along sun-shaded east and west exterior facades, adjacent to labs. Faculty offices clustered at the north have views of a formal green space. To the south, interaction space allows passersby to stop in a sunlit environment.

Typical lab floor

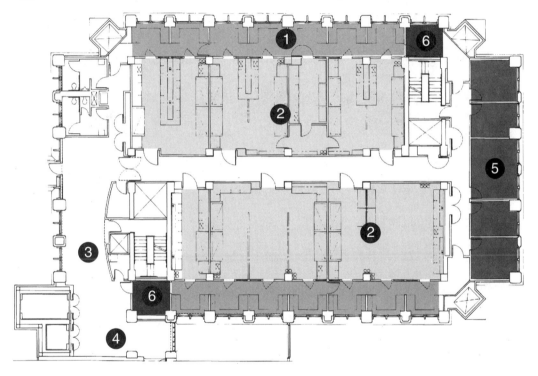

(Floor plan courtesy of Stone Marraccini Patterson.)

LEGEND—

1. Post-graduate student office and work space
2. Laboratories
3. Interaction space
4. Elevator lobby
5. Professor's office
6. Teaching assistant work space

University of California - San Francisco
Mt. Zion Research Building

Architect: Stone Marraccini Patterson, San Francisco

The typical floor plan accommodates four lab suites (each with four lab modules), clustered in pairs around common support and mechanical areas. Each suite serves three principal investigators and shares some lab functions with the adjacent suite, in order to maximize the use of common equipment. The modular design provides maximum flexibility for future changes in the type of research and space configuration.

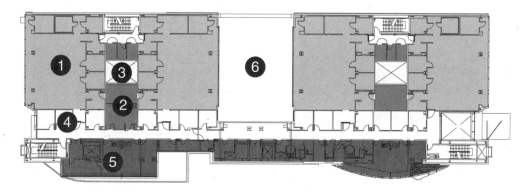

(Floor plan courtesy of Stone Marraccini Patterson.)

LEGEND—

1   Lab suite
2   Shared lab functions
    (instrument room, glass wash, etc.)
3   Shared mechanical spaces
4   Principal investigator offices
5   Common support spaces
    (Conference rooms, storage, secretarial, etc.)
6   Courtyard

The University of Chicago
The Biological Sciences Learning Center and The Jules F. Knapp Medical Research Building Complex

Prime Architect: Loebl Schlossman and Hackl, Inc., Chicago
Design Architect: The Stubbins Associates, Inc., Cambridge, Mass.

This university research center for molecular medicine is attached to the teaching center through shared atrium space which contains lounges, elevators and a 'grand' stair to encourage interaction between all facility users. A typical floor in the research center houses general laboratory spaces on two exterior walls and offices for principal researchers on a third, allowing natural light to penetrate these heavily used areas. Desk space for technicians is located within the laboratories along the windows. Shared support areas, including conference rooms, equipment rooms, environmental rooms, sterilizer and clerical spaces are clustered in the central core.

Second Level

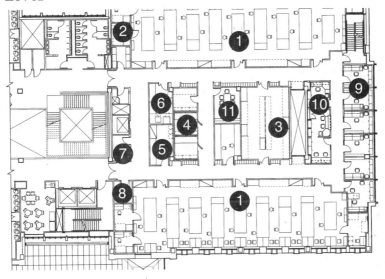

(Floor plan courtesy of Loebl Schlossman and Hackl, Inc. and The Stubbins Associates, Inc.)

LEGEND—

1 General laboratory
2 Tissue culture
3 Equipment room
4 Environmental room
5 Isotope laboratory
6 Sterilizer
7 Storage
8 X-Omat
9 Principal researcher office
10 Clerical support
11 Conference room

The University of Chicago
The Biological Sciences Learning Center and The Jules F. Knapp Medical Research Building Complex

Prime Architect: Loebl Schlossman and Hackl, Inc., Chicago
Design Architect: The Stubbins Associates, Inc., Cambridge, Mass.

Designed to embody the philosophy of a "one-room schoolhouse" for biological sciences, this teaching facility was planned to encourage interaction between students, faculty and research at all levels. A central atrium, which includes shared lounges, vertical circulation and other support spaces, connects the teaching and research areas. Each floor of the Learning Center is organized with teaching laboratories and classrooms around the perimeter, while support facilities, including darkrooms, utilities and preparation spaces, are positioned in the central core.

Second Level

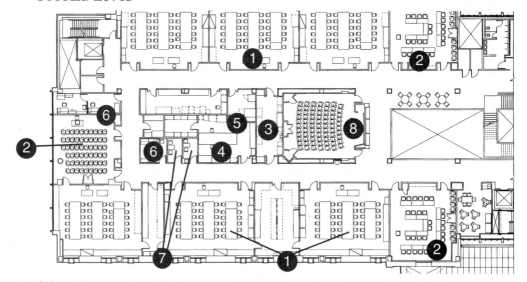

(Floor plan courtesy of Loebl Schlossman and Hackl, Inc. and The Stubbins Associates, Inc.)

LEGEND—
1   Teaching laboratory
2   Lecture/Classroom
3   Equipment room
4   Preparation
5   Sterilizer
6   Office
7   Faculty/Student conference
8   Lecture room

The University Of Chicago
The Biological Sciences Learning Center and The Jules F. Knapp Medical Research Building Complex

Prime Architect: Loebl Schlossman and Hackl, Inc., Chicago
Design Architect: The Stubbins Associates, Inc., Cambridge, Mass.

This floor of the Center houses specialized use areas in addition to lecture rooms and classroom spaces. The special use areas include animal holding facilities and a computer education suite. The computer suite includes a room of workstations for independent or group work, a lecture/training room for use of computers in biological science investigations, and staff space for curriculum development. These areas have access flooring to provide flexibility for computer installation. The arrangement of this floor follows the general building layout with laboratory and teaching spaces on the perimeter and support spaces in the central core.

Lower Level

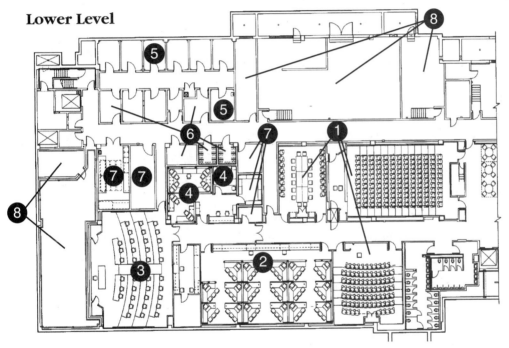

(Floor plan courtesy of Loebl Schlossman and Hackl, Inc. and The Stubbins Associates, Inc.)

LEGEND—

1 Lecture room/Classroom
2 Computer workstations
3 Computer lecture/Training
4 Curriculum development
5 Animal holding
6 Animal holding support
7 Storage
8 Utility

University of Florida, Gainesville, Fla.
Chemistry Building

Architect: Flad & Associates, Gainesville, Fla.

Laboratory Planner: Earl Walls & Associates, San Diego

This design for the department of chemistry provides wet and dry labs for laser research; magnetic-resonance imaging; mass spectrometry; electron microscopy; and physical, organic and inorganic chemistry. The plan optimizes net area through the use of a double-loaded corridor laboratory model. Offices are provided within the moduled laboratory block to maximize the direct access to the laboratories. An adjacent teaching auditorium is zoned as a separate building component to allow for virtually independent use for the college as a whole or specifically for the department of chemistry.

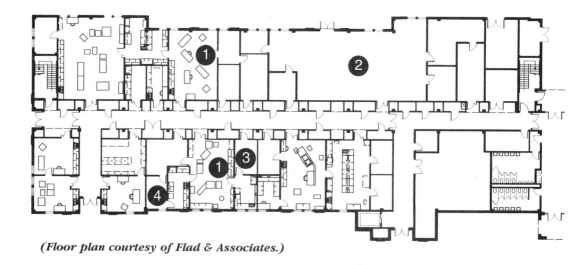

(Floor plan courtesy of Flad & Associates.)

LEGEND—

1   Laboratory
2   Main shop
3   Graduate student office
4   Faculty office

University of Maryland at Baltimore
Medical Research Building

Architect: Henningson, Durham & Richardson, Inc., Alexandria, Va.

This generic bio-medical research facility houses the department of biological chemistry and will in the future act as interim laboratories for other medical school departments. It provides spaces for specialized labs (spectroscopy), an administrative office area, meeting rooms and facility support.

All labs are located on the exterior at the front and rear and principal investigator offices are placed between the labs and the corridor system with large glass openings in both directions. Support activities are located in the interior zone. The lab modules are organized around four zones of shaft space in order to reduce duct runs and make it possible to fit within the existing 10′-8″ to 12′-0″ floor heights. Fume-hood alcoves are located adjacent to the shafts.

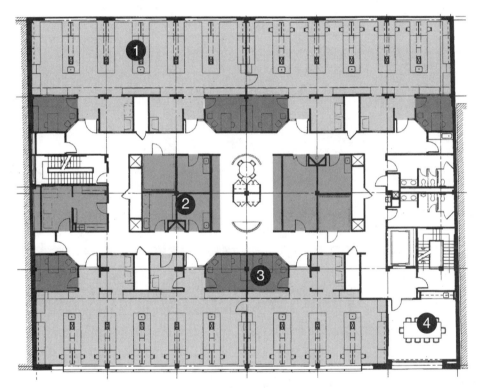

(Floor plan courtesy of Henningson, Durham & Richardson, Inc.)

LEGEND—

1 Laboratory	2 Support
3 Office	4 Conference

University of Massachusetts, Amherst, Mass. Polymer Research Center

Architect: Ellenzweig Associates, Inc., Cambridge, Mass.

This new research building is organized as a laboratory block attached to a nearly separate office block. This arrangement segregates those functions requiring heavier construction and more intensive mechanical systems from those which can be accommodated by conventional construction. This approach, well suited to laboratory facilities containing significant office and conference space, achieves substantial cost savings, increases safety and fosters interaction. The added penthouse height of the laboratory block makes an effective transition from a connecting 16-story research tower to the lower office block.

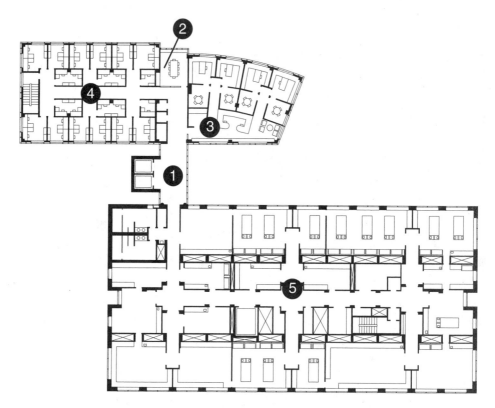

(Floor plan courtesy of Ellenzweig Associates, Inc.)

Legend—

1 Elevator lobby
2 Lounge
3 Faculty office
4 Student office
5 Research laboratories

University of Wisconsin-Madison
Grainger Hall of Business Administration

Architect: The Zimmerman Design Group, Milwaukee.

In addition to an auditorium with theater seating, Grainger Hall of Business Admin-istration contains two lecture halls, each seating about 130. Seventeen medium sized classrooms (900-1,100 sf with seating for 43-60) all feature a curved seating layout so occupants can see each other, thus fostering an interactive instructional atmosphere. Six classrooms (450-600 sf with seating for 24-27) are flat floored and have movable tables and chairs. There are also two computer classrooms on the second floor.

All classrooms are in the building's interior for better control of light, particularly during multi-media presentations. Corridors on the perimeter provide well-lit gather-ing places before and after class. To get maximum use of space, the classrooms' entrances are in the front or instructional area of the room. Rear-entry rooms require more gathering space behind the last row of tiered seats.

Second Floor

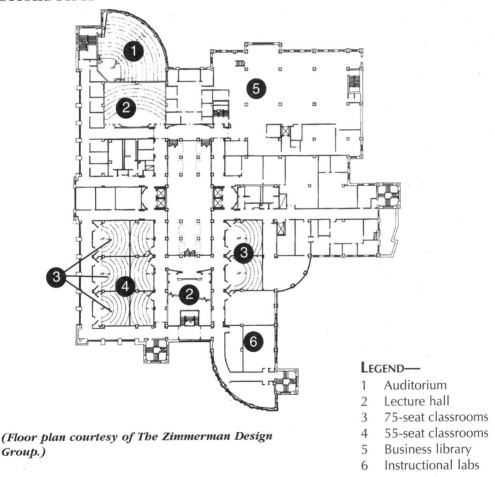

(Floor plan courtesy of The Zimmerman Design Group.)

LEGEND—

1   Auditorium
2   Lecture hall
3   75-seat classrooms
4   55-seat classrooms
5   Business library
6   Instructional labs

Virginia Commonwealth University, Richmond, Va. Medical Sciences Building

Architect: Henningson, Durham & Richardson, Inc., Alexandria, Va.

Each of the six lab floors in the Medical Sciences Building is designed with a racetrack corridor and a plan configuration that allows up to ten double-lab modules per floor. Each floor is a mix of research labs, support space and classrooms, resulting in a total of 48 generic and specialty labs. Promoting interaction between researchers, the lab modules are symmetrically located about the equipment support spine and are divided by centrally located classrooms and informal conference areas.

Offices are located adjacent to laboratories on the inside corridor, allowing the maximum penetration of natural light into the labs. Glazing in the offices provides visual connectivity to research spaces.

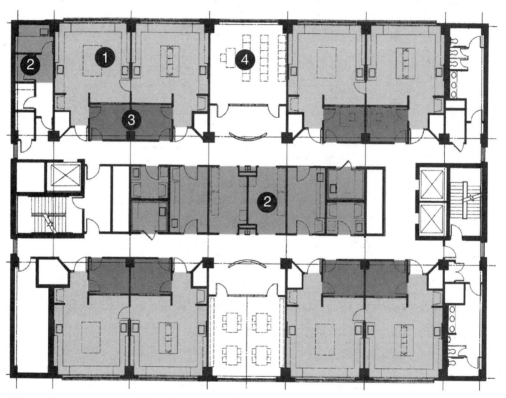

(Floor plan courtesy of Henningson, Durham & Richardson, Inc.)

LEGEND—

1	Laboratory	2	Support
3	Office	4	Classroom

Washington University Medical Center, St. Louis
Biochemistry And Molecular Biophysics Laboratories

Architect: The Christner Partnership, Inc., St. Louis

To help recruit research faculty, this laboratory suite allows tailoring to specific needs. The labs consist of two or three modules with a faculty office and instrument room. Safety issues include a safety station at the main sink and a second egress through an adjacent lab. Lighting, tack boards and writing boards outside the entry encourage communication among researchers.

Laboratory Suite

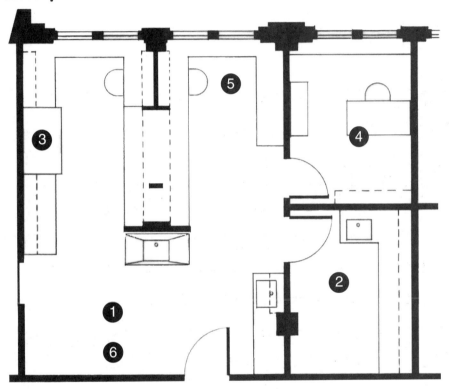

(Floor plan courtesy of The Christner Partnership, Inc.)

LEGEND—

1   Laboratory
2   Instrument room
3   Fume hood
4   Faculty office
5   Graduate student desk
6   Equipment

Facilities Planning Concepts

TABLE OF CONTENTS

Acoustics **136**
ABC's of Acoustical Design...137
Articulation Index 138
Noise Reduction Coefficient 139
Octave Band Sound Pressure 140
Word Intelligibility 141

Conceptual Project Planning..................................**142**
Creating a Total Workplace 143
Facilities Management Cycle 144
Cost Estimation—How it works 145

Healthcare Facilities **148**
Patient Exam Room Clusters 149
Mayo Clinic's Generic Standards 150
Patient-Focused Care 152
Planetree Unit 154

HVAC Systems **156**
Cold-Air HVAC System 157
HVAC Systems—Constant and Variable Volumes 158

Programming...**160**
Feasibility Evaluations 161
Focus Groups 162
Programming Methodology 163
Planning for Expansion 164
Efficient vs. Effective Space 165
Space Standards and Criteria 166

R&D Facilities **168**
R&D Facilities—Area Allocation 169
R&D Programming 170

R&D Facilities—"Cost per Square Foot" 171
R&D Facilities—Cost Dynamics 172
Light Shelf/Daylight Harvesting 173
R&D Facilities—"Kit of Parts" Approach at NIH 174
Interstitial Space 176
A Brief History of Lab Furniture 178
Moduledge 180
Energy-Conserving Building Features 182

Acoustics

ABC's of Acoustical Design

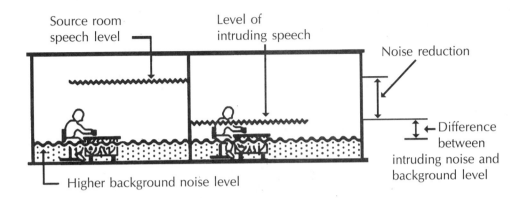

Source room speech level

Level of intruding speech

Noise reduction

Difference between intruding noise and background level

Higher background noise level

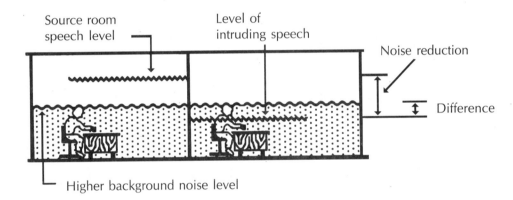

Source room speech level

Level of intruding speech

Noise reduction

Difference

Higher background noise level

In open-plan offices, speech privacy depends on the ABC's of acoustical design:

Absorbing sound with sound-absorptive finish materials.

Blocking sound paths between adjacent workstations with a barrier that interrupts the direct line between source and receiver.

Covering intruding sound by raising the background sound level (such as turning on a fan, increasing the noise generated by an HVAC system, or best of all, soundmasking).

Without changing the noise reduction of the common wall between two offices, you can improve speech privacy by providing higher background noise levels, which mask over intruding speech.

For more information, contact Carl Rosenberg, ACENTECH Inc., 125 Cambridge Park Dr., Cambridge, Mass. 02140 (617) 499-8000.

ARTICULATION INDEX

Articulation index (AI) is a number between zero and 1.0 which indicates relative levels of speech intelligibility. It is derived by comparing the level of an intruding speech signal (such as a neighbor's voice) to the level of background noise at the listener's position. An AI of zero represents no intelligibility and an AI of 1.0 represents total intelligibility.

Level differences in decibels (or dB, indicated in the figure by A,B,C,D and E) are multiplied by different weighting factors developed by Bell Telephone Labs (W_1=.002, W_2=.005, W_3=.007, W_4=.010, W_5=.008) that reflect the relative importance of that frequency for speech intelligibility. Higher frequencies carry the most meaning in speech and, hence, have the highest weighting factors.

Research has shown that an AI of 0.05 provides a confidential degree of privacy for most listeners, whereas an AI of 0.20 is equivalent to a normal degree of privacy. As the AI rises above the normal level, the intelligibility of speech increases rapidly. Once the AI reaches the 0.30 to 0.40 range, further changes in AI are of little importance in terms of relative dissatisfaction with speech privacy.

The figure below shows how AI is determined.

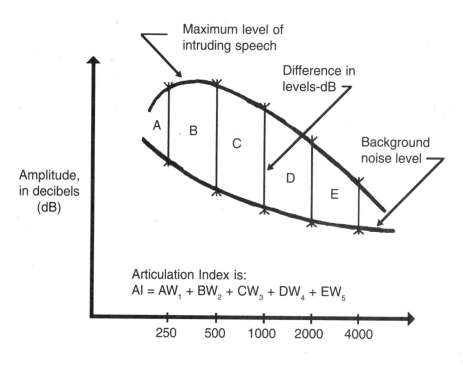

Octave Band Center Frequency

For more information, contact Carl Rosenberg, ACENTECH Inc., 125 Cambridge Park Dr., Cambridge, Mass. 02140 (617) 499-8000.

NOISE REDUCTION COEFFICIENT

The absorptive properties of all materials can be rated and compared with the single number Noise Reduction Coefficient (NRC value), which reflects the acoustical efficiency of materials at frequencies most important to human speech. This figure shows how to calculate NRC.

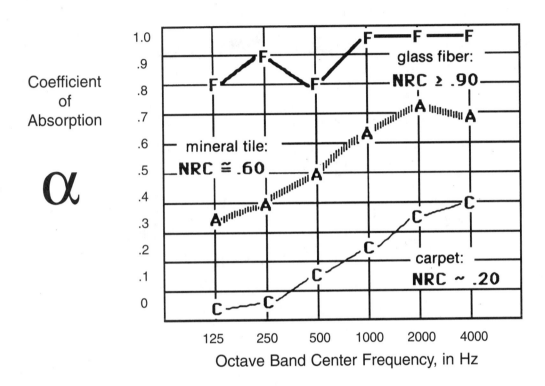

$$\frac{\alpha_{\ 250\ Hz} + \alpha_{\ 500\ Hz} + \alpha_{\ 1000\ Hz} + \alpha_{\ 2000\ Hz}}{4} = NRC$$

For more information, contact Carl Rosenberg, ACENTECH Inc., 125 Cambridge Park Dr., Cambridge, Mass. 02140 (617) 499-8000.

OCTAVE BAND SOUND PRESSURE

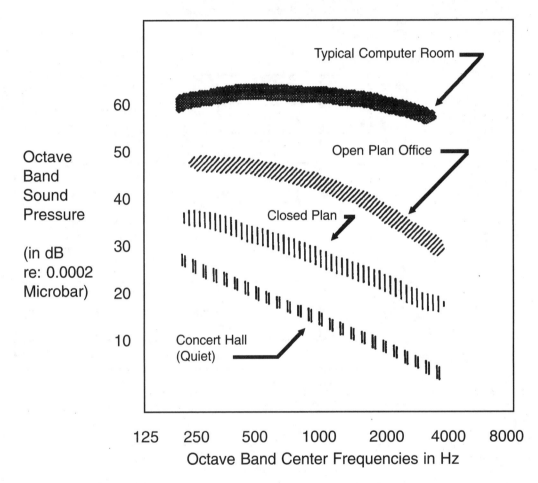

Octave Band Sound Pressure

(in dB re: 0.0002 Microbar)

Typical Computer Room

Open Plan Office

Closed Plan

Concert Hall (Quiet)

60
50
40
30
20
10

125   250   500   1000   2000   4000   8000

Octave Band Center Frequencies in Hz

This graph shows the typical spectrum and level of some common noise situations. The vertical axis shows decibels; the higher numbers are louder. The horizontal axis shows frequency or pitch, in Hertz (or cycles per second); higher frequencies are like the higher notes on a piano keyboard.

For more information, contact Carl Rosenberg, ACENTECH Inc., 125 Cambridge Park Dr., Cambridge, Mass. 02140 (617) 499-8000.

Word Intelligibility

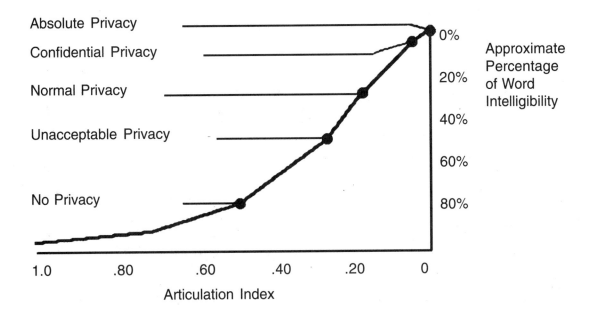

This level of intelligibility determines whether speech is distracting. In other words, a conversation will distract you if you can understand it. Speech intelligibility is based on how loud a conversation is as compared to the background sound in the listener's area. Because human perception is so clever at giving meaning to what we hear, even an Articulation Index (AI) of only .50 gives 80 percent word intelligibility. Therefore, we have to strive extra hard to achieve speech privacy with very low AI values. You will have normal speech privacy when you can work without being distracted by intruding speech. With confidential speech privacy, only occasional words or syllables are understandable.

For more information, contact Carl Rosenberg, ACENTECH Inc., 125 Cambridge Park Dr., Cambridge, Mass. 02140 (617) 499-8000.

CONCEPTUAL PROJECT PLANNING

CREATING A TOTAL WORKPLACE

Capitalizing on its new cost-saving headquarters in Pleasanton, Calif., Hexcel Corporation expects its new one-story facility to improve the way employees work.

Planners focused on creating a total workplace, as opposed to "cockpit-" type spaces for individual workers. Private offices have been moved off the perimeter to the building interior, so windows with outdoor views are no longer an exclusively executive privilege. Greatly reduced in number, managers' offices have also been trimmed in size, from a previous range of 160 to 175 sf down to a standard 120 sf. (Only the eight vice president offices, out of a total of 45 offices, depart from this standard, consisting of two 10' x 12' modules each.) All enclosed offices have an outer wall of glass.

A single main entrance funnels pedestrian traffic through a central area, increasing opportunities for interaction. A hub of support services—a travel office, copy center and mail room—located off the main reception area also multiplies the number of chance encounters.

Like the private offices, conference rooms have been pulled off the perimeter to occupy the building core and lined up on either side of the Main Street corridor.

The building also houses four 22' x 22' pavilions that serve as a communal center in each of the building's four quadrants.

—excerpted from *Facilities Planning News,* May 1993.

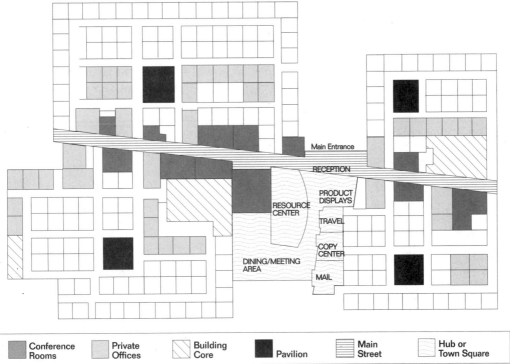

(Diagram courtesy of Hexcel Corporation.)

FACILITIES MANAGEMENT CYCLE

Increasingly, corporate management has been recognizing the need for a coordinated approach to facilities management. As the diagram above suggests, Facilities Management activities can be categorized in the following manner:

- **Planning & Evaluation**—which sets the parameters for proactive decision making.
- **Design & Construction**—which implements physical solutions to support corporate goals.
- **Asset Management**—which keeps track of property on an ongoing basis.

Integration of these activities is the key to a successful Facilities Management System, one which supports the most productive environment in the most cost-effective manner. It is not important that all these tasks be performed by every organization. What is critical is that the heart of the cycle, a system of policies and procedures, be particular to each corporation and fit into the overall management style. Depending on the size of the organization, churn rate, and other distinguishing criteria, management must make decisions about whether a task needs to be performed, whether it should be the responsibility of in-house staff or consultants and which activities should be computer supported. Together then, the manpower and computer resources of in-house staff and consultants provide the energy within the "core" to drive all activities and direct them toward the corporate goals.

For further information on Programming, contact Robert Brandt, AIA at (212) 353-4749.

Haines Lundberg Waehler
Architects Engineers and Planners
115 Fifth Avenue   New York, NY 10003
212 353 4600 Fax 212 353 4666/4667   HLW

Cost Estimation—How it works

Given the numerous components of both building and project costs and the numerous variables affecting these costs, a single estimate is inadequate. The estimating process must follow the step-by-step process of design—from general concept to specific details. As a project progresses and more information becomes available, the preliminary estimate is refined. Design professionals and professional estimators follow this sequence of stages in arriving at a final estimate for building costs. They are outlined in greater detail in the table below.

• Pre-design Budget Analysis

• Conceptual Design Estimate

• Design Development Estimate

• Final Estimate

Each stage requires a specific body of information and yields an increasingly detailed breakdown of the final building costs. The accuracy of the estimates naturally improves with the developing detail in the building design.

Although opportunities for cost control exist at each stage, the cost effectiveness of significant design changes decreases as the project advances. The design development stage is the most economical point in the project for making changes, the point at which the most information is available for the time and money expended.

Pre-Design Budget Analysis

Information Needed	Information Yielded	Accuracy
Mission/Population	Preliminary Budget Based	±20%
Approximate Building Size	on Cost per SF	
General Location		
Size of Site		
Building Quality/"Image"		

Conceptual Design Estimate

Information Needed	Information Yielded	Accuracy
Basic Building Configuration	Breakdown of CSI Component	±15%
Building Type	Costs Based on Unit Price	
General Occupancy		
Program		
Basic Materials		
Mech. Systems/Special Systems		
Site Plan		

(continued on next page)

Design Development Estimate

Information Needed	Information Yielded	Accuracy
Floor Plans/Casework	Construction Cost Breakdown	±5-10%
Sections and Elevations	by Labor and Materials	
Struct. System: Concrete or Steel		
Foundation/Footing Sizes		
Preliminary Mech./Elec. Layouts		
Site Plan		
Outline Specifications		
Soil Analysis/Site Problems		

Final Estimate

Information Needed	Information Yielded	Accuracy
Final Building Specifications	Trade Breakdown	±5%
and Working Drawings		

For further information on cost analysis and cost factors affecting your proposed or existing R&D Facility call Kenneth Drake, AIA at Haines Lundberg Waehler (212) 353-4747.

Haines Lundberg Waehler
Architects Engineers and Planners
115 Fifth Avenue   New York, NY 10003
212 353 4600 Fax 212 353 4666/4667

HLW

HEALTHCARE FACILITIES

PATIENT EXAM ROOM CLUSTERS

The building block for the Outpatient Center at The Johns Hopkins Hospital, Baltimore, is the exam cluster. It is conceived from the patient's point of view as an improvement over the labyrinthine corridors one often confronts in clinics.

In addition to exam rooms, the cluster contains a patient bathroom and a consultation room where a doctor can speak privately with a patient or relative; or where a nurse can give follow-up instructions, while the exam room is being readied for the next patient. For doctors, the cluster affords them a number of exam rooms close at hand. The consultation room is also for speaking with other doctors and students out of hearing of patients. For nursing staff, the cluster is an efficient module, with a utility storage room, and, at its entrance, an area for charting and vital signs.

For more information on exam room modules, contact:

John Wilson, AIA, Principal
Payette Associates
285 Summer Street
Boston, MA 02210
(617) 342-8200
(617) 342-8202 fax

The typical exam cluster.

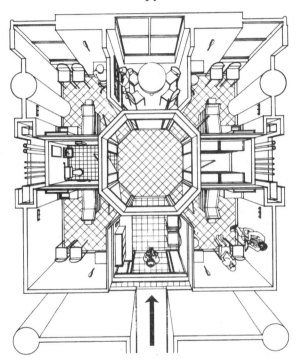

A grouping of clusters work together to form a department.

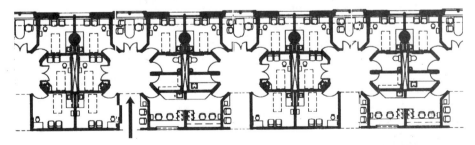

(Plans courtesy of Payette Associates Inc.)

MAYO CLINIC'S GENERIC STANDARDS

History

Principles of the first Mayo Clinic are still used today; specialists share space to facilitate consulta-tion and cross-training. Dr. Henry Plummer, one of the clinic's first physicians, devised Mayo's first group practice clinic in 1914.

"He wanted a group practice that was cooperative, with office-exam rooms in modular sections, with any physician able to use any consulting office or exam room," says Bryan McSweeney, chair of the department of engineering and facilities for the Mayo Medical Center.

This integrated group practice concept has since influenced Mayo facilities, from floor plan design to configuration of desks and custom furnishings. These standards have been tested over the years at the Rochester, Minn. campus.

Standards

In the Mayo sites, respective elements such as exam rooms have similar function and therefore similar floor plans and locations for furniture, equipment and accessories.

Mayo uses 135 to 140 sf for its tertiary care rooms, McSweeney says. The extra space accommo-dates a physician's desk, a dressing cubicle and space for a medical resident or consultant. There is also extra seating for a patient escort.

Office-exam room special features include sofas which are armless on one end, so patients can lie down if necessary, plus custom exam tables. The tables have extra storage room, adjustable backs, a flip-down kneeler and slide-out leg extensions.

Some furnishings have undergone minor revisions over the years. A file-storage sofa was developed in response to physicians' requests for more storage space.

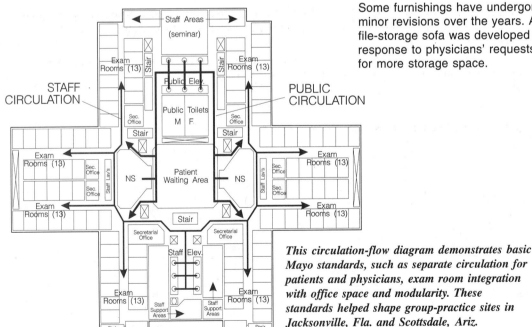

This circulation-flow diagram demonstrates basic Mayo standards, such as separate circulation for patients and physicians, exam room integration with office space and modularity. These standards helped shape group-practice sites in Jacksonville, Fla. and Scottsdale, Ariz.

Practice

Each facility's floor plan is modular, with exam rooms arrayed around a reception area or appointment desk. Early versions of the modular concept, first built in Rochester, had an H-shaped footprint, so each room could have an outside window. The more modern versions, designed after the advent of air conditioning, contain windowless interior rooms as well.

Clinic buildings for 50 and 62 doctors respectively were built on two 140-acre sites, one in Jacksonville, Fla. and another in Scottsdale, Ariz. Each site is masterplanned to eventually grow as large or larger than the 7 million-sf Rochester complex. The centers can accommodate 500 staff each and support buildings such as hospitals, research laboratories and hotels.

In both cases, the floor plan provides "great flexibility," McSweeney says. Staff can use rooms interchangeably. In some cases, as functions grow and change, a department can simply expand around the corner and move in with little, if any, remodeling.

Having interchangeable rooms was Dr. Plummer's goal: he urged facility planners to "make the right way the easy way" by letting form follow function. Plummer also wanted a highly systematic way to get doctors to patients while having patient care itself be unhurried and personal.

Modules support this goal by separating patient and staff circulation. Workers at control desks can monitor patients in exam rooms. Lights at the control desk indicate to physicians where each patient is.

Plummer was also adamant about efficient delivery of medical records. A system of record distribution using lifts, conveyor chutes and systems within and between buildings has evolved over the years.

Standards are updated by modifying or adapting existing plans "opportunistically" as new projects arise that must incorporate changes in equipment, staff, waste control or other operational features.

"Standards are really devised for reasons of efficiency," he says. "What we try to do is make our operational efficiency improve, and our efficiency improves as a result of our standards."

—excerpted from *Healthcare Facilities News*, February 1992.

PATIENT-FOCUSED CARE

"A patient who is in the hospital for three days sees about 53 different people related to their care," says Tom Fee, principal at the Washington-based consulting firm Booz-Allen & Hamilton. "They see a different nurse each day, and at the end of the stay they've been passed around from person to person and no one knows everything about their care except their doctor. It's a long, wait-intensive process, and any follow-up is done by completely different people, in the billing department and so on. The patient leaves thinking, 'I just paid $500 a night to be treated like a prisoner.'"

In 1988, Booz-Allen & Hamilton, along with planners from the Sentara Health System (Norfolk, Va.), Lakeland Memorial Hospital (Lakeland, Fla.), Vanderbilt Hospital (Nashville), St. Vincent's (Indianapolis), and Clarkson Hospital (Omaha) studied their operations in order to improve both the quality of the patient's experience and the effectiveness of their operations.

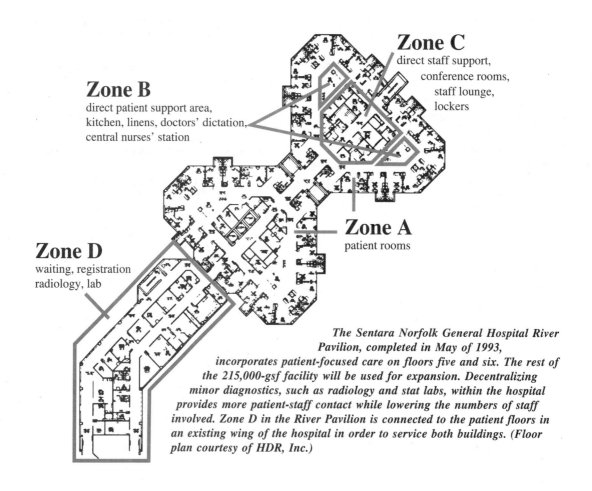

Zone C
direct staff support, conference rooms, staff lounge, lockers

Zone B
direct patient support area, kitchen, linens, doctors' dictation, central nurses' station

Zone A
patient rooms

Zone D
waiting, registration radiology, lab

The Sentara Norfolk General Hospital River Pavilion, completed in May of 1993, incorporates patient-focused care on floors five and six. The rest of the 215,000-gsf facility will be used for expansion. Decentralizing minor diagnostics, such as radiology and stat labs, within the hospital provides more patient-staff contact while lowering the numbers of staff involved. Zone D in the River Pavilion is connected to the patient floors in an existing wing of the hospital in order to service both buildings. (Floor plan courtesy of HDR, Inc.)

Defining PFC

The hospital group formulated five principles to guide them in improving quality. These constitute their definition of patient-focused care:

- streamline and simplify documentation
- place services closer to the patient
- broaden staff qualifications
- simplify processes
- focus patient populations

The hospitals plan to realize these goals by changing charting methods, making records available at the bedside, grouping patients by type, cross training staff and bringing commonly used functions such as minor testing and diagnosis nearer to the patient.

Design Implications

"Patient-focused care turns the traditional hospital on its head," says Fee. "Instead of having so many highly specialized people to perform services, a small group of cross-trained individuals can provide 95 percent of the care that the patient needs."

In order for a small group of people to care for a patient and to reduce patient travel time, routine functions of patient care are decentralized within the hospital, bringing them nearer to the patient. To place services closer to the patient, the hospital group decided to divide services into zones.

Patient rooms are placed in Zone A. Zone B comprises direct patient support to service a group of nine patients with linens, snacks, dictation and a nurses station. Staff support such as lockers, lounge and equipment supply is placed in Zone C which is designed to serve two nine-bed groups. The diagnosis and testing functions are placed in Zone D which should be able to service all the patients on the floor.

This model was used to design the patient floors of the Sentara Norfolk General Hospital River Pavilion and it has also been used to remodel patient floors at a number of hospitals.

The results of the shift to patient-focused care are dramatic, says Fee.

"We've seen two things: morale goes up—for physicians, staff and patients; and productivity (time spent caring for the patient) has gone up from 24 to 50 percent," says Fee.

—excerpted from *Healthcare Facilities News*, July 1993.

PLANETREE UNIT

Planetree, a nonprofit consumer health organization founded in 1978, seeks to inject humanity and individuality into the contemporary healthcare system. The organization takes its name from the plane tree under which Hippocrates taught medicine in ancient Greece.

Two central principles of Planetree are that education is a key step in demystifying medical care and empowering patients, and that patient comfort promotes healing. With these in mind, the organization established the Planetree Health Resource Center, an extensive public medical library in 1981. The first Planetree Model Unit opened at San Francisco's Pacific Presbyterian Medical Center (now California Pacific Medical Center) in 1985.

Since then, Planetree model units have opened at four other hospitals: San Jose Medical Center, Mid-Columbia Medical Center in The Dalles, Ore., Delano Regional Medical Center in Delano, Calif., and most recently Beth Israel Medical Center in New York. Trinity Medical Center in Moline, Ill., is currently constructing two units based on the Planetree model.

According to Laura Gilpin, Planetree's director of educational services, prime targets for a Planetree make-over are the typically low-profile medical/surgical units. These utilitarian wards fail to attract the same kind of attention or innovation that characterize specialty units like pediatrics or oncology.

"This area is typically a catchall, with stroke victims alongside pneumonia or AIDS patients and people recovering from car accidents," Gilpin says. "It's not glamorous, high-tech or fancy. We felt the least was being done here to humanize patient care."

Breaking the Institutional Grid

Architect Marc Schweitzer has done programming and concept design work for all but the first Planetree unit. He suggests several design features that help patients feel comfortable and involved. (Some of these have yet to be implemented since most Planetree units are renovations rather than new construction.)

*   Patient rooms should be large enough to include family sitting and even sleeping space. Visitors should have a chair with a reading light that doesn't disturb the resting patient.

*   Fabrics, textures and colors should create a residential, rather than a hotel-like atmosphere.

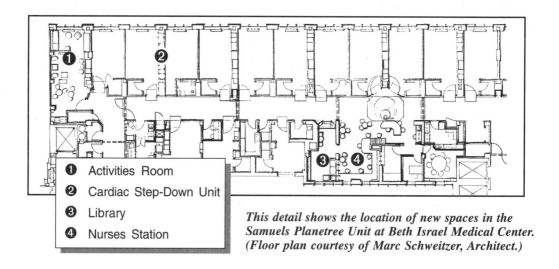

❶ Activities Room
❷ Cardiac Step-Down Unit
❸ Library
❹ Nurses Station

This detail shows the location of new spaces in the Samuels Planetree Unit at Beth Israel Medical Center. (Floor plan courtesy of Marc Schweitzer, Architect.)

Schweitzer recommends woods, veneers, fabrics (like chintz or floral patterns), artwork on the footwall and curtains at the window.

- Patients should have 24-hour access to food of their choice. A functional kitchen on the unit allows a nutritionist to prepare meals and educate patients about healthy eating.

- Interior shapes and forms should "break the grid" to reduce the institutional feel of existing facilities. For example, arcades, a bay window and several different kinds of lighting to break up the long hallways.

- Non-architectural elements of the Planetree philosophy include an active arts program, music, videos, books-on-tape and even visiting performers. A massage program is available for patients and staff.

Open nurses' stations are a central part of the Planetree philosophy. (Photo by Miller Photography, courtesy of Marc Schweitzer, Architect.)

For more information on Planetree write Laura Gilpin, Director of Educational Services, Planetree, 2300 California Street, Suite 201, San Francisco, CA 94115; or call (415) 923-3696, or Marc Schweitzer at Marc Schweitzer, Architect 246 First Street, Suite 306, San Francisco, CA 94105 (415) 512-0577.

—excerpted from *Healthcare Facilities News*, February, 1993.

HVAC Systems

Cold-Air HVAC System

Factors in Selection of Cost-Effective Cold-Air HVAC Systems for:

Office Buildings   Shopping Centers

Electric Demand Charges
Electric Time-of-Day Rates
Electric/Gas Rate Ratios
Utility Incentive Grants (Gas/Electric)
Building Size
Type of Occupancy
Weather Profile

Choice of Appropriate Cold-Air HVAC System

Basic System Variables:

All-air/air-water
Ice/other cold-air source
Electrical/partial gas

WHY COLD AIR? With the appropriate 40°F cold-air system, it is possible to reduce annual energy costs by 35% to 50%, compared to a conventional 55°F all-air VAV system—often with little or no increase in construction cost to the owner/developer.

WHICH COLD-AIR SYSTEM? The most cost effective cold-air system for a specific project depends upon the combined impact of all of the factors listed at left above. Sample conclusions based upon comparative system studies that integrate these factors for specific buildings include:

A cold air-water HVAC system often is significantly lower than a cold all-air system in both energy cost and construction cost.

An off-peak (ice thermal storage) system is often - but not always lowest in energy cost.

FOR INFORMATION AND COMPARATIVE SYSTEM STUDY: For information on alternative cold-air HVAC systems, including appropriate applications and a comparative system energy/cost study, contact Walter Janus, P.E., Gershon Meckler Associates, P.E., 590 Herndon Parkway, Suite 100, Herndon, Virginia 22070, (703) 478-9493.

HVAC Systems—Constant and Variable volumes

Constant Volume Single Duct Terminal Reheat System

Advantages:

1. System is relatively simple to balance and to maintain air balance between supply and exhaust.
2. Provides good odor control and strict temperature and humidity control.
3. Is very dependable and does not require use of complex controls.

Disadvantages:

1. Has extremely high annual energy costs, which can be reduced with the use of energy recovery.
2. No diversity in sizing equipment, which increases the system installed cost.
3. Not flexible for addition or expansion of fume exhaust system; requires rebalance of entire system.

Constant Volume Dual Duct System

Advantages:

1. Energy cost and consumption are reduced because not all supply air is cooled and reheated, only cold deck air.
2. System is all air; water piping and coils are only required at the central air handling units.
3. Diversity can be used in sizing equipment.

Disadvantages:

1. Controls and added ductwork increase system installed costs.
2. Humidity-control is not as good as single duct systems, requiring the use of a precool coil, which increases energy use.
3. Requires substantial ceiling space for ductwork and mixing boxes.

Variable Volume, Two Position (Occupied/Unoccupied) Single Duct Terminal Reheat System

Advantages:

1. Supply and exhaust air quantities are substantially reduced during unoccupied hours (approximately 3/4 of total annual operating hours) when loads and exhaust requirements are minimal, reducing energy consumption.
2. System is relatively simple to balance, and air balance is easily maintained during occupied periods.
3. Provides good odor control and strict temperature and humidity control during occupied operation.

Disadvantages:

1. No diversity in sizing equipment, which increases system installed cost.

2. Controls are somewhat more complex and require air regulators in supply and exhaust, which increases costs.

3. Not flexible for addition or expansion of fume exhaust system; requires rebalance of entire system.

Variable Volume Single Duct Terminal Reheat System

Advantages:

1. Only the necessary air is supplied to space based on cooling load or exhaust at any time, reducing energy consumption and costs substantially.

2. Can size equipment assuming diversity in loads and fume hood operation.

3. System is more flexible to changes in loads and the addition of new fume hoods.

Disadvantages:

1. System is relatively difficult to balance, and air flow rates are constantly changing during normal operation.

2. System requires complex and expensive controls.

3. Fume hood air flows vary, and hoods should be fitted with sensing devices to indicate proper exhaust air flow and face velocities.

For more information please contact John Nelson or Steve Frei at (206) 624-7588.

Affiliated Engineers, Inc.
625 North Segoe Rd.
P.O. Box 5039
Madison, WI 53705-0039
(608) 238-2616
(608) 238-2614 fax

PROGRAMMING

FEASIBILITY EVALUATIONS

Selecting the right building for a corporate relocation can have substantial financial benefits. Buildings vary in lease and building operational costs, the proportion of usable spaces ("loss factor") and the amount of construction needed to bring them up to an organization's particular standards. Long-term renovation costs will be affected by the inherent flexibility of the floorplate. Perhaps most importantly, productivity can be improved by finding a good "fit" between the space program and the building, such as effective adjacencies.

The best way to ensure that all of these items are addressed is through a team approach to evaluating potential building choices.

Programming	Urban Planning
• Space Projections • Operational Efficiency/"Fit" • Adjacencies	• Landmarks • Zoning
Design/Architecture	**Engineering**
• Aesthetic Potential • Construction/Structural Issues • Costs	• Mechanical/Electrical/Plumbing Systems Evaluations

For further information on programming, contact Robert Brandt, AIA at (212) 353-4749.

Haines Lundberg Waehler
Architects Engineers and Planners
115 Fifth Avenue   New York, NY 10003
212 353 4600 Fax 212 353 4666/4667   HLW

FOCUS GROUPS

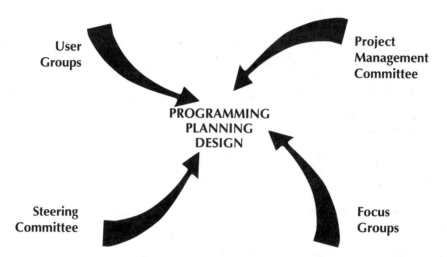

User Groups

Project Management Committee

PROGRAMMING PLANNING DESIGN

Steering Committee

Focus Groups

Successful facility programming and the design efforts that follow are dependent on quality and timely input from a myriad of sources. These sources are integrated into the committees and groups which will provide input, guidance and approvals to the project design teams. Included is a Steering Committee made of individuals chosen by administration with the role of ensuring that institution-wide goals and values are maintained. A Project Management Committee oversees and coordinates the day-to-day project planning and design efforts. User Groups represent the ultimate building occupants and are made up of department managers and selected staff members. They are involved with the Planning and Design Team throughout the programming and early design process.

One source often overlooked until late in the planning phase, and often not afforded the same level of input as other sources, is the Focus Group. Focus Groups differ from User Groups in that the individuals or departments will not necessarily occupy space in the new building. Generally, these individuals, or groups, focus on one particular area and may fulfill such a role for many other buildings within the institution's complex. These may be employed by the client institution, by independent vendors/consultants, or come from local regulatory agencies. The Focus Group's input will have a definite impact on area, site, material selection, utilities, construction costs, etc.

The Project Planner should identify the make-up of the Focus Group early in the process and seek their continual input, review and approvals or "sign-offs."

Examples of Focus Group components:

Safety	Security
Maintenance	Housekeeping
Physical/Energy Plant	Communications
Information Management	Materials Handling
Parking	Food Service/Vending
Landscaping	Local Authorities

For further information on Focus Groups, call Marty Meisel (319) 354-4700.

Hansen Lind Meyer, Inc.
Drawer 310
Plaza Center One
Iowa City, Iowa 52244-0310

HLM

PROGRAMMING METHODOLOGY

A good design program is an effective road map for the designer, helping to keep the project on track. The question is whether it is a map to success or failure after the dust has settled and the facility is functioning.

A common error is to think of programming methodology only in terms of the *expediency* of the process. The secret of success is to focus on the *validity* of the process. Even an extensive programming effort is generally less than 5% of the total design time. Given the long-term cost savings made possible by a program that supports productive operations, these planning hours are an investment well spent.

What is the key to a valid, as well as expeditious, program? Three elements integrated into the programming methodology—*Process, Issues and Team*. The *Process* must be orderly and plan for frequent, controlled interaction with the client. Issues to be addressed must include management's operational, financial and human resources goals, since these should be the basis for the staffing, adjacencies and spatial qualities. Ultimately, this challenging approach to programming demands that the right *Team* is involved, a team that has a range of expertise in operational analysis and human factors, as well as the "real world" disciplines of architecture and engineering to make sure that the program is attainable in the available space at reasonable cost.

For further information on programming, contact Robert Brandt, AIA at (212) 353-4749.

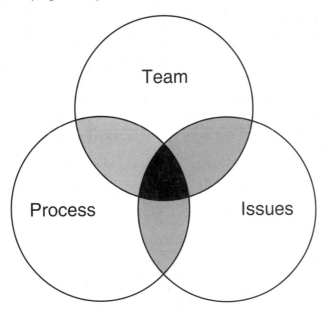

Haines Lundberg Waehler
Architects Engineers and Planners
115 Fifth Avenue   New York, NY 10003
212 353 4600 Fax 212 353 4666/4667   HLW

PLANNING FOR EXPANSION

Successful facility planning should include planning for expansion. This entails more than identifying where building additions might occur. The facility planner must identify those functions most likely to expand. Expansion spaces should be an integral part of early adjacency diagrams. In-place growth for each function should be included in initial planning.

Functional expansion may be satisfied in several ways:

- Expansion of function within existing space by increasing services, density, efficiency, etc.

IN-PLACE EXPANSION

- Expansion into adjacent space.

EXPANSION INTO ADJACENT SPACE

- Relocation of entire function to a larger space.

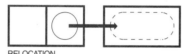

RELOCATION

- Building expansion (horizontal, vertical, or independent structure).

BUILDING EXPANSION

Spaces or services serving expandable functions should also be planned for expansion or reconfiguration. Examples include:

Offices	Circulation
Elevators and stairs	Adjacencies
Utility availability	Site
Building codes	Parking

Major building expansion should be planned to spring from functional "nodes" (i.e. office blocks, cafeteria, library, atria/courtyard, materials management, energy center, etc.) common to the basic building functions and circulation.

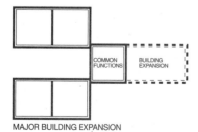

MAJOR BUILDING EXPANSION

For further information on Planning for Expansion, call Marty Meisel (319) 354-4700

Hansen Lind Meyer, Inc.
Drawer 310
Plaza Centre One
Iowa City, Iowa 52244-0310

EFFICIENT VS. EFFECTIVE SPACE

Efficient versus Effective Space—from RTKL's Architectural Programming Definitions

Space Configuration: Greater efficiency does *not* always translate into greater effectiveness. Square footage by itself is not the only factor in determining space needs. A floor plan that maximizes the perimeter may be ideal for law firms that demand private offices with windows, while a deeper floor plan that maximizes the enclosure may be more appropriate for open office plans housing studio space or clerical operations.

1. Maximize perimeter (least "efficient" but may be most effective)

1' | **100 SF**

100'

Perimeter/Enclosure Ratio = 202 LF/100 SF
- Maximal Window Potential
- Maximal Natural Light/View
- Maximal Deep Space

- Maximal Heating/Cooling Load
- Maximal Average Distance from Core

2. Maximize enclosure (most "efficient" but may be least effective)

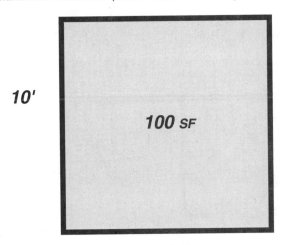

10'

100 SF

10'

Perimeter/Enclosure Ratio = 40 LF/100 SF
- Maximal Deep Space
- Minimal Heating Cooling Load
- Minimal Average Distance from Core

- Minimal Window Potential
- Minimal Natural Light/View

RTKL RTKL Associates, Inc. Baltimore • Dallas • Washington • Los Angeles • London • Tokyo
Hong Kong • Guadalajara

SPACE STANDARDS AND CRITERIA

RATIOS VS. FACTORS:

Understanding the difference between ratios and factors will help avoid common miscalculations.
Example: Using 20% Circulation

1. Ratios—To calculate efficiencies   • Reductive   • Evaluative

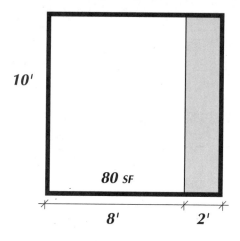

10'

80 SF

8'   2'

100%   *Total Area*
-80%   *Net Area*
20%   *Circulation Ratio*

2. Factors—To estimate area requirements   • Additive   • Planning-Oriented

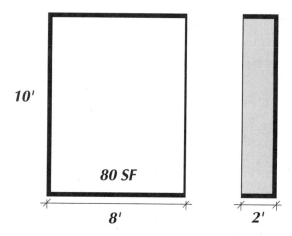

10'

80 SF

8'   2'

80 SF   *Net Area*
x 1.25   *Circulation Factor*
100 SF   *Total Area*

To obtain 20% circulation, use a factor of 1.25

For more information about RTKL's approach to architectural programming or its multi-disciplinary
design services, please call Associate Vice President Dianne Blair Black, AIA (410) 528-8600.

RTKL RTKL Associates, Inc. Baltimore • Dallas • Washington • Los Angeles • London • Tokyo
Hong Kong • Guadalajara

R&D Facilities

R&D Facilities—Area Allocation

Percent Net Area Allocation in R&D Facilities

Significant differences in distribution of net areas depend on program requirements, as shown in the graphs below.

Components that are common to the lab building itself (building services-toilets, janitor closets and administration/general support-conference rooms, administration offices, etc.) do not vary significantly.

Contact: Stanley Stark, AIA 212-353-4780

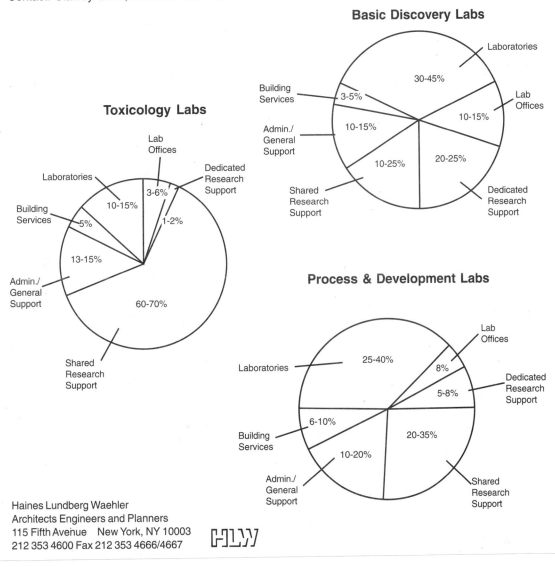

Basic Discovery Labs

Laboratories 30-45%
Lab Offices 10-15%
Building Services 3-5%
Admin./General Support 10-15%
Shared Research Support 10-25%
Dedicated Research Support 20-25%

Toxicology Labs

Lab Offices 3-6%
Dedicated Research Support 1-2%
Laboratories 10-15%
Building Services 5%
Admin./General Support 13-15%
Shared Research Support 60-70%

Process & Development Labs

Laboratories 25-40%
Lab Offices 8%
Dedicated Research Support 5-8%
Building Services 6-10%
Admin./General Support 10-20%
Shared Research Support 20-35%

Haines Lundberg Waehler
Architects Engineers and Planners
115 Fifth Avenue   New York, NY 10003
212 353 4600 Fax 212 353 4666/4667

HLW

R&D Programming

Excerpt from "From Program to Design," *Architectural Technology*, Summer 1985 (updated 1994) by Stanley Stark, AIA, partner with Haines Lundberg Waehler, a New York City-based architecture, engineering, and planning firm that specializes in the design of research facilities.

This algorithm converts the figures shown below (based on laboratory work space) to total building perfection: first, the net area per person is multiplied by the projected number of staff. This figure, together with the space required for scientific support function (related to the specific research programs) and administrative support functions (related to the other structures and activities on the site) yields the net building area. Multiplying this by a "gross factor" of 1.6-1.8 yields a "gross building area" assumption.

NET AREA (IN SQ. FT.) PER PERSON
(Predictable research functions)

Research Activity	Technicians (Labs Only)	Technicians & Scientists (Lab + Office)	Total Lab Area Including Direct Scientific Support
Basic Discovery	190	180	370
Chemistry and Analytic	150-200	140-175	300-345
Pharmaceutical Formulation & Development			
❑ Labs only	175	150	340
❑ Labs & chemical manufacturing & support	-	-	550-650
Chemical	220	180	-
Teaching Labs	50-60/station	-	100-120
Electronics & Telecom	125	-	200
Materials & Specialty	225-250	140-155	285-310

Data is based on typical R&D programs 1980-1990.

Laboratories are extremely complex buildings that must respond to many constituencies—scientists, research administrators, managers, safety officers, engineers, the neighboring public and others. Often, agendas conflict.

At the same time, laboratories must adapt to unpredictable research directions and the physical requirements they may impose. A consensus on these directions is seldom reached. Accommodating change, whether technological or organizational, is therefore always a fundamental design requirement.

Lab design is where "push comes to shove" has real meaning. Goal setting drives programming. Programming drives design. Programming for a laboratory begins with a rigorous exploration of long-term research agendas. Then, a series of operational assumptions must be made. Space standards, one of the most critical, is highlighted here.

For further information on factors affecting your proposed or existing R&D Facility call Stanley Stark at 212-353-4780.

Haines Lundberg Waehler
Architects Engineers and Planners
115 Fifth Avenue   New York, NY 10003
212 353 4600 Fax 212 353 4666/4667   HLW

R&D Facilities—"Cost per Square Foot"

You can be given no more useful caveat than this: Fully understand what costs are referred to in "costs per square foot." The costs of constructing a new facility are traditionally categorized as building costs, or the cost of the new structure itself; site development costs; and project costs, or the full scope of costs you will incur in your building project.

Building costs refer to the costs of labor and materials for the construction of the facility. Figure 1 lists building costs for a range of types of construction, from the creation of a new laboratory down to a simple cosmetic renovation. Figure 2 lists the components of building costs incurred in the construction of a new laboratory. As indicated, the costs in both lists are based on a laboratory of approximately 100,000 gross square feet built in the New York/New Jersey/Connecticut area.

Laboratory Building Costs per Sq. Ft.   Figure 1

First Quarter 1994 (New York Area)

Current Costs (not including site work) for projects of 100,000 sq. ft. or greater. For smaller projects, add a premium of 10-20%.

New Construction	$260 - 270
Addition	$210 - 235
Gut/Alteration	$180 - 210
Renovation/Existing Lab: Mechanical/Calling/Lighting	$120 - 150
Renovation/Existing Lab: Mechanical System	$80 - 100
Finish Replacement	$45 - 50

Components of Building Construction Costs   Figure 2

	Approx. %	Cost/sq.ft.
Excavation/Foundation/Structure	18%	$48
Perimeter Walls	10%	$27
Interior Finishes	4%	$11
Other General Construction	8.5%	$23
Specialties	3%	$8
Equipment & Casework	6.5%	$18
Plumbing/FD	6.5%	$18
HVAC	22.5%	$60
Electrical	13%	$35
General Condition/OH/Profit (& CM Fee)	8%	$22
	100%	$270

For further information on cost analysis and cost factors affecting your proposed or existing R&D Facility call Kenneth Drake, AIA 212-353-4747.

Haines Lundberg Waehler
Architects Engineers and Planners
115 Fifth Avenue   New York, NY 10003
212 353 4600 Fax 212 353 4666/4667   HLW

Building Costs by Region

Cost/sf and Percentage of 1994 NY Area Cost of $270/sf

In addition to an understanding of "cost per square foot" as it is used in the design and construction industries, you should be aware of the variables affecting cost in a particular place at a particular time.

Building costs can vary considerably according to region by as much as 40%. For example, in the first quarter of 1994 building costs in the New York area were 38% higher than those in Atlanta and 10% lower than those in San Francisco.

Market conditions, another powerful cost variable, are almost completely regional in nature.

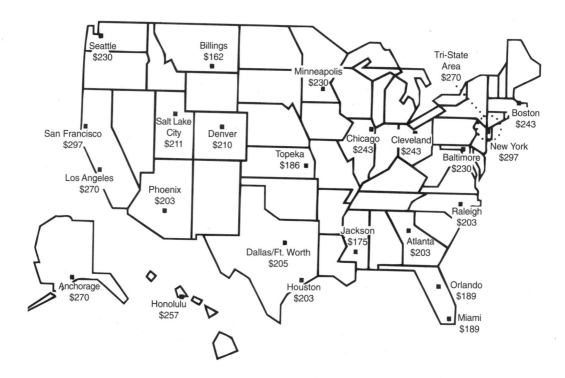

For further information on cost analysis and cost factors affecting your proposed or existing R&D facility call Kenneth Drake, AIA 212-353-4747.

Haines Lundberg Waehler
Architects Engineers and Planners
115 Fifth Avenue   New York, NY 10003
212 353 4600 Fax 212 353 4666/4667   HLW

LIGHT SHELF/DAYLIGHT HARVESTING

The light-shelf concept, when used with perimeter corridors having south, east and west exposures, can effectively be used to redistribute natural light deep into lab modules. Placement of a light shelf at approximately two feet below the adjacent ceiling plane is intended to direct daylight off the ceiling and into interior spaces while also providing some shading from direct sunlight in the summer. During winter, the low altitude of the sun would circumvent the shelf and provide solar heat to the corridor and adjacent wall. The shelf should be placed within the corridor since (from the standpoint of maintenance) any accumulation of dirt or snow will eliminate the usefulness. The shelf can also be used to incorporate an indirect lighting system, which can be controlled by a photocell to compensate for periods of poor daylight. This system also allows for maximum usage of the space above the corridor ceiling for mechanical systems.

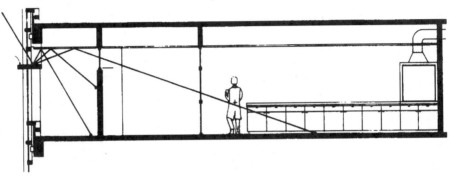

A new strategy that has recently been employed for labs with a window is the daylight harvesting concept. With this concept, three light sensors spaced equidistantly from the window are placed into the ceiling. These sensors are directly connected to electronic, dimming-style ballasts for all the light fixtures in that third of the laboratory. As the exterior light levels change, the sensors adjust the lights up or down to maintain the desired level of illumination.

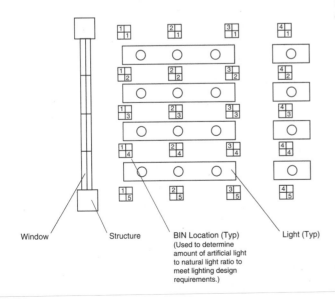

Window   Structure   BIN Location (Typ)   Light (Typ)
                                   (Used to determine
                                   amount of artificial light
                                   to natural light ratio to
                                   meet lighting design
                                   requirements.)

For further information on the Daylight Harvesting/Light Shelf Concept, call John Becker (703) 917-0500.

Hansen Lind Meyer, Inc.
1420 Beverly Road, Suite 230
McLean, VA 22101-3719

HLM

R&D Facilities—"Kit of Parts" approach at NIH

In light of anticipated frequent program shifts, a major design goal of NIH's Silvio O. Conte Building in Bethesda, Md., is to provide a combination of flexibility and standardization in the labs so alterations can be made with minimal disruption. The keys to meeting this target are strict adherence to the planning module and a generic, Kit-of-Parts approach to lab fit-out.

Labs are laid out on an 11' x 11' planning grid, which constitutes a "half-module." Most labs are double (22' x 22') or triple (22' x 33') modules, but the planning scheme also allows for occasional single- (11' x 22') and half-module units. (See plans below and opposite.) Offices are similarly planned based on 5' x 10' increments.

A custom-developed Kit-of-Parts specifies default standards for fit-up of all lab, lab support and office modules. In the labs, technician desk spaces are located in the front of the room, illuminated by clerestory windows in the wall along the personnel corridor. Benches and fume hoods or biosafety cabinets are in the back—close to utilities routed in from the service corridor, but away from traffic and disruptive air currents. The peninsula-type lab benches attach to the rear wall to facilitate utility hookups from the service corridor.

When necessary, the special requirements of individual scientists are superimposed on the generic grid. Modifications to mechanical systems are easily made.

"Comments from the maintenance people show they are very pleased with the layout of mechanical

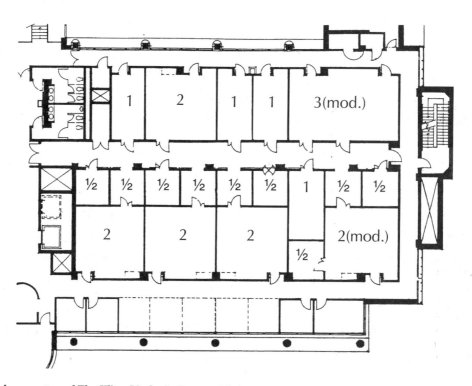

(Floor plan courtesy of The Kling-Lindquist Partnership.)

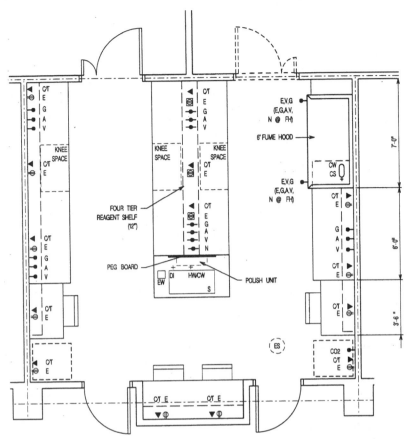

This typical double-module lab is based on the Kit-of-Parts. Some options include a 6' biosafety cabinet, a 6' fume hood, a 4' biosafety cabinet, a 2' incubator, a 4' fume hood and 3' lab bench. (Floor plan courtesy of TKLP.)

spaces and how the systems work," says Bob Thompson, project director and principal with The Kling-Lindquist Partnership (TKLP), the Baltimore-based design firm for the project.

Flexibility Tested

The flexibility of the standardized scheme has already been put to the test. After construction was completed in September 1992, two last-minute program changes occurred: electrophysiology labs were converted to house biology labs for the National Center for Human Genome Research, and the newly installed NIH Director, Harold Varmus, M.D., decided to locate his laboratories in the Conte Building. Both modifications were accomplished without delaying the June 1993 move-in schedule.

"A sign of the success of the Kit-of-Parts is that the basic configuration of the labs did not change," says Ken Schotsch, project manager with TKLP. "NIH was able to do the equivalent of casework modifications to refit the fourth floor labs for the Human Genome project without altering engineering systems. The conversion was done in-house by NIH, and the process was streamlined because the A/E did not have to redo drawings."

—excerpted from *Facilities Planning News*, October 1994.

INTERSTITIAL SPACE

Interstitial space at the Fred Hutchinson Cancer Research Center (FHCRC) in Seattle consists of a load-bearing deck hung from the structural floor above. Interstitial space houses all the mechanical and electrical equipment necessary to provide services to the lab below. Over non-laboratory spaces, interstitial space houses conference rooms, offices, lounges and locker rooms.

Labs, which measure 10'6" x 22', are located at the perimeters of the buildings. Lab support spaces, each 10' x 20', are located at the building's core. Shared equipment is located adjacent to labs.

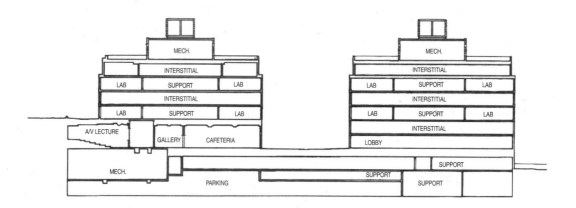

Cost Savings—Initial vs. Long Term

In addition to increasing design costs, interstitial design increased initial costs in the FHCRC project. Among them: the construction of a full walk-on deck and an extra three vertical feet of exterior wall for each interstitial floor. In addition, more structural frame, elevators, stairs and mechanical/electrical risers were added, as were lighting, HVAC and fire protection inside the interstitial space.

According to Guy Ott, vice president of facilities operations at the FHCRC, higher initial costs were mitigated during construction in the following way:

• First, by allowing work on the mechanical and electrical systems to be undertaken concurrently with the laboratory and support space buildout, the construction process can be easily fast-tracked. Ott received a letter from the project contractor indicating that the project would have taken six months longer to complete without the benefit of interstitial space.

"Time is money," says Ott. "Our costs to construct the interstitial portion of the buildings were offset almost 100% by the cost savings of getting the project finished early."

• Second, because the FHCRC has an unusually high ratio of mechanical/electrical cost (initially estimated at 50% of the project) the full, walk-on interstitial floor saves time and money by enabling the primary sub-trades to work from a floor level rather than off of scaffolding.

• Third, because utilities and services are installed in a pre-determined, orderly way, costly problems like expensive last-minute re-routing and conflicts between trades are avoided.

Interstitial Cost Savings—

Additional Building Costs $1,587,500 (2.6%)
Construction Contract Savings $1,392,000 (2.3%)
     Net Additional Cost $195,500 (0.3)

Net Cost per GSF $0.65

Additional Soft Cost Savings .... $3.6 million (4.0%)
     (6 months of interim financing x $600,000/month)

Annual Lab Alteration Savings ...... $1 million (projected)
     (200,000 sf @ 10% Churn x $50/sf)

(Courtesy of Fred Hutchinson Cancer Research Center)

• Finally, it is the FHCRC's specific program needs for highly flexible space that made interstitial design a compelling solution.

While the design increased initial construction costs by 2.6%, Ott estimates that FHCRC realized a 2.3% savings due to the shortened construction time frame. He believes more savings are likely in the future.

"One of the primary reasons to have interstitial space is to hold down the life-cycle costs of a building," says Ott. "Over the last five years, FHCRC's cost to renovate and reconfigure laboratory space has averaged in excess of $100 per nsf. Conservatively, we anticipate future renovation costs in our interstitial buildings to be less than half that amount."

For more information on interstitial space, contact Guy Ott at Fred Hutchinson Cancer Research Center, 1124 Columbia Street, Seattle, WA 98104 (206) 667-5127.

—excerpted from *Facilities Planning News*, July 1993.

A Brief History of Lab Furniture

Late 1800s:

Due to the increasing demands of universities and the fledgling domestic chemical industry, the first signs of a commercial laboratory furniture industry appear. Prior to that time, lab benches are part of a construction project's carpentry work.

Early 1920s:

By this time, several companies are offering individual cabinet units in wood and steel. A typical laboratory furniture installation involves arranging units in the desired bench configuration, then covering the assembly with a wood or stone panel cut to the desired length.

Around 1930:

The "service ledge" approach to furniture installation first appears. In order to facilitate installation of plumbing, electrical and other lab services by the multiple trades people typically involved, the benchtop is split into two sections. The freestanding "service" section of the benchtop, supported by legs made of channel-form steel, is installed in advance of the cabinets, allowing service lines to be put in place quickly and easily. Once this is completed, the cabinets and their tops are assembled in front of the ledge and all benchtop seams are sealed.

1936:

The U.S. Department of Agriculture develops a system of flexible furniture using a series of telescoping legs that allow the bench assembly to be set at various heights. When the assembly has been set at the desired height, cabinets slide into the structure like drawers. Once put in place, the assembly must be completely dismantled in order to change the height. (See illustration at right.)

1962:

The first "cantilever" system of lab furniture is developed. A structural steel cantilevered frame is used to support the combined weight of the counter top and cabinetry which, for the first time, are suspended from above rather than supported from below. Since no laboratory furniture manufacturer will agree to produce the system, early projects are built by an office furniture manufacturer. Several years later the lab furniture industry adopts the design as its own and begins to manufacture cantilever-based systems.

Department of Agriculture concept: 1. Leg supports are mounted on the floor at modular
intervals. 2. Tops are then installed and anchored in position. 3. Fixtures supplied are installed
by mechanical trades. Piping is supplied, fabricated, installed by mechanical trades. 4. Cabinets
are installed by owner's maintenance crew. (Diagram courtesy of Duralab.)

—excerpted from *Facilities Planning News*, October 1992.

Moduledge

Moduledge is a non-proprietary lab furniture system based on both traditional design concepts and radically new ones. Developed specifically to address the need for easy lab reconfiguration, it uses traditional dry wall partitions and an innovative service ledge to satisfy demands for benchtop integrity and flexibility. The term "Moduledge" was coined by Jerry Koenigsberg of GPR Planners Collaborative in White Plains, N.Y.

Service ledge design

The service ledge is 22" wide and rests on three legs instead of two, with service fittings located off-center. This allows a 6-inch drywall partition to be installed on top of the service ledge wherever necessary, extending from the top of the ledge to the ceiling, or up to the structural grid. This design permits a variety of laboratory sizes without affecting utility distribution.

Because a partition can be added or deleted without impacting utilities or benchwork, it takes the location of those partitions totally out of the planning process.

Cabinetry and benchtop design

Like traditional casework installations, its floor-mounted cabinets provide a vibration- and deflection-free work surface.

Because each cabinet has its own countertop, the system allows for quick and easy removal of cabinets—to create knee spaces at sitting-height work stations—or both cabinets and countertops to accommodate floor-standing equipment. Once cabinets and countertops are assembled in the desired

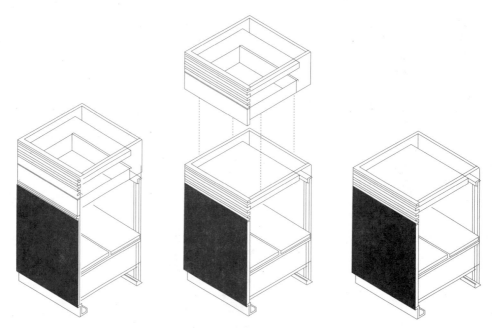

This diagram of the Mod II Furniture System with the "Add-a-Drawer" feature shows how the two cabinet components can be either stacked for full-height arrangements or the three-drawer assembly used alone for lower-height arrangements. (Diagram courtesy of GPR Planners Collaborative.)

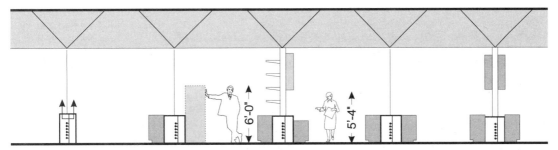

The Moduledge system can be integrated with traditional drywall partitions, allowing labs to be easily expanded and contracted according to space needs. Services are shared across partitions through a common service ledge. The Mod II design allows people of varying height to work comfortably at their benchtops. (Diagram courtesy of GPR Planners Collaborative.)

configuration all seams are caulked with silicone, providing a chemically resistant, liquid-tight seal that can be broken when necessary with a putty knife.

The system has been installed at Johns Hopkins University, Allied-Signal Corporate Technology Center and the Bevill Biomedical Science Building at the University of Alabama at Birmingham.

"We're seeing little or no cost premium for this system over traditional casework," says Steve Rosenstein, founding partner of GPR.

In some cases, he says, there has actually been a cost savings, due mainly to a reduction in the number of utility lines required. With this system, one set of utility lines can serve the labs on both sides of a partition.

Mod II

The Moduledge system was recently modified to eliminate its most significant limitation: countertops could not be raised and lowered without purchasing additional cabinetry. This modification is a response to two relatively new significant drivers in lab design: ergonomics and the Americans with Disabilities Act (ADA).

Traditional lab furniture was developed for a person 5'8" or taller. Today's laboratory population includes a significant number of shorter people who find the 36-inch average bench height awkward and "worker unfriendly." In addition the ADA requires that employers provide a customized work environment for any disabled person who can satisfactorily perform required tasks under modified conditions.

To address these demands, the frame supporting the basic standing-height cabinet (which in the original Moduledge design is a single four-drawer component) is divided to accommodate two components: a bottom three-drawer assembly and a top one-drawer assembly.

For full-height arrangements, the two components are stacked; for lower-height arrangements—including work areas for shorter or disabled workers—the top drawer assembly is simply eliminated. The counter top is then mounted directly on top of the three-drawer base cabinet. This modified system is referred to as the "Mod II Furniture System with the 'Add-a-Drawer' Feature."

For more information on Moduledge and Mod II, contact Jerry Koenigsberg or Steve Rosenstein, at GPR Planners Collaborative (914) 997-0666.

—excerpted from *Facilities Planning News,* October 1992.

ENERGY-CONSERVING BUILDING FEATURES

The National Renewable Energy Laboratory's Solar Energy Research Facility (SERF), located at the base of the South Table Mesa near Golden, Colo., provides 115,000 sf of labs and offices for research in photovoltaics (converting sunlight into electricity), high-temperature superconductivity and basic energy research.

In addition to providing a safe and efficient workplace, SERF demonstrates energy-saving technologies which can be incorporated at a relatively low cost. These include daylighting, energy-efficient fluorescent lighting, evaporative cooling, a trombe wall and an exhaust heat-recovery system. Combined, these energy-saving technologies are expected to save nearly $200,000 a year in operating expenses. Some of these technologies (direct and indirect evaporative cooling, for example) are expected to pay for themselves in three years or less.

Highlights

Lighting

Daylighting reduces the need for artificial illumination. Stepped clerestory windows in the office modules bring daylight inside to softly illuminate the work areas and brighten the corridors separating the labs from offices. Aluminum-clad trusses and roof tiers prevent sunlight from directly entering the building during the spring, summer and fall. Light passing through the clerestories strikes a white painted ceiling and northern office walls and scatters throughout the office areas. Strategically placed windows and curved alcoves disperse light down into the interior corridors. Sensors turn on lights when a person enters a room and turn them off when the room is no longer occupied.

Cooling Strategies

The SERF uses two kinds of evaporative cooling: direct and indirect. Direct evaporative cooling (also known as "swamp cooling") lowers air temperature and increases humidity. This air is then distributed throughout the building, eliminating the need to generate and distribute steam. The SERF employs indirect evaporative cooling to eliminate heat produced by mechanical equipment. In conventional facilities, mechanical chillers cool the water that circulates through and around equipment to dissipate heat. At the SERF, heated water passes through cooling towers before it reaches the mechanical chillers. Due to the area's arid climate, the cooling towers are usually sufficient to reduce the temperature. However, when the dew point is sufficiently high, the water in the towers will not evaporate quickly enough. At this point, the mechanical chillers (which use HCFC 22, a less harmful refrigerant), go to work. The cooling towers are larger than required for the building's size, allowing the water more contact with air for better cooling. This reduces the airflow pressure drop, so smaller fans can be used.

Trombe Wall

The SERF's shipping and receiving area, which has no south-facing windows, contains a trombe wall. In this passive solar technology, sunlight passes through glass and a narrow airspace to strike a 16"-thick concrete wall. A dark coating on the wall helps absorb heat, which is then radiated into the building. Heat gain during the summer is minimal because little direct sunlight hits the wall. The area is also protected by shadows in the summer.

For more information about energy-saving facilities features at SERF, contact Susan Wilcox at Anderson DeBartolo Pan
2480 North Arcadia Ave.
Tucson, AZ 85712
(602) 795-4500.

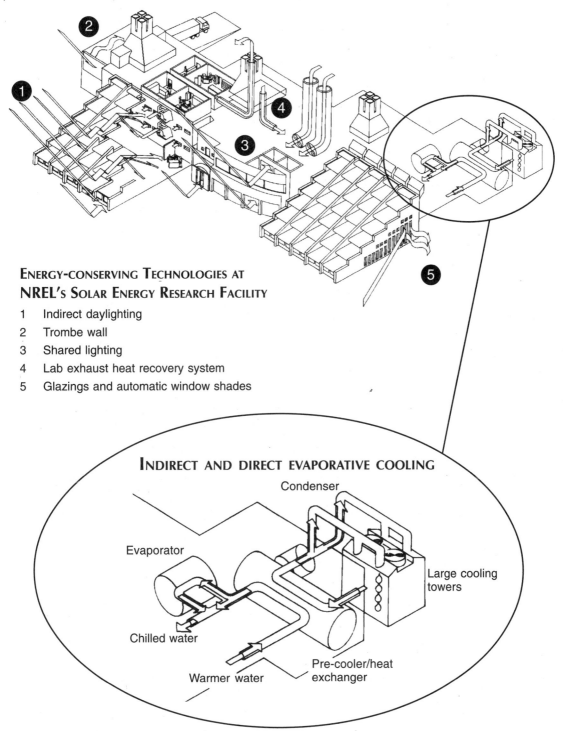

ENERGY-CONSERVING TECHNOLOGIES AT NREL's SOLAR ENERGY RESEARCH FACILITY

1   Indirect daylighting
2   Trombe wall
3   Shared lighting
4   Lab exhaust heat recovery system
5   Glazings and automatic window shades

INDIRECT AND DIRECT EVAPORATIVE COOLING

Condenser

Evaporator

Large cooling towers

Chilled water

Warmer water

Pre-cooler/heat exchanger

(Plans by NREL, courtesy of Anderson DeBartolo Pan.)

100 Recent Project Profiles

TABLE OF CONTENTS

Animal Facilities **189**
    Chicago Zoological Society 191
    United States Department of Agriculture (USDA) 191

Corporate Office/Mixed Use Facilities **195**
    Advanced Micro Devices 197
    American Family Insurance 197
    American Family Life Assurance Company (AFLAC) 198
    American Home Products 198
    Baltimore Life/Life of Maryland 199
    Champion International 200
    Howard Hughes Medical Institute 201
    Intel Corporation 201
    Irvine Ranch Water District 202
    James River Corporation 203
    Library Plaza Tower Associates (LPT) 203
    LifeScan Incorporated 204
    The Lighthouse, Inc. 205
    Los Angeles Department of Water and Power 205
    Mercantile Stores Company, Inc. 206
    O'Brien Powder Products, Inc. 207
    Proteon, Inc. 207
    Rhône-Poulenc Rorer Inc. 208
    Towers Perrin 208
    US West 209
    Vision Service Plan 210
    Walker, Richer & Quinn, Inc. 210
    West Allis Memorial Hospital 211

Healthcare Facilities **213**
    Inpatient Facilities **215**
    Baystate Medical Center 215
    Boston City Hospital 215
    Cape Cod Hospital 216
    ChildCare, Inc. 216
    Columbia Hospital Corporation 217
    Greater Baltimore Medical Center 218
    Kaiser Permanente Medical Center 218
    Passavant Hospital 219

St. Elizabeth Hospital 219
St. Luke's Medical Center 220
St. Luke's\Roosevelt Hospital Center 220

Outpatient Facilities **221**
Marin General Hospital 221
Mary Imogene Bassett Hospital 222
Mercy Hospital 222
Richland Memorial Hospital 223
Rocky Mountain Cancer Center 223
St. Elizabeth's Medical Center 224
Yale New Haven Hospital 224

Inpatient/Outpatient Facilities **225**
Pomona Valley Hospital Medical Center 225

Medical Office/Patient Education Facilities **226**
St. Thomas Hospital 226
Wake Medical Center 226

R&D Facilities **229**
Biomedical Research Facilities **231**
Alton Ochsner Medical Institutions 231
Beth Israel Hospital 231
DNAX (Schering Plough Corporation) 232
Joslin Diabetes Center 232
National Institutes of Health 233
Wadsworth Center for Laboratories and Research 234

Biotechnology Facilities **234**
Alpha-Beta Technology, Inc. 234
BASF 235
Genentech, Inc. 235
Genentech, Inc. 236

Pharmaceutical Facilities **236**
Allergan, Inc. 236
Bristol-Myers Squibb 237
Sandoz Pharmaceuticals Corporation 238
Schering-Plough Corporation 238

Miscellaneous R&D Facilities **239**
Atochem North America 239
Bell Northern Research Ltd. 239
Bristol-Myers Squibb Company 240
DowElanco 240
Eli Lilly & Company 241
Himont, USA 242

National Renewable Energy Laboratory 242
Neutrogena Corporation 243

University Facilities 245

University Biomedical Facilities 247
Hospital of the University of Pennsylvania 247
Pennsylvania State University 247
University of Maryland School of Medicine 248
University of Texas Southwestern Medical Center 249

University Healthcare Facilities 250
University of Alabama Health Services Foundation 250
University of California—Berkeley 250
University of Nebraska 251
University of Pittsburgh Medical Center 252

University Science Facilities 252
California State University at Fullerton 252
Case Western Reserve University 253
Duke University 253
Massachusetts Institute of Technology 254
Medical College of Pennsylvania 255
University of California—Berkeley 255
University of California—Davis 256
University of California—Los Angeles 257
University of Rochester 257

University Miscellaneous Facilities 258
Beaver College 258
Carleton College 258
Haverford College 259
University of California—Irvine 260
University of Washington 260
University of Wisconsin—Milwaukee 261
West Virginia University 261

Miscellaneous Facilities 265
Canadian Space Agency (CSA) 267
Child Abuse Prevention Foundation 267
General Services Administration 268
Irvine Ranch Water District 268
National Archives & Records Administration 269
United States Regulatory Commission 269
U.S. Postal Service 270

ANIMAL FACILITIES

Chicago Zoological Society

Brookfield Zoo Veterinary Care Facility
Occupancy: August 1993

Building Owner: Chicago Zoological Society
Location: Brookfield, Illinois
Project Type: New construction
Principal Building Function: Animal hospital
Project Delivery Method: General contractor
Total NSF: 12,785
  Office/Staff Support: 3,300
  Treatment, Radiology, Surgery/ICU: 3,125
  Hospitalization: 3,000
  Laboratory: 1,300
  Necropsy: 1,050
  Quarantine/Isolation: 1,010
Total GSF: 20,000
Construction Cost: $3.5 million
Project Cost: $4.5 million
Cost per SF: $175

Architect: Flad & Associates, Madison, Wis.
Mechanical/Electrical Engineer: Affiliated Engineers, Inc., Madison, Wis.
Builder: Turner Construction, Special Projects Division, Arlington Heights, Ill.

United States Department of Agriculture (USDA)

Animal Research Building
Occupancy: September 1994

Building Owner: USDA Animal and Plant Health Inspection Service
Location: Fort Collins, Colo.
Project Type: New construction
Principal Building Function: Research laboratory
Project Delivery Method: Competitive bid, general contract
Total NSF: 21,250

Total GSF: 25,000
Construction Cost: $5,168,722
Project Cost: $6,016,359
Cost per SF: $206

Architect: Hoover Berg Desmond, Denver, Colo.
Consultants:
   Civil/Structural: Boyd Brown Stude & Cambern, Englewood, Colo.
   Lab Consultant: EnvirAnQuest, Fort Collins, Colo.
   ME: Energy Masters Corporation, Overland Park, Kan.
   Prime Contractual Firm: Englewood Design Group, Overland Park, Kan.
Builder: M.A. Mortenson Company, Fort Collins, Colo.

CORPORATE OFFICE/MIXED USE FACILITIES

Advanced Micro Devices

Corporate Headquarters
Occupancy: June 1994

Building Owner: Advanced Micro Devices
Location: Sunnyvale, Calif.
Project Type: Renovation
Principal Building Function: Offices
Project Delivery Method: General contract
Total NSF: Not Available
Total GSF: 318,000
Construction Cost: $30 million
Project Cost: $41 million
Cost per SF: $129

Architect: HOK Architects, San Francisco
Consultants (all of California):
   Acoustic/Audio-Visual: Paoletti Associates, San Francisco
   Electrical: Sasco/Valley Electric, Mountain View
   Lighting: Luminae Souter, San Francisco
   Mechanical: The Linford Company, San Jose
   Structural: Martin Middlebrook Louie, San Francisco
Builder: DPR Construction Inc., Redwood City, Calif.

American Family Insurance

National Headquarters
Occupancy: February 1992: Central plant, data center/mail processing
            September 1992: Office, training education

Building Owner: American Family Insurance
Location: Madison, Wis.
Project Type: New construction
Principal Building Function: National Headquarters facility including office and
   administration, central data center and mail processing center.
Project Delivery Method: Construction management, fast-track with separate bid
   packages for major building components
Total NSF: 610,248
   Offices: 406,733
   Education & Training: 47,558
   Mail Center: 15,218
   Data Center: 46,324
   Support: 64,415

Central Utility Plant: 30,000
Total GSF: 840,000
Construction Cost: $81.4 million
Project Cost: Not Available
Cost per SF: $98 (includes site and parking facilities)

Architect and Structural Engineer: Flad & Associates, Madison, Wis.
Consultants:
   Data Center: The Austin Company, Cleveland
   MEP: Affiliated Engineers, Inc., Madison, Wis.
Construction Manager: M.A. Mortenson Company, Minneapolis

American Family Life Assurance Company (AFLAC)

AFLAC Square
Occupancy: May 1994

Building Owner: AFLAC
Location: Chofu, Japan
Project Type: New construction
Principal Building Function: Offices, data center
Project Delivery Method: Build-to-suit
Total NSF: Not Available
Total GSF: 300,000
Construction Cost: Not Available
Project Cost: $400 million (includes land and interior fit-out)
Cost per SF: $1,333

Architect: Mitsubishi Estate Company, Japan
Overall Project Manager: Satulah Group, San Francisco
General Contractors: Kajima Corporation, Taisei, Tokyu and Fujita, Japan

American Home Products

Corporate Headquarters
Occupancy: October 1993

Building Owner: American Home Products
Location: Five Giralda Farms, Madison, N.J.
Project Type: New construction
Principal Building Function: Corporate office headquarters
Project Delivery Method: Fast-track, nine bid packages
Total NSF: 380,000
Total GSF: 480,000
Construction Cost: $100 million

Project Cost: Not Available
Cost per SF: $208

Architect: The Hillier Group, Princeton, N.J.
Consultants:
  Acoustics: Shen Milsom & Wilke, New York
  Civil, Environmental, Structural: Paulus, Sokolowski & Sartor, Warren, N.J.
  Curtain Wall: Curtain Wall Design, Inc. (C.D.L.), Dallas, Texas
  Food Service: Philip C. Antico, Inc., Seacliff, N.Y.
  Lighting: David A. Mintz Incorporated, New York
  Masonry: Colin Munro, Batvia, Ill.
  MEP and Fire: R.G. Vanderweil Engineers, Inc., Princeton, N.J.
  Security Design: Schiff & Associates, Inc., Bastrop, Texas
  Telecommunications: Walsh-Lowe & Associates, Inc., Hoboken, N.J.
  Traffic: Michael Maris Associates, Inc., Glen Rock, N.J.
Builder: Sordoni Skanska Construction Company, Parsippany, N.J.

Baltimore Life/Life of Maryland
Baltimore Life Corporate Headquarters
Occupancy: December 1992

Building Owner: Baltimore Life
Location: Owings Mills, Md.
Project Type: New construction
Principal Building Function: Offices
Project Delivery Method: Construction management
Total NSF: 75,700
  Tenant Space: 15,100
  Common Support: 10,800
  Administrative Services: 9,800
  Information Systems: 8,000
  Accounting: 6,100
  Actuarial: 3,300
  Customer Service: 3,300
  Career Sales: 3,200
  Underwriting: 2,900
  General Agency: 2,700
  Executive: 2,600
  Human Resources: 1,800
  Finance: 1,500
  Claims: 900
  Legal: 800
  Other: 2,900
Total GSF: 103,000
Construction Cost: $10.3 million

Project Cost: $16.4 million
Cost per SF: $100

Architect: Ayers/Saint/Gross Architects and Planners, Baltimore
Consultants:
  Civil: Daft McCune Walker, Towson, Md.
  Interiors: Forte Design, Baltimore
  Landscape: SWA Group, Boston
  ME: James A. Posey & Associates, Baltimore
  Project Forester: Steve Clark & Associates, College Park, Md.
  Structural: LPJ, Inc., Baltimore
Builder: The Whiting-Turner Contracting Company, Baltimore

Champion International

Knightsbridge Campus, Corporate Administration
Occupancy: September 1991

Building Owner: Champion International Corporation
Location: Hamilton, Ohio
Project Type: Corporate office renovation and expansion
Principal Building Function: Corporate administrative offices, HQ
Project Delivery Method: Construction management; multiple prime contractors
Total NSF: 322,369
  Main Addition: 166,750
    Office: 87,350
    Mech./Maint./Storage/Dock: 50,000
    Cafe/Kitchen/Service: 15,500
    Atrium/Circulation: 4,800
    Conference Areas: 4,000
    Credit Union: 1,750
    Company Store: 1,350
  Renovation: 155,619
    Misc. Office: 67,116
    North Wing: 31,808
    West Wing: 28,353
    East Wing: 25,942
    Lobby: 2,400
Total GSF: 360,000
  Renovation: 175,000
  Addition: 185,000
Construction Cost: Not Available
Project Cost: $30.9 million (includes partial site work, addition, all addition furnishings)
Cost per SF: $85.8

Architect/Engineer/Interiors: Hixson Architecture/Engineering/Interiors, Cincinnati

Kitchen Consultant: Kruse Lally & Associates, Cincinnati
General Contractor: (Addition) F. Messer & Sons, Cincinnati
Construction Manager: (Renovation) Champion International, Hamilton, Ohio

Howard Hughes Medical Institute

HHMI Headquarters
Occupancy: June 1993

Building Owner: Howard Hughes Medical Institute
Location: Chevy Chase, Md.
Project Type: New construction
Principal Building Function: Offices, conference center
Project Delivery Method: General contract/GMP
Total NSF: Not Available
Total GSF: 305,000
Construction Cost: $55 million
Project Cost: $76.5 million
Cost per SF: $180.33

Architect: The Hillier Group, Princeton, N.J.
Consultants:
   Acoustics/Audio-Visual: Acentech Inc., Cambridge, Mass.
   Civil: Kamber Engineering, Gaithersburg, Md.
   Landscape: Louise Schiller Associates, Princeton, N.J. and LDR, Columbia, Md.
   MEP: Joseph R. Loring and Associates, Inc., Washington, D.C.
   Structural: Cagley and Associates, Rockville, Md.
Contractor: George Hyman Construction Co., Bethesda, Md.

Intel Corporation

SC-10 Robert N. Noyce Building
Occupancy: January 1992

Building Owner: Intel Corporation
Location: Santa Clara, Calif.
Project Type: New construction
Principal Building Function: Office, parking, dry lab, cafeteria, museum, recreation
   center
Project Delivery Method: Negotiated bid, design-build MEP, multiple bid packages
Total NSF:
   Building: 559,230
   Recreation Center: 6,150

Total GSF:
  Building: 585,240
  Garages: 569,960
  Recreation Center: 6,480
Construction Cost: $64,317,300
  Office Building (including site work): $53,664,200
  Garages: $9,689,000
  Recreation Center (including site work): $936,200
Project Cost: Not Available
Cost per SF:
  Office Building: $91.70
  Garages: $17
  Recreation Center (including site work): $144.50

Architect: Bottom Duvivier, Redwood City, Calif.
Consultants:
  Electrical: Ackerman Engineers, Palo Alto, Calif.
  Landscape: SWA, Sausalito, Calif.
  Mechanical: Practicon, Palo Alto, Calif.
  Structural: Robinson, Meier, Juilly, South San Francisco
Builder: Rudolph & Sletten, Foster City, Calif.

Irvine Ranch Water District

Corporate Headquarters
Occupancy: October 1992

Building Owner: Irvine Ranch Water District
Location: Irvine, Calif.
Project Type: New construction
Principal Building Function: Corporate headquarters
Project Delivery Method: GC
Total NSF: 55,256
  First Floor: 23,580
  Second Floor: 20,506
  Board Room/Multi-Purpose: 1,110
Total GSF: 52,300
Construction Cost: $7.3 million
Project Cost: Not Available
Cost per SF: $140

Architect: LPA, Inc., Irvine, Calif.
Consultants:
  Civil: Fuscoe Williams Lindgren & Short, Irvine, Calif.
  Electrical: R.E. Wall & Associates, Tustin, Calif.
  Landscape: The Dike Partnership, Irvine, Calif.

Mechanical: Tsuchiyama & Kaino, Inc., Irvine, Calif.
  Structural: SKT Structural Engineering, Laguna Hills, Calif.
Builder: Snyder Langston Builders, Irvine, Calif.

James River Corporation

Technology and Business Center
Occupancy: November 1992

Building Owner: James River Corporation
Location: Milford, Ohio
Project Type: New construction
Principal Building Function: Research and development labs, pilot plant, administrative functions, multimedia center, ancillary support spaces, customer support areas
Project Delivery Method: Fast-track, 10 bid packages
Total NSF: 150,500
  Labs, Office and Lab Support Technical Center: 52,000
  Offices: 50,000
  Pilot Plant: 27,600
  Warehouse: 20,900
Total GSF: 197,500
Construction Cost: $17.6 million
Project Cost: $21 million
Cost per SF: $89 (includes extensive site development and lab equipment, excludes loose furniture)

Architect: Baxter Hodell Donnelly Preston, Inc., Cincinnati
Engineer: H.A. Williams & Associates, Cincinnati
Builder: Duke Construction Management, Inc., Cincinnati

Library Plaza Tower Associates (LPT)

Plaza Park Tower
Occupancy: January 1992

Building Owner: Grosvenor International
Location: Sacramento, Calif.
Project Type: New construction, steel frame, floors of metal decking with concrete topping
Principal Building Function: Offices
Project Delivery Method: GMP
Total NSF: 401,000
Total GSF: 539,460
Construction Cost: $80 million
Project Cost: $90 million

Cost per SF: $148

Architect: Kaplan/McLaughlin/Diaz Architects, San Francisco
Consultants:
ME: Glumac & Associates, Inc., San Francisco
Structural: Buehler & Buehler, Associates, Sacramento, Calif.
Contractor: Turner Construction Company, Sacramento, Calif.

LifeScan Incorporated
LifeScan Building 3
Occupancy: Phased June-August, 1991

Building Owner: LifeScan Incorporated
Location: Milpitas, Calif.
Project Type: New construction
Principal Building Function: Healthcare manufacturing, research labs, sales, marketing, customer service, quality control and engineering departments
Project Delivery Method: Multi-phased fast-track; general contractor and design contractors preselected; other subcontracts negotiated
Total NSF: 143,480
Labs/Manufacturing: 77,138
Offices: 38,777
Warehouse: 21,563
Exercise Facility: 6,912
Total GSF: 145,802
Construction Cost:
Phase I: $814,000
Phase II: $5.9 million
Phase III: $6.1 million
Project Cost: $13 million
Cost per SF: $89.31

Architect: Briggs Associates, San Jose, Calif.
Consultants:
Civil: Kier & Wright, Santa Clara, Calif.
Electrical: BRK Associates, Alameda, Calif.
Landscape: Lauderbaugh Hill, Landscape Architects, Sunnyvale, Calif.
Mechanical: Mechanical Solutions, San Jose, Calif.
Structural: Ireland Engineering, Fremont, Calif.
Contractor: Vanderson, Inc., Fremont, Calif.

The Lighthouse, Inc.

Lighthouse National Headquarters
Occupancy: June 1994

Building Owner: The Lighthouse, Inc.
Location: New York
Project Type: Renovation, addition
Principal Building Function: Vision center, child development center, technology center, classrooms, institute for applied research, performing arts center, computer center, administrative offices
Project Delivery Method: Construction manager with a GMP
Total NSF: 101,000 (outfitted)
Total GSF: 170,000
Construction Cost: $27.5 million
Project Cost: Not Available
Cost per SF: $161

Architect: Mitchell/Giurgola Architects, New York
Consultants:
 Acoustic: Robert A. Hansen Associates, Inc., New York
 Elevator: John A. Van Deusen & Associates, Inc., Livingston, New Jersey
 MEP: Cosentini Associates, New York
 Structural: Severud Associates, New York
Builder: Barr and Barr, New York

Los Angeles Department of Water and Power

James H. Anthony Office Building
Occupancy: July 1992

Building Owner: Los Angeles Department of Water and Power
Location: Los Angeles
Project Type: New construction on 35-acre site
Principal Building Function: Offices, computer center, water-quality laboratories, telecommunications control center
Project Delivery Method: CM/GC
Total NSF: 270,000
 Computer Center: 30,000
 Laboratories: 18,000
 Cafeteria: 12,000
 Telecommunications Control Center: 12,000
 Mail Processing Center: 8,000
 Warehouse: 8,000

Employee Fitness Center: 1,500
Total GSF: 315,000
Construction Cost: $57.6 million
Project Cost: Not Available
Cost per SF: $182

Architect: The Austin Company, Santa Ana, Calif.
Consultants: None
General Contractor: McCarthy, Irvine, Calif.

Mercantile Stores Company, Inc.

Mercantile Stores University
Occupancy: September 1992

Building Owner: Mercantile Stores Company, Inc.
Location: Fairfield (Cincinnati), Ohio
Project Type: New construction (single-story)
Principal Building Function: Education and learning center
Project Delivery Method: Construction management, fast track, early bid packages for
items with a long lead time (steel, mechanical and electrical equipment, curtain wall)
Total NSF:
Phase I: 13,133
    Classrooms: 4,446
    Conference Rooms: 2,367
    Office Area: 1,787
    Breakout Area: 1,700
    Kitchen: 303
    Tel./Data Room: 160
    Other: 2,365
Phase II: 13,700
    Classrooms: 9,000
    Auditorium: 4,000
    Conference Room: 700
Total GSF: 30,000
Construction Cost:
Phase I: $1,910,500
Phase II: $1,030,200
Project Cost: $2,940,700
Cost per SF: $58

Architect: Hixson Architecture/Engineering/Interiors, Cincinnati
Consultant: Audio Visual Systems, Inc., Dayton, Ohio
Builder: Reece Campbell, Inc., Cincinnati

O'Brien Powder Products, Inc.

Headquarters Facility
Occupancy: February 1993

Building Owner: O'Brien Powder Products
Location: Houston
Project Type: New construction
Principal Building Function: Headquarters, manufacturing, warehouse
Project Delivery Method: Construction management
Total NSF: Not Available
Total GSF: 140,000
Construction Cost: $8 million
Project Cost: $10,709,000
Cost per SF: $52.01

Architect: Lockwood, Andrews and Newman, Inc., Houston
Consultants: None
Construction Manager: Gilbane Building Company, Houston

Proteon, Inc.

Headquarters and Manufacturing Facility
Occupancy: October 1992

Building Owner: The Chiofaro Co., Boston
Location: Westborough, Mass.
Project Type: New construction
Principal Building Function: Headquarters, manufacturing
Project Delivery Method: Construction management, general contract
Total NSF: 250,000
  Office: 187,500
  Manufacturing: 62,500
Total GSF: 250,000
Construction Cost: $16 million
Project Cost: Not Available
Cost per SF: $64 (including fit-up)

Architect: Symmes Maini & McKee Associates, Inc., Cambridge, Mass.
Consultants: None
Contractor: Algonquin Construction, Rumford, R.I.

Rhône-Poulenc Rorer Inc.

Corporate Headquarters/Central Research Laboratories
Occupancy:

      Headquarters: September-November 1991
      Central Research Laboratories: January-July 1992

Building Owner: Rhône-Poulenc Rorer Inc.
Location: Collegeville, Pa.
Project Type: New construction
Principal Building Function: Corporate headquarters facility for international
    pharmaceutical firm; central research laboratory
Project Delivery Method: Multi-phased fast-track; simultaneous design and
    construction with research and central utility facilities
Total NSF: 240,000
    Office Wing, Library, Conference Rooms: 191,000
    Executive Offices: 31,500
    MIS (Management Information System) Computer Room Support: 9,500
    Print Shop, Central Duplicating, Mail: 5,500
    Waiting Area/Lobby: 2,500
Total GSF: 315,000
Construction Cost: $33,500,000
Project Cost: $54,140,000
Cost per SF: $172

Architect/Engineer: CUH2A, Princeton, N.J.
Consultants:
    Audio/Visual: Norair Asadourian, Rego Park, N.Y.
    Food Service: Romano-Gatland, Lindenhurst, N.Y.
Construction Manager: Turner Construction Company, Philadelphia

Towers Perrin

Towers Perrin Office Relocation and Data Center
Occupancy: August 1991

Building Owner: Towers Perrin
Location: Philadelphia
Project Type: Renovation, new construction
Principal Building Function: Consulting offices, conference center, administrative
    support
Project Delivery Method: Fast-track, 6 bid packages
Total NSF: 340,000
    Offices: 305,000
    Administrative services: 20,000

Conference center: 15,000
Total GSF: 450,000
Construction Cost: $20 million
Project Cost: $30 million
Cost per SF: $45

Architect: The Hillier Group, Philadelphia
Consultants:
   ME: Flack + Kurtz, New York
   Structural: Cagley & Harman, King of Prussia, Pa.
Builder: Commercial Construction Group, Philadelphia

US West

Jack MacAllister Center for Advanced Technologies
Occupancy: April 1991

Building Owner: Project and Facilities Management: Betawest for US West
Location: University of Colorado Research Park, Boulder, Colo.
Project Type: New construction
Principal Building Function: Corporate headquarters, telecommunications research
Project Delivery Method: Single bid with CM/GC
Total NSF: 158,000
Total GSF: 289,249
Construction Cost: $31.5 million
Project Cost: $41.3 million
Cost per SF: $143

Architect: MBT Associates, San Francisco
Consultants:
   Acoustics: Charles Salter, San Francisco
   Audio/Visual: Robert Morris, Walnut Creek, Calif.
   Civil Engineer: Drexel Barrell, Boulder, Colo.
   Cost Estimation: Adamson Associates, San Francisco
   Elevators: Lerch Bates, Littleton, Colo.
   Landscape: EDAW, Inc., Fort Collins, Colo.
   MEP: Flack + Kurtz, San Francisco
   Soils Engineer: Chen Associates, Denver
   Structural: Forell Elsesser Engineers, San Francisco
Builder: Gerald Phipps, Inc., Denver, Colo.

Vision Service Plan

Corporate Headquarters
Occupancy: April 1993

Building Owner: Vision Service Plan
Location: Rancho Cordova, Calif.
Project Type: New construction
Principal Building Function: Offices, customer service, data processing, shipping
Project Delivery Method: Negotiated design/build
Total NSF: 132,000
Total GSF: 153,200
Construction Cost: $9 million (includes shell and site improvements)
Project Cost: Not Available
Cost per SF: $53 (shell)

Architect: LPA, Inc., Sacramento
Consultants: (all of Sacramento)
  Civil: Psomas & Associates
  Electrical: Rex Moore
  Mechanical: MDG
  Structural: Culp & Tanner
Contractor: Camray Construction, Sacramento

Walker, Richer & Quinn, Inc.

West Lake Union Center
Occupancy: March 1994

Building Owner: Fisher Properties, Inc.
Location: Seattle
Project Type: New construction
Principal Building Function: Office space, retail, parking
Project Delivery Method: Negotiated contract
Total NSF: 104,400
Total GSF: 112,000
Construction Cost: $3,657,890
Project Cost: $3,839,111
Cost per SF: $32.82

Architect: NBBJ, Seattle
Consultant: ABKJ, Seattle
Builder: Turner Construction, Seattle

West Allis Memorial Hospital

West Allis Renovations
Occupancy: March 1994

Building Owner: West Allis Memorial Hospital
Location: West Allis, Wis.
Project Type: Renovation/expansion
Principal Building Function: Administrative offices
Project Delivery Method: "Flad Track" (negotiated fast-track construction)
Total NSF: 119,700
Total GSF: 174,800
Construction Cost: $29.8 million
Project Cost: $36.5 million
Cost per SF: $170

Architect: Flad & Associates, Madison, Wis.
Consultants:
   Engineering: Affiliated Engineers, Inc., Madison, Wis.
   Masterplanning: Space Diagnostics, Inc., Madison,Wis.
General Contractor: C.G. Schmidt, Milwaukee

HEALTHCARE FACILITIES

INPATIENT
OUTPATIENT
INPATIENT/OUTPATIENT
MEDICAL OFFICE/PATIENT EDUCATION

Baystate Medical Center

Wesson Women and Infants Unit
Occupancy: January 1992

Building Owner: Baystate Medical Center
Location: Springfield, Mass.
Project Type: New construction and renovation
Principal Building Function: Maternity/perinatal center
Project Delivery Method: Fast-track, sequenced
Total NSF: 68,485
  New: 46,060
  Renovation: 22,425
Total GSF: 113,000
Construction Cost: $18.7 million
Project Cost: $23.4 million
Cost per SF: $166

Architect: TRO/The Ritchie Organization, Newton, Mass.
MEP: R.G. Vanderweil Engineers, Boston
Construction Manager: Gilbane Building Company, Providence, R.I.

Boston City Hospital

Inpatient Addition
Occupancy: January 1994

Building Owner: Boston City Hospital
Location: Boston
Project Type: New construction
Principal Building Function: Clinical labs, emergency facilities, trauma center,
  surgical suites
Project Delivery Method: Publicly bid/general contract
Total NSF: Not Available
Total GSF: 349,000
Construction Cost: Not Available
Project Cost: $63.5 million
Cost per SF: $182.16

Architect: Hoskins Scott & Partners, Inc.; CANNON (both of Boston)

Consultants: (all of Boston)
  Civil: ASEC Corporation
  Geotechnical: McPhail Associates
  HVAC/Electrical: BR+A Consulting Engineers
  Plumbing: Robert W. Sullivan
  Structural: McNamara/Salvia
General Contractor: Peabody Construction Company, Boston

Cape Cod Hospital

Lyndon P. Lorusso Emergency Center
Occupancy: September 1993

Building Owner: Cape Cod Hospital
Location: Hyannis, Mass.
Project Type: New construction
Principal Building Function: Emergency care
Project Delivery Method: General contractor
Total NSF: 20,000
Total GSF: 32,000
  New construction: 25,000
  Renovation: 7,000
Construction Cost: $5,734,000
Project Cost: Not Available
Cost per SF: $179

Architect: Hoskins Scott & Partners Inc., Boston
Consultants:
  Landscape: The Halvorson Company, Inc., Boston
  MEP: Thompson Consultants Inc., Marion, Mass.
  Structural: McNamara/Salvia, Boston
General Contractor: Westcott Construction Company, Attleboro, Mass.

ChildCare, Inc.

Minneapolis Children's Medical Center
Occupancy: Phased Fall 1991—April 1993

Building Owner: ChildCare, Inc., Minneapolis
Location: Minneapolis
Project Type: New construction and renovation
Principal Building Function: Children's medical center
Project Delivery Method: Phased, multiple-bid packages with construction management
Total NSF: 157,247

New: 99,112
　Renovated: 58,135
Total GSF: 237,691
　New: 150,717
　Renovated: 86,974
Construction Cost: $30,572,928
　General: $13,645,021
　Mechanical: $7,024,054
　Electrical: $6,294,139
　Sitework: $329,040
　Signage: $128,714
　Other: $3,151,960
Project Cost: $33,199,707
Cost per SF: $129

Architect: Hansen Lind Meyer Inc., Iowa City, Iowa
Food Service Design: Robert Rippe & Associates Inc., Minneapolis
Construction Manager: M.A. Mortenson Company, Minneapolis

Columbia Hospital Corporation

Bay Area Medical Center
Occupancy: September 1993

Building Owner: Columbia Hospital Corporation
Location: Corpus Christi, Texas
Project Type: New construction
Principal Building Function: Acute-care hospital and MOB
Project Delivery Method: General contractor
Total NSF: 301,292
　Hospital: 180,000
　Medical Office Building: 112,923
Total GSF: Not Available
Construction Cost: $33 million
Project Cost: $50 million
Cost per SF: $96

Architect: The Stichler Design Group, San Diego
Consultants:
　Civil: Urban Engineering, Corpus Christi, Texas
　Electrical: Semenza Engineering, San Diego
　Interiors: Watkins, Carter, Hamilton Architects, Bellaire, Texas
　Landscape: The Dike Parternship, San Diego
　Lighting: Ericson Heinrichs Lighting Design, San Diego
　Medical Equipment: Health Facility Consultants, Houston
General Contractor: Fulton Construction Corporation, Corpus Christi, Texas

Greater Baltimore Medical Center

Greater Baltimore Medical Center Addition
Occupancy: November 1993 (Phase I)

Building Owner: Greater Baltimore Medical Center
Location: Baltimore
Project Type: New construction
Principal Building Function: Community hospital
Project Delivery Method: Construction manager with GMP, 8 bid packages
Total NSF: 154,262
  Surgery/PACU/Support: 34,139
  LDR/Delivery/OB: 20,867
  M/S Nursing Units: 20,204
  ICU'S: 15,000
  Post-partum: 13,540
  Cafeteria/Dietary: 10,805
  Nursery/NICU: 10,159
  Department of Medicine/Cardiology: 8,279
  Radiology: 5,381
  Support: 15,888
Total GSF: 180,000
Construction Cost: $28 million (1992 dollars)
Project Cost: $35 million (1992 dollars)
Cost per SF: $146

Architect: RTKL Associates, Baltimore
Consultants:
  Civil Engineer/Landscape: Daft McCune Walker, Baltimore
  Parking Structure: Walker Parking Consultants/Engineers, Inc., West
  Conshohocken, Penn.
Builder: J. Vinton Schafer & Sons, Inc., White Marsh, Md.

Kaiser Permanente Medical Center

North Wing Addition
Occupancy: June 1992

Building Owner: Kaiser Foundation Hospitals
Location: San Francisco
Project Type: Addition, renovation
Principal Building Function: Acute hospital/administration
Project Delivery Method: Design/build
Total NSF: 114,000

Total GSF: 132,000
Construction Cost: $34 million
Project Cost: $59 million
Cost per SF: $257

Architect: Hospital Designers Inc., St. Louis
Structural Engineer: Thompson LaBrie, Pasadena, Calif.
Builder: Hospital Building and Equipment Co., St. Louis

Passavant Hospital

Additions and Renovations
Occupancy: December 1994

Building Owner: Passavant Hospital
Location: Pittsburgh
Project Type: New construction, renovations
Principal Building Function: Healthcare
Project Delivery Method: Fast track with GMP (construction management)
Total NSF: 216,626
   New Construction: 187,848
   Renovation: 28,778
Total GSF: 187,848
Construction Cost: $39,420,732
Project Cost: $60 million
Cost per SF: $170

Architects: Williams Trebilcock Whitehead, Pittsburgh and Ellerbe Becket, Washington, D.C.
Consultants:
   Electrical: Carl J. Long, Pittsburgh
   Mechanical: Dodson Engineering, Pittsburgh
   Site Development: Chambers Vukich, Zelienople, Penn.
   Structural: Watson Engineering, McMurray, Penn.
Builder: Turner Construction Company, Pittsburgh

St. Elizabeth Hospital

St. Elizabeth Hospital Tower for Care
Occupancy: April 1994

Building Owner: St. Elizabeth Hospital
Location: Elizabeth, N.J.
Project Type: New construction
Principal Building Function: Emergency, surgery, LDRs/nurseries, patient care units,

operating rooms, patient beds
Project Delivery Method: GMP with construction manager
Total NSF: 187,000
New: 137,000
Renovation: 50,000
Total GSF: 187,000 (includes renovation and new central utilities plant)
Construction Cost: $41 million (includes equipment)
Project Cost: $58 million
Cost per SF:
Construction only: $217
Project Cost: $309

Architect/MESP/Fire Protection/Interiors: Ballinger, Philadelphia
Consultants: None
Construction Manager: Gilbane Building Company, Northeast Office, Princeton, N.J.

St. Luke's Medical Center

Knisley Building Addition
Occupancy: March 1993

Building Owner: St. Luke's Medical Center
Location: Milwaukee
Project Type: New construction and renovation
Principal Building Function: Inpatient bed tower
Project Delivery Method: Contract manager, multiple bid packages
Total NSF: 34,700 (departmental)
Total GSF: 51,000 (departmental)
Construction Cost: $14,215,883
Project Cost: $16,888,244
Cost per SF: $222.99 (includes systems retrofit and use of crane for all building materials)

Architect: Hammel Green & Abrahamson, Inc., Milwaukee
Consultants: (both of Milwaukee)
Electrical: Leedy & Petzhold
Mechanical: Ring & DuChateau
Builder: Boldt Construction, Milwaukee

St. Luke's\Roosevelt Hospital Center

Roosevelt Hospital
Occupancy: April 1993

Building Owner: St. Luke's\Roosevelt Hospital Center

Location: New York
Project Type: New construction
Principal Building Function: Acute-care hospital
Project Delivery Method: Construction management
Total NSF: Not Available
Total GSF: 589,280
Construction Cost: $150 million
Project Cost: Not Available
Cost per SF: $254

Architect: Skidmore Owings Merrill, New York
Consultants:
  Acoustic: Cerami & Associates, New York
  Equipment: Equipment Planners, Inc., Summit, N.J.
  Kitchens: Romano Gatland, Lindenhurst, N.Y.
  Lighting: Fischer Marantz, New York
  ME: Jaros Baum and Bolles, New York
Construction Manager: Lehrer McGovern Bovis, Inc., New York

OUTPATIENT FACILITIES

Marin General Hospital

Marin General Cancer Center
Occupancy: January 1993

Building Owner: Western Investments
Location: Larkspur, Calif.
Project Type: Renovation of existing medical office building
Principal Building Function: Medical office building for outpatient cancer treatment
Project Delivery Method: GC, negotiated contract
Total NSF: 5,520
Total GSF: 10,000
Construction Cost: $3.7 million
Project Cost: $6.5 million
Cost per SF: $370

Architect: Kaplan/McLaughlin/Diaz, San Francisco
Consultants: (all of San Francisco)
  Electrical: Cammisa & Wipf
  Mechanical: Guttmann and MacRitchie
  Structural: Dasse Design

Builder: Mayta & Jensen, San Francisco

Mary Imogene Bassett Hospital

The Bassett Clinic and Energy Center
Occupancy: August—December 1992

Building Owner: The Mary Imogene Bassett Hospital
Location: Cooperstown, N.Y.
Project Type: New construction, renovation
Principal Building Function: Ambulatory clinic, laboratories, energy center
Project Delivery Method: CM, traditional bid
Total NSF:
   Clinic: 115,000
   Energy Center: 11,000
Total GSF:
   Clinic: 135,000
   Energy Center: 14,000
Construction Cost: $24 million
Project Cost: Not Available
Cost per SF: $161

Architect/MES/Interiors: CANNON, Grand Island, N.Y.
Consultants:
   Hardware: Tatara Enterprises, Akron, N.Y.
   Radiation Therapy: Jack S. Kromer, Georgetown, Texas
Construction Manager: McCarthy, Inc., St. Louis

Mercy Hospital

Mercy Hospital and Health Campus
Occupancy: July 1992

Building Owner: Mercy Healthcare Systems
Location: Bakersfield, Calif.
Project Type: New construction
Principal Building Function: Hospital, medical offices, emergency services
Project Delivery Method: Design/bid
Total NSF: 69,135
Total GSF: 127,000
Construction Cost: $18,425,000
Project Cost: $29 million
Cost per SF: $148

Architects: Kaplan/McLaughlin/Diaz, San Francisco; BFGC Architects, Bakersfield

Consultants:
  ME: Syska & Hennessy, San Francisco
  Structural: Butzbach/Bar-Din/Dagan, San Francisco
General Contractor: Centex Golden, San Diego

Richland Memorial Hospital

Center for Cancer Treatment and Research
Occupancy: April 1992

Building Owner: Richland Memorial Hospital
Location: Columbia, S.C.
Project Type: New construction
Principal Building Function: Ambulatory Cancer Center
Project Delivery Method: GC, 13 bid packages
Total NSF: 130,000 (estimated)
Total GSF: 170,000
Construction Cost: $19,775,089
  Main Project: $15,732,409
  General Conditions: $1,236,000
  Excavation/Foundation: $840,919
  Site Mechanical: $612,954
  Site Work: $200,000
Project Cost: $32 million
Cost per SF: $116.32

Architect: Hansen Lind Meyer Inc., Orlando, Fla.
Consultants:
  Radiation: Jimmy O. Fenn, Radiation Consultant, Columbia, S.C.
  Structural/Civil: Stevens & Wilkinson Inc., Columbia, S.C.
Builder: Barton-Malow, Columbia, S.C.

Rocky Mountain Cancer Center

Rocky Mountain Cancer Center
Occupancy: April 1994

Building Owner: Rocky Mountain Cancer Center L.L.C.
Location: Denver
Project Type: New construction
Principal Building Function: Outpatient medical oncology, pediatric oncology and
  radiation oncology
Project Delivery Method: Design-build
Total NSF: 34,000
Total GSF: 39,000

Construction Cost: $3.8 million
Project Cost: $7.4 million
Cost per SF: $97

Architect: H+L Architecture Ltd., Denver
Consultants (both of Denver):
  ME: McFall, Konkel & Kimball
  Structural: Bierbach Consulting Engineers
Builder: The Neenan Company, Denver

St. Elizabeth's Medical Center

St. Margaret's Center for Women and Infants
Occupancy: June 1993

Building Owner: St. Elizabeth's Medical Center
Location: Boston
Project Type: New construction
Principal Building Function: Women's and infants' outpatient services
Project Delivery Method: Fast-track
Total NSF: 70,000
Total GSF: 91,500
Construction Cost: $16 million
Project Cost: $22 million
Cost per SF: $160

Architect: TRO/The Ritchie Organization, Newton, Mass.
Consultants:
  Civil: Daylor Consulting Group, Boston
  Equipment Planners: Gene Burton & Associates, Nashville, Tenn.
  Landscape Architect: Mason & Frey, Belmont, Mass.
  MEP: R.G. Vanderweil Engineers, Inc., Boston
  Structural: Chapin Associates, Norwood, Mass.
Builder: Jackson Construction Company, Dedham, Mass.

Yale New Haven Hospital

West Pavilion
Occupancy: June 1993

Building Owner: Yale New Haven Hospital
Location: New Haven, Conn.
Project Type: New construction
Principal Building Function: Hospital services

Project Delivery Method: Construction management (GMP), phased construction (fast-track)
Total NSF: 230,350
Total GSF: 445,000
Construction Cost: $96.3 million
Project Cost: $121.8 million
Cost per SF: $185

Architect: Shepley Bulfinch Richardson and Abbott, Boston
Consultants:
  Acoustical: Cavanaugh Tocci Associates, Inc., Sudbury, Mass.
  Equipment Planning: Heinemann Associates, Eden Prairie, Minn.
  Food Service: Food Facilities Concepts, Inc., Carnegie, Penn.
  Functional Planning: M. Bostin & Associates, Elimsford, N.Y.
  Heliport: Design Build International, Inc., Bloomfield, Conn.
  Interior Furnishings & Coordination: Rosalyn Cama Design Associates, Inc., New Haven, Conn.
  Landscape Architect: Rolland/Towers, P.C., New Haven, Conn.
  ME: BR + A Consulting Engineers Inc., Boston
  Plumbing/Fire Protection: Robert W. Sullivan Inc., Boston
  Signage: Jon Roll Associates, Cambridge, Mass.
  Structural: Spiegel Zamecnik & Shah, Inc., New Haven, Conn.
  Vertical Transportation: LeVee & Associates, Bowie, Md.
  Waterproofing: Simpson Gumpertz & Heger, Inc., Arlington, Mass.
 Builder: Turner Construction Company, Sheldon, Conn.

Inpatient/Outpatient Facilities

Pomona Valley Hospital Medical Center
Women's Center Phase I Addition
Occupancy: January 1992

Building Owner: Pomona Valley Hospital Medical Center
Location: Pomona, Calif.
Project Type: New construction
Principal Building Function: Women's Center (inpatient/outpatient)
Project Delivery Method: General contractor
Total NSF: 133,000
Total GSF: 190,000
Construction Cost: $39,634,489
Project Cost: $50 million
Cost per SF: $263

Architect/Interior/Landscape: NBBJ, Seattle
Consultants:
  MEP: Popov Engineering, Newport, Calif.
  Structural: Taylor & Gaines, Pasadena, Calif.
General Contractor: McCarthy/Pacific, Irvine, Calif.

MEDICAL OFFICE/PATIENT EDUCATION FACILITIES

St. Thomas Hospital
Support and Education Building
Occupancy: May 1994

Building Owner: St. Thomas Hospital
Location: Nashville, Tenn.
Project Type: New construction
Principal Building Function: Support/education spaces, library, offices, patient hotel
Project Delivery Method: Construction management
Total NSF: Not Available
Total GSF: 106,730
Construction Cost: $11,071,000
Project Cost: $11,071,000
Cost per SF: $103

Architect/Engineer: Henningson, Durham & Richardson, Inc., Omaha, Neb.
Consultants: None
Construction Manager: Turner Construction Company, Nashville, Tenn.

Wake Medical Center
Wake Medical Education Institute
Occupancy: March 1994

Building Owner: Wake Medical Center
Location: Raleigh, N.C.
Project Type: New construction
Principal Building Function: Clinics, offices, parking, conference center
Project Delivery Method: Public bid, 4 prime contracts
Total NSF: 62,900
  AHEC Clinics (2nd-3rd floor): 30,800
  AHEC Offices (4th floor): 13,400
  Conference Center/Medical Library (1st floor): 18,700

Total GSF: 121,500 (plus 72,990 parking)
Construction Cost: $13 million
Project Cost: $16.9 million
Cost per SF: $107 (excludes parking)

Architect: Freeman-White Architects, Inc., Charlotte, N.C.
Engineer: DSA Design Group of NC Inc., Raleigh, N.C.
Contractor: Davidson and Jones, Raleigh, N.C.

R&D FACILITIES

BIOMEDICAL RESEARCH
BIOTECHNOLOGY
PHARMACEUTICAL
MISCELLANEOUS

Biomedical Research Facilities

Alton Ochsner Medical Institutions

Research/Clinical Facility
Occupancy: March 1993

Building Owner: Alton Ochsner Medical Institutions
Location: New Orleans
Project Type: New construction
Principal Building Function: Research and clinical laboratories
Project Delivery Method: Traditional single prime contract
Total NSF: 50,829
Total GSF: 112,338
Construction Cost: $12,286,740
Project Cost: $14,622,068
Cost per SF: $109

Architect: Hansen Lind Meyer, Iowa City, Iowa
Associate Architect: Kessels-Diboll-Kessels, New Orleans
Vibration Consultant: Environmental Services, Inc., Minneapolis
Builder: T.L. James & Company Inc., Building Division, New Orleans

Beth Israel Hospital

Research North
Occupancy: March 1994

Building Owner: Beth Israel Hospital
Location: Boston
Project Type: Renovation
Principal Building Function: Research laboratory
Project Delivery Method: Construction management with GMP
Total NSF: 85,610
Total GSF: 114,000
Construction Cost: $19.4 million
Project Cost: Not Available
Cost per SF: $170

Architect: Tsoi/Kobus & Associates, Inc., Boston
Consultants:
  Civil: Vanasse Hangen Brustlin, Inc., Watertown, Mass.

Development: Boston Properties, Inc., Boston
Electrical: Lottero + Mason Associates, Inc., Boston
Landscape: John Copley & Associates, Inc., Boston
Mechanical: TMP Consulting Engineers, Inc., Boston
Specifications: Richard D. White, Weston, Mass.
Structural: McNamara/Salvia, Inc., Boston
Tenant: Lab Designs, Newton Highlands, Mass.
Builder: Turner Construction Company, Boston

DNAX (Schering Plough Corporation)

DNAX Research Institute
Occupancy: 1983, 1987, September 1992

Building Owner: DNAX (Schering Plough Corporation)
Location: Palo Alto, Calif.
Project Type: Multi-phased renovation of warehouse shell space into research wet lab
and support
Principal Building Function: Biomedical research, scale-up laboratories, animal
facilities and administrative support
Project Delivery Method: Bid and negotiation
Total NSF: 60,000
Total GSF: 70,000
Construction Cost: $9.45 million
Project Cost: Not Available
Cost per SF: $135

Architect: Kornberg Associates, Menlo Park, Calif.
Consultants:
Randall Lamb Associates, San Francisco
Rinne & Peterson, Palo Alto, Calif.
Builders (all of California)**:**
1983 Phase: Swensen, San Jose
1987 Phase: Rudolph & Sletten, Foster City
1992 Phase: Howard J. White, Mountain View

Joslin Diabetes Center

Research and Clinical Facility Expansion
Occupancy: Phased July 1993--April 1994

Building Owner: Joslin Diabetes Center
Location: Boston
Project Type: New construction and renovations
Principal Building Function: Research for vascular biology, transgenics, molecular

biology and clinical research; lab support spaces, administrative spaces
Project Delivery Method: Construction management
Total NSF:
  New: 77,000
Total GSF:
  New: 93,000
  Renovated: 17,000
Construction Cost: $18.2 million
Project Cost: Not Available
Cost per SF: $165 (includes new and renovated space)

Architect: Ellenzweig Associates, Inc., Cambridge, Mass.
Consultants:
  Code Consultant: Hal Cutler, P.E., Sudbury, Mass.
  Cost Estimating: Vermeulens, Inc., Boston
  Landscape Architect: The Halvorson Company, Boston
  ME: BR + A Consulting Engineers, Inc., Boston
  Plumbing/Fire Protection: Robert W. Sullivan, Inc., Boston
  Specification Writer: Gui Specifications, Belmont, Mass.
  Structural: LeMessurier Consultants, Inc., Cambridge, Mass.
Builder: George B.H. Macomber Construction Company, Boston

National Institutes of Health

Building 5
Occupancy: September 1992

Building Owner: National Institutes of Health
Location: Bethesda, Md.
Project Type: Renovation, additions
Principal Building Function: Basic and theoretical research
Project Delivery Method: General contract
Total NSF: 44,900
  Laboratories: 26,710
  Support Space: 7,740
  Offices: 7,730
  Lab and Seminar Room: 2,720
Total GSF: 88,700
Construction Cost: $15 million
Project Cost: Not Available
Cost per SF: $175

Architect: A.M. Kinney, Cincinnati
Asbestos Consultant: Aerosal Monitoring and Analysis Inc., Lanham, Md.
Builder: Walsh Construction Company, Trumbull, Conn.

Wadsworth Center for Laboratories and Research

David Axelrod Institute for Public Health
Occupancy: October 1992 (phased)

Building Owner: Wadsworth Center for Laboratories and Research
Location: Albany, N.Y.
Project Type: New construction
Principal Building Function: Medical laboratory
Project Delivery Method: Construction management, owner agent
Total NSF: 120,000
Total GSF: 250,000
Construction Cost: $46 million
Project Cost: $65 million
Cost per SF: $184

Architect: Urbahn Associates, Inc., N.Y.
Engineer: STV Group, New York
Construction Manager: McCarthy Bros. Co., St. Louis

BIOTECHNOLOGY FACILITIES

Alpha-Beta Technology, Inc.

Bipharmaceutical Manufacturing Facility
Occupancy:
    Offices and Labs: March 1994
    Manufacturing: May 1994

Building Owner: Alpha-Beta Technology
Location: Smithfield, R.I.
Project Type: New construction
Principal Building Function: Quality control labs, sterile manufacturing, production
Project Delivery Method: Construction management
Total NSF: 54,000
Total GSF: 57,000
  Clean Manufacturing Space: 20,000
  Administrative/Office Area: 10,000
  Laboratory Areas: 9,000
  Warehouse Space: 18,000

Construction Cost: $17 million
Project Cost: $34 million
Cost per SF:
  Warehouse: $50
  Manufacturing: $750

Engineer: John Brown E & C, Chicago
Owner Consultant: Cutler Associates, Worcester, Mass.
Construction Manager: Gilbane Building Company, R.I.

BASF

Biomedical Research Center
Occupancy: September 1993

Building Owner: BASF
Location: Worcester, Mass.
Project Type: New construction
Principal Building Function: Pharmaceutical and biotechnology R & D
Project Delivery Method: Construction management
Total NSF: 213,000
Total GSF: 372,000
Construction Cost: $68.5 million
Project Cost: $83.7 million
Cost per SF: $225

Architect: Smith, Hinchman & Grylls Associates, Inc., Detroit
Consultants:
  Environmental Permits/Survey/Civil: Daylor Consulting, Boston
  Landscape: Johnson, Johnson & Roy/inc., Ann Arbor, Mich.
  Process: Triad Technologies, Inc., Newcastle, Del.
Construction Manager: Marshall Contractors, Rumford, R.I.

Genentech, Inc.

Building 3B
Occupancy: April 1993

Building Owner: Genentech, Inc.
Location: San Francisco
Project Type: New construction
Principal Building Function: Multi-use pharmaceutical manufacturing
Project Delivery Method: GMP contract
Total NSF: 23,500
Total GSF: 27,400

Construction Cost: $21 million
Project Cost: $30 million
Cost per SF: $700

Architect:
   Building Shell: Fluor Daniel, Redwood City, Calif. (shell designed in 1986)
   Engineer: Bechtel Corporation, San Francisco
Consultants: None
Builder: Dome Construction, San Francisco

Genentech, Inc.

Founders Research Center
Occupancy: September 1992

Building Owner: Genentech, Inc.
Location: South San Francisco, Calif.
Project Type: New construction
Principal Building Function: Biotechnology research labs, offices, support space
Project Delivery Method: Negotiated contract
Total NSF: 162,500
Total GSF: 303,500
Construction Cost: $68,920,000
Project Cost: $70,400,000
Cost per SF: $227

Architect: SRG Partnership, PC, Portland, Ore.
Consultants:
   Lab Planning: Richard R. Rietz, Foster City, Calif.
   ME: Affiliated Engineers, Inc., Madison, Wis.
   Structural: KPFF Consulting Engineers, Portland, Ore.
Builder: Rudolph & Sletten, Inc., Foster City, Calif.

PHARMACEUTICAL FACILITIES

Allergan, Inc.

Research and Development Facility II
Occupancy: May 1993

Building Owner: Allergan, Inc.

Location: Irvine, Calif.
Project Type: New construction
Principal Building Function: Biological, chemical and pharmaceutical research and safety evaluation
Project Delivery Method: General contract/GMP with pre-construction services
Total NSF: 93,940
Total GSF: 154,000
Construction Cost: $33.3 million
Project Cost: $40 million (includes design, programming, city and county fees and office furniture)
Cost per SF: $216.23

Architect: The Blurock Partnership, Newport Beach, Calif.
Consultants:
  Engineer: Affiliated Engineers, Madison, Wis.
  Lab Planner: Earl Walls Associates, San Diego
Contractor: Turner Construction, Orange County, Calif.

Bristol-Myers Squibb

U.S. Pharmaceuticals Division Headquarters
Occupancy: May 1993

Building Owner: Bristol-Myers Squibb
Location: Plainsboro, N.J.
Project Type: New construction
Principal Building Function: Offices, TV studio, training rooms, conference room, parking
Project Delivery Method: General contract/GMP
Total NSF: Not Available
Total GSF: 690,000
Construction Cost: $87,135,000
Project Cost: $100 million
Cost per SF: $145

Architect: The Hillier Group, Princeton, N.J.
Consultants:
  Acoustics: Shen Milsom & Wilke, New York
  Civil: Van Note-Harvey Associates, Princeton, N.J.
  Geotechnical: Melick-Tully & Associates, Inc., South Bound Brook, N.J.
  Interiors: KPA Design Group, Philadephia
  Land Planners: Wells-Larsen-Appel, Haddonfield, N.J.
  MEP: Flack + Kurtz, New York
  Structural: DiStasio & Van Buren, Union, N.J.
Construction Contractor: Sordoni Skanska Construction, Parsippany, N.J.

Sandoz Pharmaceuticals Corporation

Research and Development Building 405
Occupancy: March 1992

Building Owner: Sandoz Pharmaceuticals Corporation, Sandoz Research Institute
Location: East Hanover, N.J.
Project Type: New construction
Principal Building Function: Pharmaceutical research and development
Project Delivery Method: One fixed-price lump-sum bid
Total NSF: 91,400
Total GSF: 177,000
Construction Cost: $44 million
Project Cost: $50 million
Cost per SF: $248

Architect: A.M. Kinney Associates, Architects, Engineers, Cincinnati
Consultants: Not Available
Builder: Walsh Construction Company, Trumbull, Conn.

Schering-Plough Corporation

Drug Discovery Facility (DDF)
Occupancy: December 1992

Building Owner: Schering-Plough Research Institute
Location: Kenilworth, N.J.
Project Type: New construction
Principal Building Function: Pharmaceutical research
Project Delivery Method: Construction manager/modified fast track/multiple MEP
packages, multiple overall bid packages
Total NSF: 552,700
  Lab Blocks: 320,100
  Administrative Offices: 104,000
  Animal Facility: 75,100
  Administrative Support: 47,700
  Building Support: 5,400
Total GSF: 985,500
Construction Cost: $245 million (includes built-in equipment but not furnishings)
Project Cost: $300 million
Cost per SF: $248

Architect: Haines Lundberg Waehler

Consultants:
  Controls: Electronic Systems Associates, New York
  Cost Estimating: Federman Construction Consultants, New York
Construction Manager: Torcon, Inc., Westfield, N.J.

MISCELLANEOUS R&D FACILITIES

Atochem North America

Research Laboratory—Building #9
Occupancy: June 1992

Building Owner: Atochem North America, a division of Elf-Aquataine
Location: King of Prussia, Pa.
Project Type: New construction
Principal Building Function: Research laboratory
Project Delivery Method: CM
Total NSF: 24,441
  First floor: 16,745
  Second floor: 7,696
Total GSF: 43,700
Construction Cost: $7.3 million
Project Cost: $9.1 million
Cost per SF: $208

Architect: H2L2 Architects/Planners, Philadelphia
Consultants:
  Acoustical: Robert Hansen, New York
  Civil: Pennoni Associates, Inc., Philadelphia
  Lighting: Lighting Design Collaborative, Inc., Philadelphia
  ME: DLB Associates, Inc., Wanamassa, N.J.
  Structural: A.W. Lookup Co., Conshohocken, Pa.
Builder: Sordoni-Skanska Construction Company, Parsippany, N.J.

Bell Northern Research Ltd.

Carling Lab 5
Occupancy: October 1993

Building Owner: Bell Northern Research Ltd.
Location: Ottawa, Canada

Project Type: New construction
Principal Building Function: Labs, offices, multi-purpose tower
Project Delivery Method: Construction management
Total NSF: 496,358
Total GSF: 600,000
Construction Cost: $75 million
Project Cost: $100 million
Cost per SF: $125
(all cost information in Canadian dollars)

Planning/Design: CRSS Architects, Inc., Houston
Consultant: Giffels Associates, Ltd., Toronto, Ontario
Construction Manager: Giffels Associates

Bristol-Myers Squibb Company

Bristol-Myers Squibb Chemical Development Laboratory
Occupancy: July 1991

Building Owner: Bristol-Myers Squibb Company
Location: New Brunswick, N.J.
Project Type: New construction
Principal Building Function: Process research and development
Project Delivery Method: Phased, construction management, individual bid packages
    assembled by CM
Total NSF: 51,474
   Labs: 26,170
   Offices: 14,106
   Lab support: 5,050
   Other: 6,148
Total GSF: 97,785
Construction Cost: $25.5 million
Project Cost: $31 million
Cost per SF: $261

Architect: The Kling-Lindquist Partnership, Inc., Philadelphia
Consultants: Not Available
Builder: The Gilbane Building Company, Princeton, N.J.

DowElanco

Research and Development Center
Occupancy: November 1992

Building Owner: DowElanco

Location: Indianapolis
Project Type: New construction
Principal Building Function: Agricultural chemical research and development laboratories for discovery, process research, biology and environmental chemistry
Project Delivery Method: Phased multiple contracts: general, contractor, plumbing, etc.
Total NSF: 353,194
    Laboratories: 140,219
    Lab Support: 65,763
    Greenhouses (Labs): 53,465
    Offices: 50,402
    Other: 43,345
Total GSF: 610,125
Construction Cost: $42 million
Project Cost: $65 million
Cost per SF: $107

Architect: JBA Architects, P.C., Newark, Ohio
Consultant: Korda/Nemeth Engineering, Columbus, Ohio
Builder: Whittenberg Construction Company, Louisville, Ky.

Eli Lilly & Company

C93 Research Facility
Occupancy: July 1993

Building Owner: Eli Lilly & Company
Location: Clinton, Ind.
Project Type: New construction
Principal Building Function: Labs and offices
Project Delivery Method: Construction manager
Total NSF: 38,800
    Mechanical/Electrical: 16,200
    Lab: 7,700
    Offices: 7,100
    Lab Support: 3,700
    Other: 4,100
Total GSF: 51,325
Construction Cost: $10,250,000
Project Cost: $13,000,000
Cost per SF: $199.70

Architect: CSO Architects, Inc., Indianapolis
Engineer: CUH2A, Princeton, N.J.
Builder: Gilbane Building Company, Chicago

Himont, USA
North American Research & Development Center
Occupancy: April 1992

Building Owner: Himont, USA
Location: Elkton, Maryland
Project Type: New construction
Principal Building Function: Research and development, conference facilities, administration, library
Project Delivery Method: Design-build
Total NSF: 115,000
Total GSF: 175,000
  Lab/Office/R&D Wings: 91,000
  Atrium/Conference: 35,000
  High-Bay: 20,000
  Central Utility Plant: 16,000
  Pilot Plant: 10,000
  Atrium: 3,000
Construction Cost: $25 million
Project Cost: $30 milion
Cost per SF: $143

Architect/Interiors/Engineer: Ballinger, Philadelphia
Consultants: None
Builder: Henderson Corporation, Raritan, N.J.

National Renewable Energy Laboratory
Solar Energy Research Facility
Occupancy: Phased October 1993—April 1994

Building Owner: Department of Energy
Location: Golden, Colo.
Project Type: New construction
Principal Building Function: Materials science research, photovoltaics, high-temperature superconductivity
Project Delivery Method: General contractor
Total NSF: 77,050
Total GSF: 115,000
Construction Cost: $17.3 million
Project Cost: $19.6 million
Cost per SF: $150

Architect: Anderson De Bartolo Pan, Inc., Phoenix
Consultants:
  Civil: Drexel Barrell, Boulder, Colo.
  Fire Protection: Rolf Jensen & Associates, Concord, Calif.
  Lab Design: Research Facilities Design, San Diego
  Landscape: EDAW, Inc., Fort Collins, Colo.
Builder: G.E. Johnson, Colorado Springs, Colo.

Neutrogena Corporation

Skin Care Research Facility
Occupancy: April 1994

Building Owner: Neutrogena Corporation
Location: Los Angeles
Project Type: Renovation
Principal Building Function: Cosmetic and skin care product research and development
Project Delivery Method: General contract/GMP with pre-construction services
Total NSF: 16,000
Total GSF: 32,000
Construction Cost: $3.15 million
Project Cost: $4.5 million
Cost per SF: $98.75

Architect: The Blurock Partnership, Newport Beach, Calif.
Consultants:
  Electrical: Frederick Brown Associates, Newport Beach, Calif.
  Mechanical: Tsuchiyama & Kaino, Irvine, Calif.
  Structural: John A. Martin & Associates, Los Angeles
Contractor: Kitchell Contractors, Irvine, Calif.

UNIVERSITY FACILITIES

BIOMEDICAL
HEALTHCARE
SCIENCE
MISCELLANEOUS

University Biomedical Facilities

Hospital of the University of Pennsylvania

Institute for Human Gene Therapy Research Laboratory
Occupancy: April 1993

Building Owner: Hospital of the University of Pennsylvania
Location: Philadelphia, Pa.
Project Type: Renovation (includes building system upgrades)
Principal Building Function: Genetics research lab, administration
Project Delivery Method: Construction management, fast-track
Total NSF: Not Available
Total GSF: 5,300
  Administration/Service: 2,900
  Lab: 2,400
Construction Cost: $1,998,500
Project Cost: $2.5 million
Cost per SF: $377

Architect/Engineer/Interior Design: Vitetta Group Incorporated, Philadelphia
Consultants: None
Construction Manager: L.F. Driscoll Co., Bala Cynwyd, Pa.

Pennsylvania State University

Biomedical Research Building, Hershey Medical Center
Occupancy: November 1992

Building Owner: The Pennsylvania State University
Location: Hershey, Pa.
Project Type: New construction
Principal Building Function: Research laboratory
Project Delivery Method: General contractor, single lump-sum bid
Total NSF: 137,814
  Departmental Breakdown:
    Medicine: 31,741
    Surgery: 29,806
    Anesthesiology: 18,906
    College Shell: 16,796
    College Assigned: 12,376
    Pediatrics: 11,973
    Pathology: 8,013

Microbiology: 6,265
Opthamology: 1,938
Functional Breakdown:
Assigned Lab: 61,223
Assigned Office: 49,506
College Shell Lab: 7,275
College Shell Office: 6,325
Classroom/Seminar: 6,223
College Shell Office/Lab: 3,196
Student Lockers/Lounges: 2,852
Lobby/Waiting: 1,154
Total GSF: 250,435
Construction Cost: $38,338,813
Project Cost: $39,046,188
Base Building: $81,979,435
Lab/Office Fitup: $6,359,378
Utility Construction Costs: $707,375
Cost per SF: $154

Architect: Geddes Brecher Qualls Cunningham, Philadelphia
Consultants:
The Sigel Group, Narbeth, Pa.
Civil: Gannett Fleming, Harrisburg, Pa.
Cost Consultant: Wolf & Company, Pleasantville, N.Y.
Laboratory Planning/Design: Earl Walls Associates, San Diego
Landscape: Louise Schiller Associates, Princeton, N.J.
Structural: Brecher Associates, Philadelphia
Builder: H.B. Alexander, Harrisburg, Pa.

University of Maryland School of Medicine
Biomedical Research Facility
Occupancy: October 1992

Building Owner: University of Maryland at Baltimore
Location: Baltimore, Md.
Project Type: Renovation
Principal Building Function: Provide lab "swing" space for researchers representing
numerous specialties
Project Delivery Method: CM
Total NSF: 31,848
Total GSF: 57,740
Construction Cost: Not Available
Project Cost: $8.4 million
Cost per SF: $145

Architect: Henningson, Durham & Richardson Inc., Alexandria, Va.
Consultants: None
Construction Manager: Lehrer McGovern Bovis, New York

University of Texas Southwestern Medical Center

Simmons Biomedical Research Building
Occupancy: April 1993

Building Owner: University of Texas System/University of Texas Southwestern
  Medical Center
Location: Dallas
Project Type: New construction
Principal Building Function: Biomedical research
Project Delivery Method: General contractor, competitive bidding, multiple-bid
  packages
Total NSF:
  Research: 204,313
  Parking: 67,762
Total GSF:
  Research Building and Lecture Facility: 412,688
  Energy Plant: 16,753
Construction Cost: $55,754,000 (includes site work, utilities and separate thermal en-
  ergy plant)
Project Cost: Not Available
Cost per SF:
  Lab Building: $125
  Thermal Energy Plant: $272

Architect: F & S Partners Incorporated, Dallas
Consultants:
  Acoustics: Acoustic Design Associates, Dallas
  Civil: Huitt-Zollars Civil Engineers, Dallas
  Consulting Architect: Edward Larrabee Barnes/John M.Y. Lee Architects, New York
  Laboratory Planning and Design: Earl Walls Associates, San Diego
  Lighting: Archillume Lighting Design, Austin, Texas
  MEP: Gaynor & Sirmen Engineers, Inc., Dallas
  Structural: Datum Engineering Inc., Dallas
  Transportation and Traffic Engineering/Planning: Deshazo Starek and Tang, Dallas
Builder: Dal-Mac Construction Company, Dallas

University of Alabama Health Services Foundation

The Kirklin Clinic
Occupancy: June 1992

Building Owner: The University of Alabama Health Services Foundation
Location: Birmingham, Ala.
Project Type: New construction
Principal Building Function: Ambulatory patient care
Project Delivery Method: Construction management, fast-track with GMP
Total NSF: 318,515
Total GSF: 415,821
Construction Cost: Clinic and Deck: $61.4 million
  Clinic: $50.7 million
  Deck, plus 18,000 sf of retail area and central plant: $10.7 million
Project Cost: $125 million
Cost per SF: $118

Architects:
  TRO/The Ritchie Organization, Birmingham, Ala.
  Pei; Cobb Freed & Partners, New York
  Garikes Wilson Atkinson, Inc., Birmingham, Ala.
Consultants:
  Acoustics: Acentech Inc., Cambridge, Mass.
  Civil: Walter Schoel, Birmingham, Ala.
  Equipment Planner: Earl Meyer & Associates, Birmingham, Ala.
  Furnishings & Equipment: Mitchell International, Chicago
  Geotechnical: Bhata Engineering Corp., Birmingham, Ala.
  Interiors: Moody & Associates, Birmingham, Ala.
  Landscape: Nimrod Long & Assoc., Birmingham, Ala.
  Lighting: William Lamb, Cambridge, Mass.
  ME: Newcomb & Boyd, Atlanta
  Signage: Lorenc Design, Atlanta
  Structural: Lane/Bishop/York/Delahay, Inc., Birmingham, Ala.
Builder: Brasfield & Gorrie/BRIC Inc. of Detroit (joint venture), Birmingham, Ala.

University of California—Berkeley

Tang Center
Occupancy: December 1992

Building Owner: University of California

Location: Berkeley, Calif.
Project Type: New construction
Principal Building Function: Outpatient student/faculty clinic
Project Delivery Method: Fast track, four bid packages
Total NSF: 47,200 (assignable)
Total GSF: 74,800
Construction Cost: $11.1 million
Project Cost: Not Available
Cost per SF: $148

Architect: Anshen + Allen, San Francisco
Consultants:
  Acoustical: Charles M. Salter & Associates, San Francisco
  Electrical: The Engineering Enterprise, Alameda, Calif.
  Elevator: Lerch Bates, Novato, Calif.
  Mechanical: Guttmann & MacRitchie, San Francisco
  Structural and Civil: Forell/Elsesser Engineers, San Francisco
Builders:
  Earthwork & Foundation Package: EMSCO, Oakland, Calif.
  Final Package: Hensel Phelps Construction Company, Santa Clara, Calif.
  Pre-Construction Services: Swinerton & Walberg, San Francisco

University of Nebraska

Outpatient Care Center
Occupancy: March 1993

Building Owner: University of Nebraska Medical Center
Location: Omaha, Neb.
Project Type: Renovation and new construction
Principal Building Function: Outpatient care/teaching hospital
Project Delivery Method: General contractor
Total NSF:
  New: 145,268
  Renovation: 9,795
Total GSF:
  New: 221,500
  Renovation: 15,114
Construction Cost: $26,731,501
Project Cost: Not Available
Cost per SF: $112.93 (includes current estimate of renovation cost)

Architect: Hansen Lind Meyer Inc., Iowa City, Iowa
Associate Architect: Robert D. Nelson Company, Omaha, Neb.

Consultants:
  Cost Estimation and Planning: Cost, Planning & Management International, Des
    Moines, Iowa
  Healthcare Planning: Deloitte Touche, Houston
Builder: Kiewit Construction Co., Omaha, Neb.

University of Pittsburgh Medical Center

Magnetic Resonance Center Building
Occupancy: May 1992

Building Owner: Presbyterian University Hospital
Location: Pittsburgh
Project Type: New constuction/fit-up
Principal Building Function: Magnetic Resonance Department
Project Delivery Method: Traditional
Total NSF: 25,162
Total GSF: 35,440
Construction Cost: (Base) $12,269,000
Project Cost: Approximately $16 million (w/magnets)
Cost per SF: $451

Architect and MEP: Burt Hill Kosar Rittelmann Associates, Butler, Pa.
Structural Engineer: Dotter Engineering, Inc., Pittsburgh
Builder: Ross and Kennedy, Pittsburgh

UNIVERSITY SCIENCE FACILITIES

California State University at Fullerton

Science Building Addition
Occupancy: January 1994

Building Owner: California State University
Location: Fullerton, Calif.
Project Type: New construction
Principal Building Function: Research, teaching, support/equipment space
Project Delivery Method: Competitive bid, general contract
Total NSF: 60,000
Total GSF: 98,000
Construction Cost: $19,307,000

Project Cost: $25,805,000
Cost per SF: $186

Architect: Anshen + Allen, Los Angeles
Lab Planner: Research Facilities Design, San Diego
General Contractor: McCarthy/Pacific, Irvine, Calif.

Case Western Reserve University

Kent Hale Smith Engineering & Science Building
Occupancy: July 1994

Building Owner: Case Western Reserve University
Location: Cleveland
Project Type: New construction
Principal Building Function: Educational and research activities
Project Delivery Method: Construction management, GMP
Total NSF: 54,230
NSF included:
  Lab Space: 30,365
  Office Space: 11,300
  Conference Rooms: 1,955
  Classrooms: 1,560
Total GSF: 93,000
Construction Cost: $18,174,500
Project Cost: $24 million
Cost per SF: $195

Architect: Shepley Bulfinch Richardson and Abbott, Boston
Consultants:
  Electrical/Plumbing/Fire Protection: Beyers Engineering Co, Cleveland
  HVAC: TMP Consulting Engineers, Boston
  Landscape: The Halvorson Company, Inc., Boston
  Structural: Zaldastani Associates, Inc., Boston
Construction Manager: The Albert M. Higley Company, Cleveland

Duke University

Levine Science Research Center
Start of Phased Occupancy: May 1994

Building Owner: Duke University
Location: Durham, N.C.
Project Type: New construction

Principal Building Function: Labs, School of the Environment, interdisciplinary research
Project Delivery Method: General contract
Total NSF: 199,652
  Basic Science: 51,122
  School of the Environment: 41,771
  DCMB: 24,689
  Computer Science: 19,756
  ID Centers/Industry: 12,021
  Engineering: 9,671
  Teaching: 3,405
  Shared Space: 37,217
Total GSF: 334,903
Construction Cost: $56 million
Project Cost: $77 million
Cost per SF: $167

Architect and Lab Planner: Payette Associates, Inc., Boston
Consultants:
  Civil: Bass, Nixon & Kennedy, Raleigh, N.C.
  Landscape: Carol Johnson & Associates, Cambridge, Mass.
  MEP: R.G. Vanderweil Engineers, Boston
  Structural: Simpson, Gumpertz & Heger, Arlington, Mass.
Builder: Centex-Simpson of Fairfax, Va.

Massachusetts Institute of Technology
Biology Building
Occupancy: May 1994

Building Owner: Massachusetts Institute of Technology
Location: Cambridge, Mass.
Project Type: New construction
Principal Building Function: Research laboratories
Project Delivery Method: GC, bid of plans and specs
Total NSF: 147,250
Animal: 28,700
Laboratories: 46,550
Lab Support: 23,000
Office: 20,951
Other: 28,050
Total GSF: 244,800
Construction Cost: $55 million
Project Cost: 70 million
Cost per SF: 286

Architect: Goody, Clancy & Associates, Boston
Consultants:
  MEP: R.G. Vanderweil Engineers, Boston
  Programming: Cambridge Laboratory Consultants, Weston, Mass.
  Structural: LeMessurier Consultants, Cambridge, Mass.
General Contractor: George B.H. Macomber Company, Boston

Medical College of Pennsylvania
Queen Lane Campus Building
Occupancy: November 1992

Building Owner: Medical College of Pennsylvania
Location: Philadelphia
Project Type: Renovation, addition
Principal Building Function: Education and research
Project Delivery Method: CM, GMP, two phases: education (I) and research (II)
Total NSF: 150,000
  Education: 82,500
  Research: 67,500
Total GSF: 213,800
  Education: 117,700
  Research: 96,100
Construction Cost: $27.4 million
  Education:
    General Trades: $6,747,000
    HVAC and Plumbing: $4,939,000
    Electrical: $1,760,000
  Research:
    HVAC and Plumbing: $6,407,000
    General Trades: $6,343,000
    Electrical: $1,740,000
Project Cost: $43 million
Cost per SF: $114 (I) and $146 (II)

Architect: Ewing Cole Cherry Brott, Philadelphia
Acoustical Consultant: Acentech Inc., Cambridge, Mass.
Builder: McCarthy Construction, St. Louis

University of California—Berkeley
Valley Life Sciences Building
Occupancy: September 1994

Building Owner: Regents of the University of California
Location: Berkeley, Calif.
Project Type: Renovation and new construction
Principal Building Function: Research and teaching laboratories, museums
Project Delivery Method: Owner PM, general-contract fee bid, subcontract bids
Total NSF: 269,500
Total GSF: 408,500
  Renovation: 339,400
  New Construction: 69,100
Construction Cost: Not Available
Project Cost: $58 million
Cost per SF: $145

Architect: The Ratcliff Architects, Emeryville, Calif.
Consultants:
  Acoustical: Walsh/Norris & Associates, San Francisco
  Electrical: The Engineering Enterprise, Alameda, Calif.
  Lab Consultant: Research Facilities Design, San Diego
  Landscape: Haygood & Associates, Berkeley, Calif.
  Mechanical: Gayner Engineers, Inc., San Francisco
  Structural: H.J. Degenkolb, San Francisco
Construction Manager: Ehninger, Fetzer, Tholen, Salt Lake City
Contractor: Perini Corporation, San Francisco

University of California—Davis

Engineering Unit II
Occupancy: June 1993

Building Owner: University of California, Davis
Location: Davis, Calif.
Project Type: New construction
Principal Building Function: Teaching, research, administration, support
Project Delivery Method: General contractor
Total NSF: 150,000
Total GSF: 185,000
Construction Cost: $26.9 million
Project Cost: Not Available
Cost per SF: $145

Architect, Lab Planner and Engineer: Erlich-Rominger, Los Altos, Calif.
Consultants:
  Civil: Morton & Pitalo, Sacramento, Calif.
  Electrical: Ackerman Engineers, Palo Alto, Calif.
  Mechanical: Mechanical Planning, Inc., San Jose, Calif.

Soils: Kleinfelder, Sacramento, Calif.
Structural: Rinne & Peterson, Palo Alto, Calif.
Vibration/Acoustics: Acentech, Inc., Canoga Park, Calif.
Contractor: Sundt Corp., Sacramento, Calif.

University of California—Los Angeles

Molecular Sciences Building
Occupancy: September 1993

Building Owner: Regents of the University of California
Location: Los Angeles
Project Type: New construction
Principal Building Function: Research laboratory
Project Delivery Method: Competitive bid, general contract
Total NSF: 88,973
  Chemistry Wing: 66,340
  Microbiology Wing: 22,633
Total GSF: 159,880
  Chemistry Wing: 112.469
  Microbiology Wing: 47,411
Construction Cost: $40.7 million
Project Cost: $49 million
Cost per SF: $258

Architect: Anshen + Allen, Architects, Los Angeles
Consultants:
  Building Engineers: Ove Arup & Partners, California Ltd., Los Angeles
  Laboratory Planners: McLellan & Copenhagen, Cupertino, Calif.
Builder: Robert E. McKee, Inc., Los Angeles

University of Rochester

Center for Optoelectronics and Imaging
Occupancy: November 1992

Building Owner: University of Rochester
Location: Rochester, N.Y.
Project Type: New construction
Principal Building Function: Laser/optics energetics, research labs, support space
Project Delivery Method: General contract
Total NSF: 70,000
Total GSF: 96,000
Construction Cost: $13.4 million
Project Cost: $13.4 million

Cost per SF: $140

Architect: SWBR Architects, P.C., Rochester, N.Y.
Consultants: (all of Rochester, N.Y.)
  Civil: Joseph C. Lu, P.E., P.C.
  ME: Robson and Woese, Inc.
  Structural: Donald Jensen & Associates
Contractor: The Pike Company, Rochester, N.Y.

UNIVERSITY MISCELLANEOUS FACILITIES

Beaver College
Health Sciences Building
Occupancy: September 1994

Building Owner: Beaver College
Location: Glenside, Pa.
Project Type: New construction and renovations
Principal Building Function: Faculty offices, teaching and research laboratories, practice clinic space
Project Delivery Method: Fast-track, construction management
Total NSF: Not Available
Total GSF: 19,000
Construction Cost: $2 million
Project Cost: Not Available
Cost per SF: $105

Architect: The Hillier Group, Philadelphia
MES Engineering: Pennoni Associates, Inc., Philadelphia
Construction Manager: Nason & Cullen, Inc., Wayne, Pa.

Carleton College
Center for Math and Computing
Occupancy: September 1993

Building Owner: Carleton College
Location: Northfield, Minn.
Project Type: New construction
Principal Building Function: Classroom, laboratory

Project Delivery Method: Negotiated bid with construction management firm
Total NSF: 26,000
Total GSF: 37,000
Construction Cost: $4.3 million
Project Cost: Not Available
Cost per SF: $116

Architects: Cambridge Seven Associates, Cambridge, Mass. and SMSQSE, Northfield, Minn.
Consultants:
  ME: R.G. Vanderweil Engineers, Inc., Boston
  Structural: Weidlinger Associates, Cambridge, Mass.
Builder: CMPI, Bloomington, Minn.

Haverford College

Sharpless Hall Addition
Occupancy: September 1992

Building Owner: The Trustees of Haverford College
Location: Haverford, Pa.
Project Type: New construction and renovation
Principal Building Function: Biology labs, library, auditorium, classrooms
Project Delivery Method: Fast-track, CMG
Total NSF:
  Existing Building: 20,000
  Addition: 15,000
Total GSF:
  Existing: 32,000
  Addition: 18,000
Construction Cost: $5,060,000
  General Construction: $3,438,000
  Mechanical: $1,231,000
  Electrical: $391,000
Project Cost: $5,977,000
Cost per SF: $121

Architect: The Hillier Group, Philadelphia
Consultants:
  ME: Vinokur-Pace, Jenkintown, Pa.
  Structural: Cagley & Harman, Inc., King of Prussia, Pa.
Builder: Lehrer McGovern Bovis, Princeton, N.J

University of California—Irvine

Science Library
Occupancy: May 1994

Building Owner: Regents of the University of California
Location: Irvine, Calif.
Project Type: New construction
Principal Building Function: Science library
Project Delivery Method: Competitive hard bid
Total NSF: Not Available
Total GSF: 189,000
Construction Cost: $25 million
Project Cost: Not Available
Cost per SF: $125

Architects: James Stirling/Michael Wilford and Associates of London, England in
  conjunction with IBI Group, Newport Beach, Calif.
Consultants:
  Civil: Hall & Foreman, Costa Mesa, Calif.
  Elevator: Lerch Bates and Associates, Mira Loma, Calif.
  Fire Prevention: Rolf Jensen and Associates, Concord, Calif.
  Landscape: Burton & Spitz, Santa Monica, Calif.
  Library Consultant: Nancy McAdams, Austin, Texas
  MES: Ove Arup & Partners, Los Angeles
Construction Manager: McCarthy, Irvine, Calif.

University of Washington

H-Wing Addition
Occupancy: July 1994

Building Owner: University of Washington
Location: Seattle
Project Type: New construction
Principal Building Function: Pharmacy school, lab/office space, classrooms, support
  space
Project Delivery Method: Competitive bid (assignable)
Total NSF: 85,930
Total GSF: 210,000
Construction Cost: Not Available
Project Cost: $33 million
Cost per SF: $162

Architect: TRA, Seattle
Consultants:
  Acoustics: Michael Yantis and Associates, Bellevue, Wash.
  Food Service: Manahan & Cleveland, Seattle
  Lab Consultant: McLellan & Copenhagen, Seattle
  Landscape: Lee and Associates, Seattle
General Contractor: SDL, Bellevue, Wash.

University of Wisconsin—Milwaukee

School of Architecture and Urban Planning
Occupancy: Fall 1993

Building Owner: University of Wisconsin—Milwaukee
Location: Milwaukee
Project Type: New construction
Principal Building Function: Research, classrooms, offices, studios, labs
Project Delivery Method: Bid
Total NSF: 85,000
Total GSF: 140,000
Construction Cost: $13 million
Project Cost: $18 million
Cost per SF: $92

Architects: Holabird & Root, Chicago, in association with Eppstein Keller Uhen, Inc.,
  Milwaukee
Consultants:
  Electrical: Dolan and Dustin, Wauwatosa, Wis.
  HVAC/Plumbing/Fire Protection: PSJ Engineering, Milwaukee, Wis.
  Structural: Graef Anhalt & Schloemer, Milwaukee
Contractor: J.H. Findorff & Son Inc., Madison, Wis.

West Virginia University

Software Independent Verification and Validation Facility
Occupancy: October 1993

Building Owner: West Virginia University Research Corporation
Location: Fairmont, West Virginia
Project Type: New construction
Principal Building Function: Data processing center
Project Delivery Method: Modified construction management with GMP
Total NSF: 35,600
Total GSF: 55,000
Construction Cost: $12 million

Project Cost: $12 million
Cost per SF: $218

Architect: Hayes Large Architects, Pittsburgh
Consultants:
  Engineer: Dynamic Design Engineering, Johnstown, Pa.
  Geotechnical: GAI Consultants, Inc., Charleston, W. Va.
  Programming: Goddard Space Flight Center (Maryland) and Boeing Corporation, Fairfax, W. Va.
Construction Manager: Turner Construction, Pittsburgh

MISCELLANEOUS FACILITIES

Canadian Space Agency (CSA)

Headquarters
Occupancy: June-August 1993

Building Owner: Canadian Space Agency
Location: St-Hubert, Quebec, Canada
Project Type: New construction
Principal Building Function: Ground control for Radarsat satellite; ground control
and simulation for the mobile service system; astronaut training center; space
technology and space science lab; agency headquarters; conference center
Project Delivery Method: Phased general contract
Total NSF: Not Available
Total GSF: 300,000
Construction Cost: $53 million
Project Cost: $80.5 million
Cost per SF: $268

Architect: Lemay & Associates and Webb Zerafa Menkes Housden Architects (both of
Montreal)
Consultants: Not Available
General Contractor: Magil Construction Ltd., Montreal

Child Abuse Prevention Foundation

A. B. and Jessie Polinsky Children's Center
Occupancy: October 1994

Building Owner: Child Abuse Prevention Foundation
Location: San Diego
Project Type: New construction
Principal Building Function: Treatment of abused children, administration, residen-
tial cottages, community center, classrooms
Project Delivery Method: Conventional
Total NSF: 91,897
Total GSF: 92,000
Construction Cost: $10.3 million
Project Cost: $16 million
Cost per SF: $174

Architect/MPS: The Stichler Design Group, Inc., San Diego
Consultants: (all of San Diego)
Civil: BSI Consultants, Inc.

Electrical: BDK Engineering
Landscape: Marum Associates
Builder: Centex-Golden Construction, San Diego

General Services Administration

Oakland Federal Building
Occupancy: October 1993

Building Owner: General Services Administration
Location: Oakland, Calif.
Project Type: New construction
Principal Building Function: Courtrooms, conference space, retail, offices
Project Delivery Method: Design/bid with lease back financing
Total NSF: 860,000
Total GSF: 1 million
Construction Cost: $150 million
Project Cost: $191 million
Cost per SF: $150

Architect: Kaplan/McLaughlin/Diaz, San Francisco
Consultants:
  Civil: Jordan Associates, Oakland, Calif.
  Landscape: POD, Inc., San Francisco
  ME: Syska & Hennessy, San Francisco
  Structural: Cygna, San Francisco
General Contractor: Walsh Construction, Sacramento, Calif.

Irvine Ranch Water District

Water Quality Laboratory
Occupancy: September 1994

Building Owner: Irvine Ranch Water District
Location: Irvine, Calif.
Project Type: New construction
Principal Building Function: Operations, administration and water quality control
Project Delivery Method: General contract/GMP with pre-construction services
Total NSF: 6,600
Total GSF: 8,900
Construction Cost: $1.9 million
Project Cost: $10.5 million
Cost per SF: $213.60

Architect: The Blurock Partnership, Newport Beach, Calif.

Consultants:
Electrical: Frederick Brown Associates, Newport Beach, Calif.
Mechanical: Tsuchiyama & Kaino, Irvine, Calif.
Structural: Culp & Tanner, El Toro, Calif.
Contractor: Turner Construction Co., Orange County, Calif.

National Archives & Records Administration

Archives II
Occupancy: October 1993

Building Owner: National Archives & Records Administration
Location: College Park, Md.
Project Type: New construction
Principal Building Function: Records storage, research, office
Project Delivery Method: 7 bid packages
Total NSF: 1,332,049
Archival Storage: 691,572
Offices: 351,000
Laboratories: 104,200
Research Complex: 60,247
Total GSF: 1,839,497
Construction Cost: $244 million
Project Cost: $265 million
Cost per SF: $133

Architects: Hellmuth, Obata & Kassasbaum with Ellerbe Becket, both of Washington
D.C. (joint venture)
Consultants:
Acoustics/Audio-Visual/Video: Joiner Consulting Group, Arlington, Texas
Civil: Greenhorne & O'Mara, Inc., Greenbelt, Md.
Cost Estimating: MMP International, McLean, Va.
Lab Planner: GPR Planners Collaborative, Inc., White Plains, N.Y.
Lighting Design: Coventry Lighting Associates, Washington, D.C.
Security/Fire Protection: Gago-Babcock & Associates, Inc., Vienna, Va.
Contractor: George Hyman Construction Co., Bethesda, Md.

United States Regulatory Commission

Two White Flint North
Occupancy: April 1994

Building Owner: Lerner Enterprises/The Tower Companies
Location: North Bethesda, Md.
Project Type: New construction

Principal Building Function: Operations Center, headquarters, labs, offices
Project Delivery Method: GMP
Total NSF: Not Available
Total GSF: 364,000
Construction Cost: $21 million
Project Cost: Not Available
Cost per SF: $57

Architect: Dewberry & Davis, Fairfax, Va.
Consultants:
  ME: TOLK, Inc., Washington, D.C.
  Structural: Severud Associates, New York
Builder: Lerner Enterprises/Tower Companies, North Bethesda, Md.

U.S. Postal Service

General Mail Facility
Occupancy: January 1993

Building Owner: U.S. Postal Service
Location: New York
Project Type: New construction, renovations
Principal Building Function: Mail processing
Project Delivery Method: Design/build
Total NSF: Not Available
Total GSF:
  New: 850,000
  Renovation: 300,000
Construction Cost: Not Available
Project Cost: $225 million
Cost per SF: $195

Architect/MEPS: Lockwood Greene Engineers, New York
Design/Builder: Crow Construction Company, New York
Construction Manager: Tishman Construction, N.Y.

U.S. Postal Service

Margaret Sellers Mail Processing and Distribution Center
Occupancy: September 1993

Building Owner: United States Postal Service
Location: San Diego
Project Type: New construction

Principal Building Function: Mail processing and distribution with public services
Project Delivery Method: General contractor
Total NSF: Not Available
Total GSF: 634,914
  Work Room: 295,550
Construction Cost:
  Phase I (site preparation): $1,676,730
  Phase II (construction): $43 million
  Fixed mechanization: $4.88 million
Project Cost: $49,556,730
Cost per SF: $78.05

Architect/MEP: The Stichler Design Group, Inc., San Diego
Consultants:
  Civil: Holtman Engineers, Lakeforest, Calif.
  Cost Estimating: Lee Saylor, Inc., Carlsbad, Calif.
  Electrical: Van Buuren Kimper Associates, San Diego
  Landscape: Marum Associates, San Diego
  Roofing: Professional Services Inc., Lafayette, Calif.
  Structural: Flores & Ng, San Diego
Builder: Swinerton & Walberg Co., Fresno, Calif.

Facilities Organization and Management Profiles

The following profiles give the organizational structure and scope of facilities management functions at a range of companies and corporations across the nation.

These profiles are compiled from Facilities Planning News *as well as from Tradeline Management Conference presentations. All profiles published in* Facilities Planning News *before November, 1993 have been updated to reflect the most current data.*

TABLE OF CONTENTS

3M Austin Center, Austin, Texas 276
Amdahl Corporation, Inc., Sunnyvale, Calif. 278
Baltimore Gas & Electric Company 280
Charles Schwab & Co., Inc., San Francisco 282
Compaq Computer Corporation, Houston 284
Hewlett-Packard Company 288
Lawrence Livermore National Laboratories 290
The National Institutes of Health 292
Xerox Corporation 294

FACILITY ORGANIZATION AND MANAGEMENT

3M Austin Center, Austin, Texas

Statement

Corporate Management Philosophy:

3M is an organization of employees and stockholders who have combined their resources to pursue common goals in providing useful products and services, creating rewarding employment, assuring an adequate return to investors and contributing to a better social and economic environment for the general public.

Facilities Management Philosophy:

Our mission is to provide quality facilities and support services that help our internal 3M customers meet their business and operating objectives.

We endeavor to hire and retain "world-class" employees, providing them with the necessary resources to attain the highest achievements possible. We maintain a core group of 3M employees and complement their time and skills with qualified external contractors and consultants.

Facilities Philosophy:
- Internal Funding
- No Financial Partners

- Internal Design Direction
- Retain Consultants as Appropriate
- High Standard 3M Specification
- Use of Interim Leased Space
- Build for Long Term Investment and Occupancy
- Incremental Size for Five Years' Needs

Overview

Name of Company: 3M Company, St. Paul, Minn.

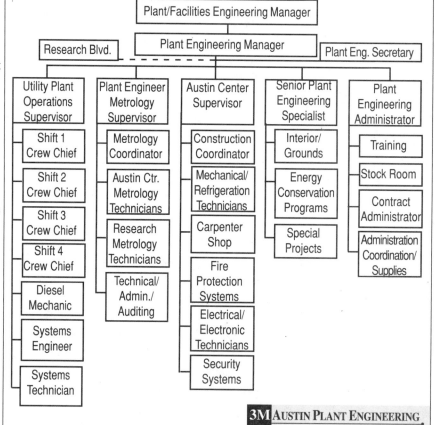

Type of Business: Manufacturing

Locations Covered by Facilities Management: 3M Austin Center, Austin, Texas

Scope of Facilities Under Management:
Total GSF: 1,300,000 gsf (excluding 500,000 sf of parking ramp structure)

Owned Facilities: 1,300,000 gsf

Leased Facilities: None

Number of Employees: 1,400 (as of August 1, 1994)

Number of Separate Buildings: 9 interconnected, plus separate central utility plant building and separate parking structure.

Total Acreage Under Management: 158

Allocation of Space by Function:
Administrative Space: 50%
Research Labs: 50%

Functions Performed Under Plant and Facilities Group:
Capital Budgeting
New Construction Planning and Management
Contract Negotiation and Management
In-house Detailed Design for New Construction
Site Development Masterplanning
Routine Renovation and Maintenance Projects
Furniture and Equipment Inventory and Management
Personnel Moves and Relocations
Waste Management and Recycling
Site Utilities (power, steam, air conditioning, etc.)
Design Support to Other Site Locations

Annual 1994 Plant and Facilities Budget:
$12,600,000 (excluding capital expenditures)

Items Included in the Annual Budget:
Facilities Management and Technical Staff/ Wages/Benefits
Travel, Training, Publications
Hourly Service, Maintenance, Tradespeople
Repairs and Maintenance
Rearrangements and Relocations
Site and Building Utilities
Instrument Calibration Shop
Major Contracted Services (see below)

Total Facilities-Related Headcount: 61
50 Plant Engineers and Administration
5 Facilities Engineers and Administration
4 Facilities Administrators
2 Environmental Engineers

Major Contracted Services/Outsourcing:
Interior and Exterior Landscaping
Pest Control
Elevator Maintenance
Water Treatment (utility plant)
Computer Hardware Servicing

Profile Information Provided By: Warren E. Johnson, Engineering Manager, Plant and Facilities Engineering

3M AUSTIN PLANT AND FACILITIES ENGINEERING

FACILITY ORGANIZATION AND MANAGEMENT

Amdahl Corporation, Inc., Sunnyvale, Calif.

Statement
Corporate Management Philosophy:

Quality, innovation and caring are the hallmarks of the Amdahl philosophy. These characterize our dealings with our employees, customers, stockholders and the communities where we live and work.

General Facilities Management Philosophy:

To provide a physical environment and supporting services that fulfill the clearly defined requirements of the company's customers, products and employees.

To contribute to the company's continued success and profitability through the effective management of facilities resources—combining outside contractors, buy/lease, etc.

Overview
Name of Company: Amdahl Corporation, Inc.

Headquarters: Sunnyvale, Calif.

Type of Business: With annual sales of approximately $2 billion, Amdahl is a major supplier of mainframe computers, data storage systems and software, in addition to educational and consulting services.

Number of Employees: 6,000

Total Facilities-Related Headcount: 70 (excluding contract employees)

Locations Covered by Facilities Management Function:

Amdahl has manufacturing and customer service operations worldwide, including Silicon Valley, Calif., and the United Kingdom.

Scope of Facilities Under Management:

Total Worldwide GSF: 3 million
Total Silicon Valley GSF: 2 million
Owned Facilities: 400,000
Leased Facilities: 1,600,000

Number of Separate Buildings: 29 (Silicon Valley)

Total Acreage Under Management: 137

Allocation of Space by Function:

Research/Labs: 70%
Manufacturing: 20%
Administrative Space: 10%

Functions Performed Under Facilities Group:

Capital Budgeting
Leasing and Lease Management
New Construction Planning
Contract Negotiation and Management
Site Development Masterplanning
Planning Routine Renovation and
    Maintenance Projects
Renovations and Maintenance
Furniture Equipment Inventory and
    Management
Personnel Moves and Relocations
Cleaning/Trash Removal

Annual 1993 Facilities Budget: $70 million (including depreciation and capital expenditures)

Items included in the Facilities Budget:

Facilities Management and Technical Staff/ Wages/Benefits
Travel, Training, Publications

Hourly Service/Maintenance/Tradespeople
Maintenance and Cleaning Supplies
Janitorial
Security
Repairs and Maintenance
Rearrangements and Relocations
Safety
Site and Building Utilities

Lease Expenses

Major Contracted Services/Outsourcing:
1. Janitorial
2. Grounds
3. Security

Profile Information Provided By: Gerald Hummel, Director of Facilities

FACILITIES RELATIVE TO TOP CORPORATE MANAGEMENT STRUCTURE AT AMDAHL

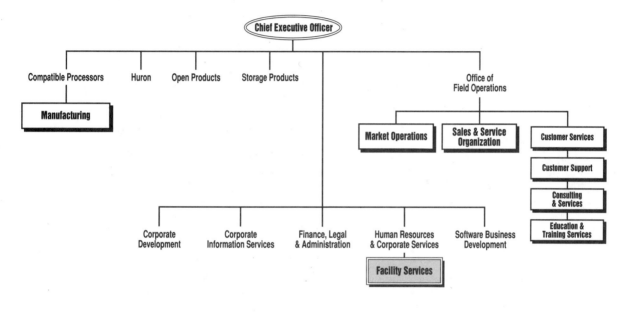

ORGANIZATION OF THE FACILITIES GROUP AT AMDAHL

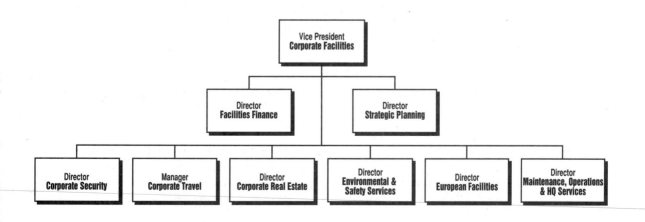

FACILITY ORGANIZATION AND MANAGEMENT

Baltimore Gas & Electric Company

Statement

Corporate Management Philosophy:

By performing as a world-class energy company, Baltimore Gas & Electric is dedicated to achieving complete customer satisfaction by providing superior energy products and services.

Facilities & Fleet Services Philosophy:

Our facilities mission is to provide and manage the land, facilities and related services that are needed to support the company's operations. Facilities & Fleet Services is a service organization which provides and manages the land and facilities needed to support BGE's operations. Beyond this basic mission, Facilities & Fleet Services also provides several services to a variety of internal customers including Employee Protection Services, Executive Security Services, Security Investigations, Substation Grounds Maintenance, Food Services and Recreational Services.

Facilities & Fleet Services values safety, cost effectiveness, quality, customer satisfaction and environmental responsibility. The department operates with the belief that the company is best served by having centralized real estate and facilities services and that Facilities & Fleet Services is the provider of choice for such services. To remain flexible and responsive to company needs, Facilities & Fleet Services utilizes a mix of BGE and contractor employees and also a mix of BGE-owned and leased facilities.

Facilities & Fleet Services has identified nine facilities-related business functions:
- strategic facility planning
- real estate operations
- facility construction
- customer-requested facility modifications
- facility maintenance
- facility operations
- property protection
- corporate security services
- facilities-related services.

It is the intent of Facilities & Fleet Services to identify costs associated with its products and services and to charge the appropriate business functions, or to directly charge the end users for these products and services, where appropriate. Facilities & Fleet Services pursues leasing revenue from company properties where it is appropriate.

Overview

Name of Company: Baltimore Gas & Electric Company

Type of Business: Gas and Electric Utility

Locations Covered by Facilities Management Function:

Calvert Cliffs: 1,656 employees
Gas & Electric Building: 1,370
Rutherford Business Center: 970
Distribution Service Centers: 836
Fossil Power Plants: 725
Spring Gardens: 610
Smallwood Center: 447
Front Street: 454
Timonium: 232
Dorsey: 141
Merchandise Stores: 115
All Others: 365
Total Employees: 7,921

Employees in BGE facilities: 7,021

Employees in leased facilities: 900

Scope of Facilities Under Management:
Total Gross Square Feet: 3,235,000

Owned Facilities: 2,855,000
Leased Facilities: 380,000
Number of Separate Buildings: 112
Total Acreage Under Management: 15,000

Allocation of Space by Function:
Administrative Space: 58%
Warehouse: 26%
Shops/Labs: 13%
Retail: 3%

Functions Performed Under Facilities Group:
Capital Budgeting
Leasing and Lease Management
New Construction Planning
Contract Negotiation and Management
Site Development Masterplanning
Planning Routine Renovation and Maintenance Projects
Renovations and Maintenance
Furniture Equipment Inventory and Management
Personnel Moves and Relocations

Cleaning/Trash Removal
Property Protection
Corporate Security Services
Food Services

Annual 1994 Facilities Budget: $21.5 million (excluding capital expenditures)

Items Included in the Facilities Budget Corresponding to the Above Annual Budget Figure:
Facilities Management and Technical Staff/Wages
Travel, Training, Publications
Hourly Service/Maintenance/Tradespeople
Maintenance & Cleaning Supplies
Janitorial
Security
Repairs and Maintenance
Rearrangements & Relocations
Safety
Site and Building Utilities
Lease Expenses

Total Facilities-Related Headcount: 155 employees/287 FTE contractors

Major Contracted Services/Outsourcing:
Custodial Services
Security Services

Profile Information Provided By: Stephen C. Roth, Director, Real Estate and Facilities Planning

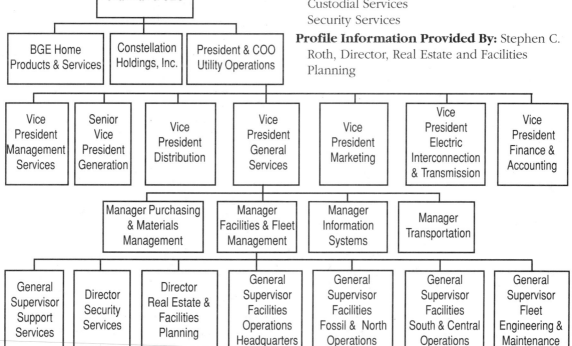

FACILITY ORGANIZATION AND MANAGEMENT

Charles Schwab & Co., Inc., San Francisco

STATEMENT

Corporate Management Philosophy:

Respect for the individual, respect for the dignity and the rights of each person in the organization.

Customer Service: To give the best customer service of any company in the world.

Excellence: The conviction that an organization should pursue all tasks with the objective of accomplishing them in a superior way.

Facility Mission Statement:

To support our company's business and strategic decisions, we will be a leader in providing:

- Safe, secure, timely and functional facilities.
- Value added professional property and design expertise.
- A facilities asset and cost control environment and process that contributes to profitable growth and operating stability.
- A facility masterplan reconciled with the business plan on quarterly basis.
- Prudent property management to limit both physical and financial risk.

This will be accomplished in such a manner that we are recognized as valued business partners by our customers and as a rewarding work-environment provider by our employees.

Facilities Management Philosophy:

Our policy is driven by customer service. In order to remain flexible in providing customer service we have chosen to lease the majority of our space in lieu of owning it.

OVERVIEW

Name of Company: Charles Schwab & Co., Inc.

Type of Business: Broker trader business

Location(s) Covered by Facilities Management Function:

4 headquarters locations in the Greater Bay Area (San Francisco)
210 branch locations throughout the U.S.
4 major customer service centers nationally
2 limited international locations

Scope of Facilities Under Management:
Total GSF: 1,900,000 gsf
  Owned Facilities: 2%
  Leased Facilities: 98%
Number of Employees: 6,800 nationwide

Allocation of Space by Function:
Commercial Office: 55%
Warehouse: 20%
Administrative Space: 15%
Dedicated (trading, broker, etc...): 7%
Research/Labs: 3%

Functions Performed Under Facilities Group:
Capital Budgeting
Leasing and Lease Management
New Construction Planning
Contract Negotiation and Management
In-house Detailed Design for New
  Construction
Site Development Masterplanning
Planning Routine Renovation and
  Maintenance Projects
Renovations and Maintenance
Furniture Equipment Inventory and
  Management
Personnel Moves and Relocations

Cleaning/Trash Removal
Branch Expansion/Development

Annual 1992 Facilities Budget for San Francisco Headquarters: (excluding capital expenditures) $20,000,000

Items included in the Facilities Budget Corresponding to the Above Annual Budget Figure:
Facilities Management and Technical Staff
Wages/Benefits
Travel, Training, Publications
Hourly Service/Maintenance/Tradespeople
Maintenance & Cleaning Supplies
Janitorial
Security

Repairs and Maintenance
Rearrangements & Relocations
Safety
Site and Building Utilities
Lease Expenses
Rent

Total Facilities-Related Headcount: (excluding contract employees)
21 facilities staff
16 security staff

Major Contracted Services/Outsourcing:
Architecture
Specialized Engineering

Profile Information Provided By: C. Norman Vaughn, V.P. Corporate Facilities Management

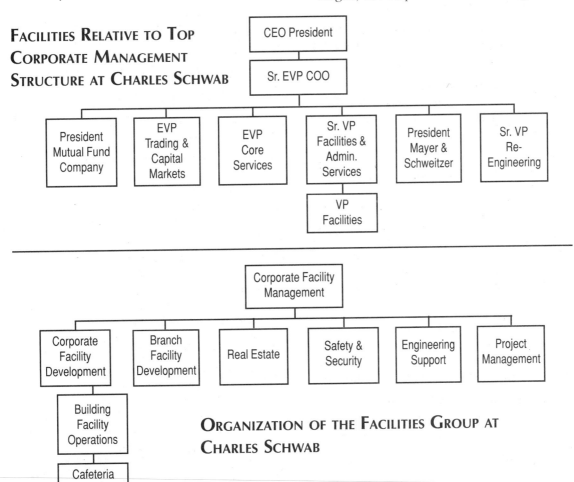

FACILITIES RELATIVE TO TOP CORPORATE MANAGEMENT STRUCTURE AT CHARLES SCHWAB

CEO President
Sr. EVP COO
President Mutual Fund Company
EVP Trading & Capital Markets
EVP Core Services
Sr. VP Facilities & Admin. Services
President Mayer & Schweitzer
Sr. VP Re-Engineering
VP Facilities

Corporate Facility Management
Corporate Facility Development
Branch Facility Development
Real Estate
Safety & Security
Engineering Support
Project Management
Building Facility Operations
Cafeteria

ORGANIZATION OF THE FACILITIES GROUP AT CHARLES SCHWAB

FACILITY ORGANIZATION AND MANAGEMENT

Compaq Computer Corporation, Houston

Statement

Responding to Compaq Computer's exceptional growth in the personal computer market during its first decade, the Operating Services organization has managed the design, construction and operations of over 5,000,000 sf of administration and manufacturing space in Houston, Scotland and Singapore. We currently have several major projects in Europe. The facilities group has grown from one staff member to 210 in less than 10 years.

Several key components of our management philosophy made it possible to successfully provide facilities during this expansion.

First, our corporate culture: We organized and managed from the beginning as a large company in its formative stages rather than as a small growing company. The core culture principles are common sense, teamwork, consensus decision-making and enjoying our work. We encourage decision-making even at the lowest possible levels in the organization.

Compaq's culture has allowed us to attract and retain a professional and competent staff. We seek qualities such as respect for the individual, integrity, honesty, the ability

ORGANIZATION OF OPERATING SERVICES AT COMPAQ

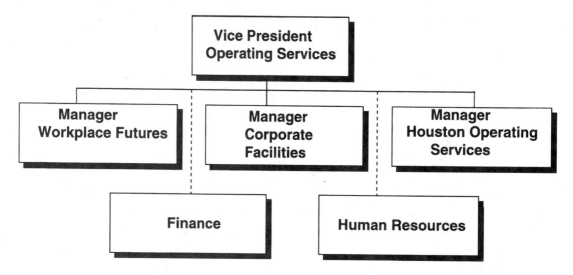

COMPAQ

to say "I don't know" and not being afraid to make a mistake.

Operating Services' goals are quality (meeting the customer's requirements), flexibility (being able to meet new requirements easily) and cost. These design priorities parallel business goals which also include preserving the natural environment and efficient use of energy and resources. Problem-solving teams of facilities architects and engineers, as well as users and outside consultants, negotiate these design and business issues on every project.

Offices are viewed as tools to help do one's job. Virtually all offices are constructed of full-height demountable partitions with doors. We employ very few open furniture systems domestically. Office size is based on need. It is not uncommon for staff and secretarial offices to be as large or larger than a manager's office. Furniture is also ordered on the basis of need, so there is no "standard" configuration.

Requested maintenance and preventative

ORGANIZATION OF THE CORPORATE FACILITIES GROUP AT COMPAQ

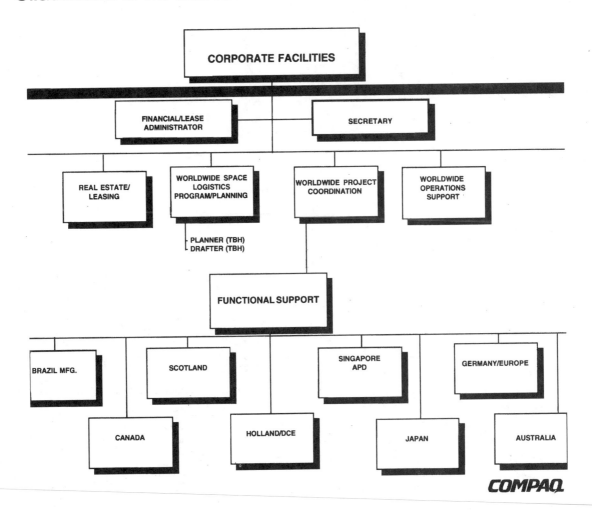

maintenance are performed by an in-house staff of technicians. Contract labor is used to complement staff skills as well as ensure short cycle time in filling customer requests. Operations personnel are involved in new building design teams, establishing operations programs for international projects and corporate metrology.

Open communication is the key to our success and is the focus of our department; it is the thread that links our culture, functional organizations and processes together. Electronic mail, roundtables, newsletters, department meetings and an open-door policy maintain the flow of information. We use AutoCAD software to allow our staff and key consultants to quickly, consistently and accurately transmit drawing information to

each other. We recently sent a videotaped presentation of our European Distribution Center design programming requirements to one of our overseas subsidiaries when travel was considered unwise due to conflict in the Middle East.

OVERVIEW

Name of Company: Compaq Computer Corporation

Type of Business: Personal Computer Manufacturing

Locations Covered by Facilities Management: Worldwide

Scope of Facilities Under Management:
Total GSF: 8,382,000 gsf
Owned Facilities: 5,320,000 gsf

ORGANIZATION OF THE HOUSTON OPERATING SERVICES GROUP AT COMPAQ

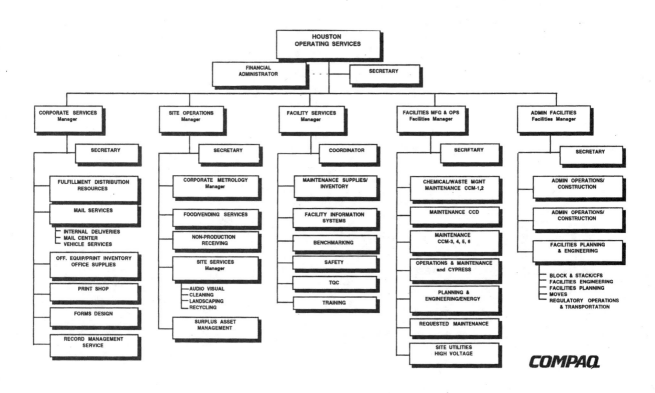

Leased Facilities: 3,062,000 gsf
Number of Employees: 10,000
Number of Separate Buildings: 35, with 86 field office locations
Total Acreage Under Management: 1000+

Allocation of Space by Function:
Administrative Space: 46%
Manufacturing: 54%

Functions Performed Under Facilities Group:
Capital Budgeting
Leasing and Lease Management
New Construction Planning
Contract Negotiation and Management
Site Development Masterplanning
Planning Routine Renovation and Maintenance Projects
Renovations and Maintenance
Furniture Equipment Inventory and Management
Personnel Moves and Relocations
Cleaning/Trash Removal

Annual Facilities Budget:
Approximately $50 million (excluding capital expenditures)

Items Included in the Facilities Budget Corresponding to the Above Annual Budget Figure:
Facilities Management and Technical Staff/ Wages/Benefits
Hourly Service, Maintenance, Tradespeople
Lease Expenses
Maintenance and Cleaning Supplies
Janitorial
Rearrangements & Relocations
Repairs and Maintenance
Safety
Site and Building Utilities
Travel, Training, Publications

Total Facilities-Related Headcount: 210
(excluding contractors)

Major Contracted Services/Outsourcing:
Landscape Maintenance
Cleaning

Profile Information Provided By: Karen D. Walker, Vice President, Operating Services

FACILITY ORGANIZATION AND MANAGEMENT

Hewlett-Packard Company

Statement

Corporate Management Philosophy:

Hewlett-Packard Company (HP) was founded in 1939 on the concept of "Management by Objective," which is still the company's primary philosophy. Line managers have considerable authority to manage their product families in support of growth and technology objectives. Respect for the individual and support for the development of employees is a fundamental tenant.

General Facilities Management Philosophy:

Facility Management at HP is a decentralized function that reports to business unit management at individual sites. Facility Management focuses on asset management (protection of long-term asset value), property management (assuring the property, plant and equipment can support HP's business needs on a reliable basis) and customer services (responding to internal requests that improve overall productivity).

HP management wants flexible cost structures in all expense areas. Therefore, a downsizing trend is occurring as facility managers define the core competencies to be managed with HP employees. The remaining services are often best managed through strategic service partnerships and through leveraged contracts with regional or national suppliers.

Most sites utilize CAFM tools to manage customer requests, maintain equipment, manage energy use, generate space plans and perform cost charge-backs.

Overview

Name of Company: Hewlett-Packard Company

Type of Business: HP designs, manufactures and services electronic products and systems for measurement, communication and computation. HP's basic business purpose is to create information products that accelerate the advancement of knowledge and improve the effectiveness of people and organizations. The company's products and services are used in industry, business, engineering, science, medicine and education. Total company revenue for FY 1993 was $20.3 billion.

Number of Employees: 96,200 worldwide

Total Facilities-Related Headcount: 2,500 (excluding contract employees)

Locations Covered by Facilities Management Function: HP has manufacturing and sales operations in 100 countries.

Scope of Facilities Under Management:
Total GSF: 40 million
Owned Facilities: 30 million gsf
Leased Facilities: 10 million gsf

Number of Separate Buildings: 800

Leased: 500

Owned: 300

Total Acreage Under Management:
Operations: 6,300 acres
Recreation: 8,000 acres
Vacant: 1,600 acres

Allocation of Space by Function:
Office space: 75%
Labs, processing: 25%

People Density:
Overall density is 440 gsf/person worldwide. Sales offices use less space per person (285 gsf/person) than the manufacturing facilities.

Functions Performed by Facility Manage-

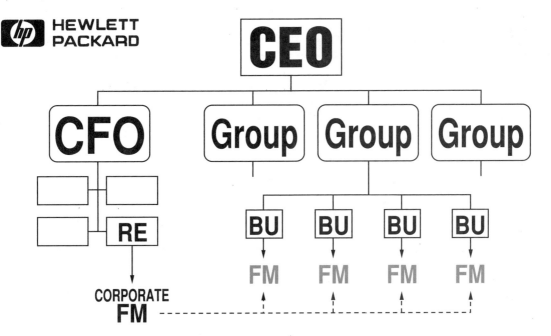

HEWLETT PACKARD

CEO
- CFO
  - RE → CORPORATE **FM**
- Group
- Group
  - BU → FM
  - BU → FM
  - BU → FM
  - BU → FM
- Group

ment: Each site FM team is organized to respond to the business unit's needs at that location. Most site FM teams perform the following functions:

- Building and Equipment Maintenance
- Capital Budgeting
- Cleaning and Trash Removal
- Contract Negotiation and Management
- Environmental
- Furniture Inventory and Management
- Health and Safety
- In-house Detailed Design for Outfitting
- Project Management
- Leasing and Lease Management
- New Construction Planning
- Planning Routine Renovation and Maintenance Projects
- Personnel Moves and Relocations
- Security
- Site Development Masterplanning
- Some teams have the additional responsibilities of administrative services (mail, copy, travel, cafe, etc.)

Annual 1994 Facilities Budget: (capital and depreciation costs included)

Overall occupancy cost: $824 million/year

(4.5% of HP's total cost structure)

Ownership cost: $365 million/year

Operating cost: $460 million/year

Items Included in the Facilities Budget:

- Facilities Management and Technical Staff's Wages and Benefits
- Hourly Service, Maintenance, Tradespeople
- Janitorial
- Lease Expenses
- Landscaping and Grounds Maintenance
- Maintenance and Cleaning Supplies
- Repairs and Maintenance
- Rearrangement and Relocation Planning
- Safety
- Security
- Site and Building Utilities
- Travel, Training, Publications

Major Contracted Services/Outsourcing:

- Custodial: 95% outsourced
- Grounds: 90% outsourced
- Security: 95% outsourced
- Mail: 95% outsourced
- Copy Centers: 95% outsourced

Profile Information Provided By: Kit Tuveson, CFM, Corporate Facility Operations Manager

FACILITY ORGANIZATION AND MANAGEMENT

Lawrence Livermore National Laboratories

Statement

Corporate Management Philosophy:

Lawrence Livermore National Laboratory (LLNL) is organized on the matrix concept in order to rapidly respond to establishing multidisciplinary project teams for large science research projects.

General Facilities Management Philosophy:

In-house work force does all routine maintenance and minimal repair, plus modifications and alterations less than $20K. When cost effective, outside contractors are used for these efforts, which include elevator maintenance, crane certification and carpet laying. Response time on small jobs and those critical to the programs is rapid. Plant engineering staffs only for the lowest level of expected work that can be done in a cost-effective manner by the in-house work force.

Overview

Name of Institution: Lawrence Livermore National Laboratory

Type of Business: Research and development for national defense, energy and environment.

Location Covered by Facilities Management Function: Livermore site and a high explosive test site, 17 miles east of the main site.

Scope of Facilities Under Management:
Total Gross Square Feet: 6,329,711
Owned Facilities: 6,091,000
Leased Facilities: 235,000

Number of Employees 10,000
Number of Separate Buildings 573
Total Acreage Under Management 7,713

Allocation of Space by Function:
Administrative Space: 48%
Research/Labs: 38%
Shops: 10%
Computer: 4%

Functions Performed Under Facilities Group:
Capital Budgeting
Leasing and Lease Management
New Construction Planning
Contract Negotiation and Management
In-house Detailed Design for New Construction
Site Development Masterplanning
Planning Routine Renovation and Maintenance Projects
Renovations and Maintenance
Cleaning/Trash Removal
Utilities Distribution On-site
Grounds Care

Annual 1994 Facilities Budget: (excluding capital expenditures)
$39.9 million, plus $23.5 million purchased utilities cost

Items Included in the Facilities Budget Corresponding to the Above Annual Budget Figure:
Facilities Management and Technical Staff/ Wages/Benefits
Travel, Training, Publications
Hourly Service/Maintenance/ Tradespeople
Maintenance & Cleaning Supplies

Janitorial
Repairs and Maintenance
Safety Site and Building Utilities
Lease Expenses

Total Facilities-Related Headcount: 1,100
(excluding contract employees)

Major Contracted Services:
Repairs and construction greater than $20K
Most major design

Profile Information Provided By: Jan Cook,
Deputy Associate Director of Plant Engineering

LLNL ORGANIZATION

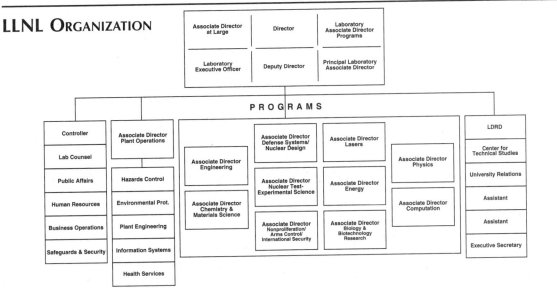

LLNL PLANT ENGINEER-ING ORGANIZATION

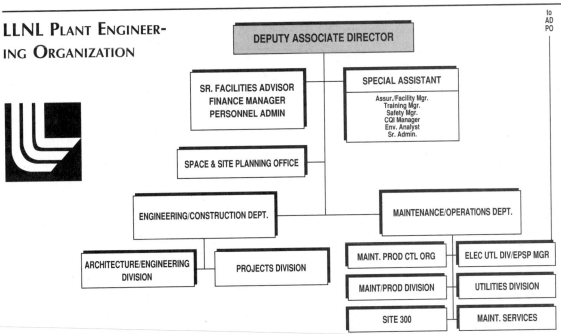

FACILITY ORGANIZATION AND MANAGEMENT

The National Institutes of Health

Statement

Statement of Corporate Management Philosophy:

The mission of the National Institutes of Health is to uncover new knowledge that will lead to better health for everyone.

General Facilities Management Philosophy:

The mission of the Division of Engineering Services is to provide a world-class physical environment to support biomedical research through a commitment to excellence and complete customer satisfaction achieved by timely delivery of quality services and effective management of resources.

Overview

Name of Institution: The National Institutes of Health

Type of Business: Biomedical Research

Locations Covered by Facilities Management Function:

Bethesda, Md. (Main Campus)
Poolesville, Md. (NIH Animal Center)
Research Triangle Park, N.C. (National Institutes of Environmental Health Sciences)
Hamilton, Mont. (Rocky Mountain Laboratories)
Baltimore, Md. (Gerontology Research Center)
Perrine, Fla. (Perrine Primate Center)
New Iberia, La.
Frederick, Md. (Frederick Cancer Research and Development Center)
Sábana Seca, Puerto Rico

Scope of Facilities Under Management:

Total GSF: 10,700,000
Owned Facilities: 9,800,000 gsf
Leased Facilities: 900,000 gsf
Number of Employees: 24,000
Number of Separate Buildings: 200
Total Acreage Under Management: 800

Allocation of Space by Function:

Research/Labs: 66%
Administrative Space: 13.5%
Service: 7.5%
Other: 13%

Functions Performed Under Facilities Group:

Capital Budgeting
New Construction Planning
In-house Detailed Design for New Construction
Site Development Masterplanning
Planning Routine Renov. and Maint. Projects
Renovation and Maintenance.
Grounds Maintenance and Landscaping
Facilities Operations (central heat, cooling plants)
Warehouse Function to Support Station Maintenance and Shops
Project Management of A/E Construction Contracts and Renovation Projects

Annual 1993 Building and Facilities Budget:

$114 million (New construction and major renovations, environmental and safety programs.)

Annual Operating Budget: $106.2 million (Bethesda, Md. and Poolesville, Md. Campus, excluding capital expenditures)

Total Annual Budget: $220.2 million

Items Included in the Operating Budget Corresponding to the Above Annual Budget Figure:
Facilities Management and Technical Staff/ Wages/Benefits
Travel, Training, Publications
Hourly Service/Maintenance/Tradespeople
Maintenance and Cleaning Supplies
Repairs and Maintenance
Rearrangements and Relocations
Safety
Site and Building Utilities
Other Facility Support and Maintenance Contracts
Other Procurement Services

Other Facility Studies and Masterplanning

Total Facilities-Related Headcount: 646
(excluding contract employees)

Major Contracted Services:
Professional A/E design services for major renovations and new construction
Construction management services for capital projects
Construction of major renovations and capital projects
Turf maintenance
Facility maintenance support contracts for special equipment including some elevators

Profile Information Provided By: Myrna Lopez, Management Analyst

DIVISION OF ENGINEERING SERVICES ORGANIZATION
(#) indicates number in department

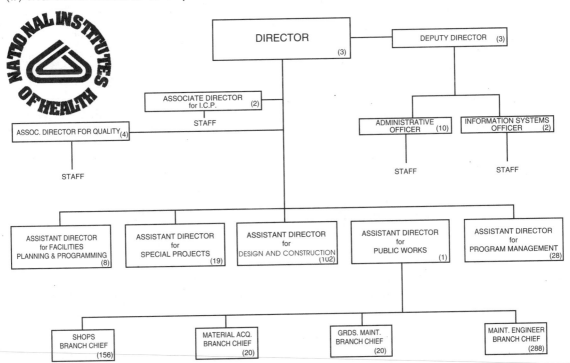

FACILITY ORGANIZATION AND MANAGEMENT

Xerox Corporation (Monroe County, N.Y. locations)

Statement

Corporate Management Philosophy:

Xerox will implement our Strategic Direction by focusing on two vital areas:

Growth—
Increase customer satisfaction worldwide
Increase market share.

Productiveness—
Increase productivity
Improve return on assets.

General Facilities Management Philosophy:

To provide facilities and related services which meet the Xerox Operating Group's business requirements for quality, cost and delivery.

In general, Xerox has an in-house operation at this location which makes extensive use of consultants, A&E firms and construction firms to augment a core competency.

Overview

Name of Company/Institution: Xerox Corp.

Type of Business: Business equipment, R&D, manufacturing and sales

Locations Covered by Facilities Management Function:
Monroe County and vicinity (New York State)

Scope of Facilities Under Management:
Total GSF: 8.9 million
Owned Facilities: 7.0 million
Leased Facilities: 1.9 million
Number of Employees: 15,000
Number of Buildings under Management: 150
Total Acreage Under Management: 1,187

Allocation of Space by Function:
Manufacturing: 48%
Administrative: 28%
Research/Labs: 14%
Special Purposes: 10%
Computer Center
Cafeterias
Parking Garage
Recreation
Substations

Functions Performed Under Facilities Group:
Capital Budgeting
New Construction Planning
Contract Negotiation and Management
In-house Detailed Design for New Construction
Site Development Masterplanning
Planning Routine Renovation and Maintenance Projects
Renovations and Maintenance
Furniture Equipment Inventory and Management
Personnel Moves and Relocations
Cleaning/Trash Removal

Annual 1994 Facilities Budget: $150 million (excluding capital expenditures)

Items Included in the Facilities Budget Corresponding to the Above Annual Budget Figure:
Facilities Management and Technical Staff/Wages/Benefits
Travel, Training, Publications
Hourly Service/Maintenance/Tradespeople
Maintenance and Cleaning Supplies
Janitorial
Security
Repairs and Maintenance

Rearrangements and Relocations
Safety
Site and Building Utilities
Lease Expenses
Other Depreciation (Buidings, tenant
   improvements, some furniture and fixtures)
Other Taxes and Insurance

Total Facilities-Related Headcount: (excluding contract employees) 730

Major Contracted Services/Outsourcing:
1. Construction (partial)
2. Architectural and Engineering services (partial)
3. Interior design (partial)

Profile Information Provided By: Jean Boles, Manager: Business and Strategic Planning Corporate Real Estate—Monroe County.

FACILITIES RELATIVE TO TOP CORPORATE MANAGEMENT STRUCTURE AT XEROX

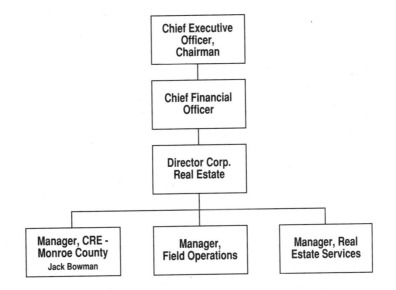

ORGANIZATION OF THE FACILITIES GROUP AT XEROX

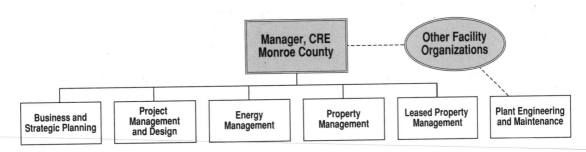

Key Facilities Terms and Issues:

A Concise Guide to Facilities Planning and Management Terminology

"Needless to say, we did some pretty serious value engineering"

Absorption Chiller   A machine which produces chilled water typically for facility air conditioning. An absorption chiller utilizes physical and chemical process for the compression cycle normally found in a refrigeration cycle.

Accelerated Cost Recovery System (ACRS)   ACRS is a standard employed by the Internal Revenue Service to establish useful lives for most depreciable property placed in service after 1980 for the purpose of recovering the property's capital cost through depreciation allowances. This system establishes recovery periods of 3, 5, 10, 15 and 18 years, and various methods of accelerated depreciation depending on the type of property.

Acceptable Thermal Environment   An indoor building environment with a temperature thermally acceptable to 80 percent of the building's occupants (per *ASHRAE* Standard-1981).

Access Floor   A raised-floor system used in computer installations and open-plan offices to provide under-floor space for wire distribution and, in some applications, distribution of conditioned air; it allows outlets to be located anywhere in the room. The system consists of metal or concrete panels supported at each corner by adjustable pedestals that rest on the structural slab. Floor coverings must be carpet tiles, laminated tiles or some other material that can be removed in sections. Panels are situated 4 to 18 inches above the structural floor, are usually 2' x 2' and are removable to allow access to the underlying power, telephone and coaxial cables. Activations are through pedestal service fittings or through panel holes and boxes attached to the panels' undersides. Power cables are distributed under the access floor through conduit or manufactured wiring systems. In access floors that are used for air return, data and phone cables are encased in conduits or raceways; in non-environmental applications (or when plenum cable is used), cables lie on the floor.

Acid Aerosol   Acidic liquid or solid particles that are small enough to become airborne. High concentrations of acid aerosols can be irritating to the lungs and have been associated with some respiratory disorders such as asthma.

Acid Waste Vent   Drains and vents designed for the disposal of acid-based industrial fluids and sediments.

ACRS   See Accelerated Cost Recovery System.

Active Construction Management (ACM)   An approach to hazardous materials remediation contracting created by Terra Insurance Company. It permits consulting engineers to head up the equivalent of a design/build site remediation project team without having to establish separate contracting and engineering firms.

Active Ingredient   In pesticides, the component that kills or otherwise controls the target pests. Pesticides are regulated primarily on the basis of active ingredients.

ADA   See Americans with Disabilities Act.

Adhesive Failure   Loss of bond between a sealant and a substrate where the sealant itself remains intact.

Adsorption   A method of treating waste in which activated carbon removes organic matter from wastewater.

Aerobic   Life or processes that require, or are not destroyed by, the presence of oxygen.

Affiliated-Party Contracts   Contracts between partnerships, parent companies and subsidiaries, or between otherwise affiliated parties. In negotiating contracts for construction services, full disclosure of all affiliated-party subcontracts is important to determine the contractor's avenues of compensation and to assure competitive bids.

Agency Construction Management   A construction management technique in which a third party acts in a fiduciary role as the owner's agent during the tenure of a project. The agency construction manager—a member of the project delivery team along with the design professional and the owner—does not become engaged in any other project delivery function, such as providing design services, contracting or performing construction work with his or her own employees.

Aggregate   In its plainest sense, an aggregate is the sum or total of a group of numbers. In insurance, aggregate limit, the total amount payable under an insurance policy regardless of the number of claims. Also refers to crushed stone, crushed slag or water-worn gravel used for surfacing a built-up roof. Can also refer to any granular mineral material.

AGVs   See Automatic Guided Vehicle Systems.

Air Challenges   Air turbulence in laboratories, specifically near a fume hood, created by the movement of people, doors opening, etc.

Air Changes   The rate of air ventilation expressed as the number of times per hour that the air volume in a given room or building is changed by an HVAC system. Equals the cubic-feet-per-hour of air flow in and out of a specified space divided by the cubic feet of the space.

Air Cushion Delivery   Another term for pneumatic tubes.

Air Flow   The direction of air movement in a building or area. It can be managed by creating areas of higher or lower pressure with respect to the surroundings.

Air Foil   Curved or angular members at a *fume hood* entrance that are positioned on the sides and at benchtop level of the fume hood to decrease the chance of hazardous fumes escaping into lab areas.

Air Lock   In general, a small room in a R&D facility with two doors that are mechanically or electrically interlocked to limit access between contaminated laboratories and corridors.

Air Quality Standards   The level of pollutants that may not be exceeded in a given time and place.

Air-Dried   Coatings that normally reach a desired hardness without external heat.

Air-Exchange Rate   The frequency with which all of the air in a building is replaced with outside air. See also *Air Changes*.

Air Plenum   Any space used to convey air in a building, furnace, or structure. The space above a suspended ceiling is often used as an air plenum.

Air-to-Air Heat Exchanger   A ventilation device that warms incoming air with latent heat in exhaust air.

Air-to-Air Heat Pump   A refrigeration or air-conditioning system that removes heat from one air source and transfers it to another air stream. It is usually applied to heat inside air by cooling outside air. When operated in reverse, the system will perform like a typical air conditioning system that cools inside air by rejecting heat to the outside air.

Allergens   Substances that cause an allergic reaction. Allergens are especially problematic in facilities housing rodents and mice.

Allergic rhinitis   An allergic reaction where the mucous membranes of the nose become inflamed.

Alligatoring   The cracking of the surfacing bitumen on a built-up roof, producing a pattern of cracks similar to an alligator's hide. The cracks may or may not extend through the surfacing *bitumen*.

Alternate Bid   An amount that is to be added or deducted from the stated bid amount if the bidder's proposed changes in project scope, materials and/or methods of construction are accepted.

Alternative Officing   In response to the competing demands of reduced occupancy costs, improved productivity and increased worker satisfaction, many organizations are turning to "alternative officing." This concept is an umbrella term for an evolving spectrum of approaches to how, when and where people work. Many organizations have made significant savings by implementing telecommuting, office sharing, hoteling and satellite office programs among other strategies. See also *Telecommuting, Hoteling*.

Ambient Air   Any unconfined portion of the atmosphere: open air, surrounding air.

Ambient Illumination   The level of diffuse, background light (as opposed to light directed in one spot or task lighting).

Americans with Disabilities Act (ADA)   The Americans with Disabilities Act of 1990 (Public Law 101-336) provides wide-ranging civil-rights protection for people with disabilities in the areas of employment and accessibility to public and private services. Disabilities include but are not limited to mobility, sight, hearing, speech, dexterity and mental or psychological disorders.

Titles I-III of the ADA are of most interest to facilities professionals:

- **Title I—Employment**
  For all businesses with more than 15 employees, the law prohibits employment discrimination against qualified individuals with disabilities. In addition, the employer must adapt facilities to make the workplace physically accessible and safe for employees with disabilities.

- **Title II—State and local government services**
  State and local governments must ensure accessibility to all services, programs and activities. The subject of accessibility at existing facilities must be addressed immediately. Major structural changes may be postponed if resources are limited, but no later than January 26, 1995.

- **Title III—Public accommodations and services operated by private entities**
  All physical and communication barriers that prevent access to goods and services for people with disabilities must be removed. Public accommodations include places such as hotels, restaurants, theaters, doctors' offices, retail stores, etc.
  In each of the cases above, the organization should have a barrier-removal plan that identifies barriers and addresses immediate or eventual removal. All new facilities and alterations to existing facilities must meet the ADA Accessibility Guidelines (ADAAG). These guidelines describe minimum accessibility requirements, including slope ratios for ramps, sidewalks and parking lots; door widths, operating force and hardware; bathroom space, fixtures and fixture locations; telephone accessibility, including provisions for hearing- or sight-impaired users;

signage; visible and audible fire alarms; areas of "rescue assistance" and so forth.

Although wide in scope, the ADA strives to be business-friendly. Changes to meet ADA guidelines must be "readily achievable," that is, they must not cause "undue burden" to a business. Businesses need not adhere strictly ADA guidelines if doing so would cause an unreasonable financial burden or significantly alter the nature of the business. However, a business must still meet the needs of people with disabilities using other methods—for instance, if automatic doors aren't feasible, an easily accessible door bell will suffice.

For more information, contact a regional Disability and Technical Assistance Center. For the one nearest you, call (800) 949-4232.

For a free copy of the ADAAG, contact the U.S. Architectural and Transportation Barriers Compliance Board at (800) 872-2253.

Anaerobic   A process or organism that occurs in the absence of oxygen.

Androgynous   Having male and female characteristics (andro/man + gyneka/woman). In reference to office furniture, indicates that a particular design can accommodate a wide range of body weights and body types to suit both males and females. Androgynous furniture designs are becoming increasingly important.

Anechoic Chamber   A room padded with material that prevents sound and radiation from entering or escaping. Sensitive electronic equipment, such as that used in airplane radar systems, is often tested in anechoic chambers because there is negligible electromagnetic interference.

Animal Dander   Tiny flakes of animal skin.

Anthropometric   Relating to the study and application of human measurements. Anthropometric design is based on how people will use things. It affects such design elements as table and desk heights, door and door knob locations, lines of sight from workstations and the placement of furniture and equipment.

Antigen   A substance that triggers the production of antibodies when introduced into the body of an individual.

Apple Talk   A local area network proprietary to Apple Computer Corporation. Unlike other systems which require networking equipment, AppleTalk is "free," in the sense that it's built into every Apple Macintosh sold since the MacPlus. For this reason, it is very common. Most complex user groups are using a system with more features, but there are still a large number of AppleTalk *LANs* in use and this is not likely to change.

Applications Processor   The brain of an integrated building system that collects and stores data and runs various software programs using the data.

Approved Equal   Material, equipment or methods approved by the architect for use in a construction project as being acceptable as the equivalent in essential attributes to the material, equipment or methods specified in the contract documents.

Aquifer   A geological formation, group of formations or part of a formation capable of yielding water to a well or spring.

Arbitrageur   A person who makes a profit from purchasing a product or security in one market and then reselling the same product or security at a higher price in another market. While true arbitrage involves no risk or speculation, the term is commonly used to describe individuals who buy stocks targeted for takeovers, hoping to profit from a finalized deal at a later date.

Arbitration   A means of resolving contractual disputes, without recourse to the courts, by presenting the facts of the dispute as viewed by each party to an impartial arbiter or panel of arbiters, usually arranged under the auspices of the American Arbitration Association. The general conditions of the A.I.A. provide for disputes to be submitted to arbitration. Generally, arbitration findings may not be appealed in court, but awards made by arbiters may be enforced by courts if not paid. Some clients, particularly government agencies with attorneys on staff, prefer not to submit to arbitration.

Architect's Project Representative   An observer of the construction process on-site who acts for and is employed by the project architect to augment the services provided by the construction administrator. Normally, an on-site project representative is not provided under an architect's basic services agreement, but may be provided for an additional fee when requested by a client.

Areaway   An open below-grade space next to a building used to admit light or air. May also be used as an entrance to a basement or crawl space.

Articulation Index   A weighted fraction (i.e., a value between 0 and 1.0) that represents the effective portion of a speech signal capable of conveying intelligible speech to a listener. It can be calculated if enough information is available or measured using a reader, a list of random words and listeners who are unfamiliar with the material. The index is useful in estimating privacy or its converse, communication. See page 138 in the Facilities Planning Concepts section for more information.

Artificial Membrane   A liner placed beneath a surface impoundment or landfill that restricts the escape of waste or its constituents from the impoundment or landfill.

Aseptic Area   A space constructed of nonporous, easily cleanable surfaces that provides an environment free of viable microorganisms. The area is supplied with *HEPA*-filtered laminar flow air and is pressurized to prevent contamination.

Aseptic Surgeries   In animal research, these are surgeries that approach the standards set for human surgeries. Also called survival surgeries.

ASHRAE   American Society of Heating, Refrigerating and Air-Conditioning Engineers.

Aspect Ratio   A measure of the proportions of an image (width to height) expressed in either whole numbers or decimals. For example, standard TV has an aspect ratio of 12:9 (or 1.33:1) while HDTV currently in use has an aspect ratio of 16:9 (or 1.78:1).

Aspirating Diffuser   Mixes incoming air with ambient air via high velocity aspirating air streams. Frequently, this type of diffuser causes drafts within animal rooms with cages on racks.

Assumption of Risk   In contracts and insurance policies, an agreement, expressed or implied, which makes one party responsible for the risk involved in fulfilling the contract. Insurance claimants who have assumed the risk cannot collect damages if it can be reasonably assumed that they were aware that a hazard existed yet proceeded with action.

Atrium   Space located in the interior of a building that is lit by natural light entering the building through a light opening in the roof. Atria are often used for public areas. Tests at the University of California, Berkeley, sky-simulation facility have produced concrete data on atria design: 1) the addition of an atrium doesn't necessarily provide good light to adjacent workspaces, 2) in atria more than five stories high, it is difficult to provide the daily 100 to 200 foot candles of natural light required to keep many plants alive at the first-floor level and 3) multiple roof monitors are the best method of filtering light during the summer months when the sun is at its peak.

Attainment Area   An area considered to have air quality as good as or better than the national ambient air quality standards as defined in the Clean Air Act. An area may be an attainment area for one pollutant and a non-attainment area for others.

Attractant   A chemical or agent that lures insects or other pests by stimulating their sense of smell.

Audio Conferencing   Group voice communication relying on exchanges among more than two participants. Microphones and loudspeakers replace telephone handsets so that groups of people in one or more remote locations can participate. Audio conferencing sometimes includes a capability to send written materials over a normal telephone line, called "audio plus graphics" conferencing. Standard touch-tone telephones can be used for remote control of special graphics projectors on the receiving end of an audio conference.

Autoclave   An industrial appliance that uses pressurized steam to sterilize surgical or laboratory instruments, glassware and other hard materials. Sizes range between counter-top models to pit-mounted units capable of handling entire carloads of materials. In R&D facilities, autoclaves are a source for waste heat recovery. Autoclaves are often used in hospitals to sterilize waste before disposal.

Automatic Guided Vehicle Systems (AGVs)   Remote-controlled vehicles used in automated plants.

Axial-Flow Fan   A fan that is contained in a cylindrical housing. Air flows through an impeller (the rotating element in a fan) parallel to the fan axis.

B

B/NBC   See Basic/National Building Code.

BACM   See Best Available Control Measures.

Baghouse Filter   Large fabric bag, usually made of glass fibers, used to eliminate intermediate and large (greater than 20 microns in diameter) particles. This device operates like the bag of an electric vacuum cleaner, passing the air and smaller particles while entrapping the larger ones.

Bag In, Bag Out   A method of introducing and removing items from a contaminated enclosure that prevents the spread of contamination or opening of the contaminated space to the atmosphere through the use of plastic bagging material.

Ballast   A device that modifies incoming voltage and controls current to provide the electrical conditions necessary to start and operate electric discharge lamps.

Ballast factor   The ratio of the *lumen* output of a lamp operated by a commercial ballast with respect to the lumen output of the same lamp operated on a reference circuit.

Balun   A device that is used to interconnect dissimilar cable types.

Bandwidth   In terms of single frequency, the range between the lowest and highest frequencies used to transmit a signal from one site to another. Bandwidth is a measure of an analog signal and is measured in *Hertz*.

Banquette   A bench-like upholstered seat used in restaurant booths and facility dining areas.

Barrier Housing   Housing for research animals that protects them from outside contamination through both procedure and facility design. In contrast, *containment housing* protects the outside environment from contaminants within the animal housing facility.

Base Isolation   A structural design of a building in which the building's major support columns are separated from the foundation or piers by flexible couplings. The design changes the resonant frequency of the building/foundation system and isolates the building from certain frequencies of ground vibrations.

Baseband   A communications channel in which signal transmission takes place without modulation. Also used to describe conductors with a *bandwidth* capability of less than 300 kHz. See also *Broadband*.

Basic/National Building Code (B/NBC)   The B/NBC and the Standard Building Code (SBC) are the model building codes predominately adopted and used in the eastern half of the United States.

Basis Points   The annual interest rates on financial instruments. Defined as the fraction of one percent per annum expressed in hundredths. For example, 35 basis points means 0.35 percent. Two hundred basis points means 2 percent.

Bay Spacing   The spacing between the structural elements of a building.

Beam Spread   The vertical and horizontal displacement of a beam of light in degrees, bounded by the angle at which 10 percent of maximum candlepower occurs. (Maximum candlepower is the highest intensity in the beam.)

Bench Coat   A thick paper with a terry cloth-like nap and plastic coating on one side used to cover lab countertops. The bench coat absorbs spills and provides an abrasive surface to reduce the movement of countertop instruments during an earthquake.

Benchmarking   The continuous process of measuring a company's performance, products, services or practices against world-class companies and adapting that information to produce superior performance within your own organization.
    Benchmarking concentrates more on process than product, allowing generic comparisons between dissimilar industries. Before the 1980s, a rudimentary form of benchmarking existed, sometimes referred to as "competitive analysis" or "marketing intelligence." Much narrower in scope than the current definition, this form of benchmarking focused almost entirely on a competitor's finished product. Many experts cite Xerox Corp., a leading manufacturer of photocopiers, as the company most responsible for promoting benchmarking's current definition. During the 1980s, Xerox led the way in generic benchmarking when it compared its distribution process to that of L.L. Bean, a mail-order distributor and recognized leader in order fulfillment and warehousing.
    For more information, contact the International Benchmarking Clearinghouse in Houston: Telephone (713) 685-4666 or fax (713) 681-5321.

Best Available Control Measures (BACM)   A term used to refer to the most effective measures (according to EPA guidance) for controlling small or dispersed particulates from sources such as roadway dust, soot and ash.

Bimetal   Beverage containers with steel bodies and aluminum tops; must be processed for recycling differently than pure aluminum.

Bio-Accumulate   The tendency of certain elements or compounds to accumulate or build up in the tissues of living organisms. Bio-accumulation is a health concern, particularly with respect to elements such as *heavy metals*.

Biodegradable   Capable of decomposing under natural conditions.

Biologicals   Vaccines, cultures and other preparations made from living organisms and their products, intended for use in diagnosing, immunizing, or treating humans or animals, or in related research.

Bioprocess   A process in which living cells or the components of living cells are used to produce an end product.

Bioremediation   Using living organisms to break down toxic compounds.

Biosafety Cabinet   A special exhaust hood with an enclosed work surface used for biological testing and experiments. Biosafety cabinets protect experiments from contaminants in the surrounding room, and they protect workers from hazardous materials being used in the cabinet. They also include features that prevent cross contamination within the cabinet. Conventional fume hoods afford protection only for the room environment. Biosafety cabinet ventilation systems provide a flow of air from the room and through the fume hood face opening as well as *HEPA* filtering of exhaust and recirculating air. Reference National Sanitation Foundation (NSF) Standard Number 49. See also *Fume Hood*.

Biosafety Levels   Designations for laboratory types based on NIH guidelines. Each designation specifies laboratory practices, control of access, containment and special laboratory design. Also known as BL 1-4.

- **BSL1**: With respect to facilities design, a BSL1 lab has no particular facility standards other than those dictated by common decontamination and access control practices.

- **BSL2** requires that there be an autoclave for sterilization of wastes and contaminated materials in the same building.

- **BSL3** has special requirements for disposal of contaminated materials, lab access control, ventilation and air filtration, discharges, containment equipment, designs for easy and rapid decontamination and facility sealing.

- **BSL4** requirements (Formerly P1-P4) are similar to BSL3, but they are more stringent and the lab area itself must be constructed to form a sealed internal shell allowing vapor-phase decontamination.
  To decontaminate filter housings and rooms in BSL4 areas, CDC uses an

electrically operated portable paraformaldehyde generator that converts liquid formaldehyde to a gaseous vapor which is released into the containment area atmosphere. Surfaces are wiped free from any residual condensate after the required exposure time.

The big jump from BSL3 to BSL4 areas is the use of a space suit. Both areas use the same lab procedures, but in BSL4 areas, the workers have to wear the suit. A worker would never use a full body suit except when absolutely necessary because it makes work slower and requires more experience.

Biosorption Passive process in which metal ions bind to a substance in the microbial cell surface; a low-cost, effective treatment for cleaning up heavy-metal waste.

Biotechnology Industrial Biotechnology Association defines biotechnology as "The development of products by a biological process." Production may be carried out by using intact organisms, such as yeasts or bacteria, or by using natural substances from organisms. See also, *Bioprocess.*

Biotechnology Facilities Many biotech firms contact the FDA when their facilities are in the design stage even though the FDA does not require a pre-construction review. If the company desires, FDA personnel will "walk through" proposed floor plans and systems. The FDA will generally spend less time reviewing the establishment application if it has previewed a facility design.

It is critical to think about validating facilities and systems during the planning stage. Once construction is completed on a biotechnology facility, make sure it is operating in compliance with Good Manufacturing Practices before the investigator from the Food & Drug Administration comes out to look at it.

Concurrent validation makes good business sense. It is a way of validating the people as well as the process. During the inspection of facilities for approval of a drug product, the FDA investigators will ask to see written procedures, test methods, specifications, sampling plans and test results to see if the operation is in compliance with GMPs. At the conclusion of the inspection, they will discuss their findings with the facility manager. This is where to ask questions. Ask them to clearly articulate the problems, then determine a strategy for correcting the problems as quickly as possible.

Biotech products are particularly sensitive to microorganism contamination, and temperature levels of 2°C to 10°C may be necessary to prevent contamination. Temperature control of heat-sensitive biological products is frequently insufficient in biotech manufacturing facilities. Temperature controls must be taken into consideration at all levels including production, purification, formulation, filling, packaging and storage.

A manufacturing process that works successfully in a pilot plant may be difficult to size up to large-scale manufacturing for commercial distribution. You have to assure yourself and the FDA that you are making the exact product you made at the pilot plant. It sounds simple, but problems can arise, for instance, in going from a 1- to a 1,000-liter fermenter.

Easily accessible mechanical equipment increases the probability that FDA validation will occur quickly.

Bitumen   In roofing, a class of amorphous, black or dark-colored (solid, semisolid or viscous) cementitious substances, natural or manufactured, that are composed principally of high molecular weight hydrocarbons and are soluble in carbon disulfide. Bitumens are found in asphalts, tars, pitches and asphaltites. The term can also be used generically to denote any material composed principally of bitumen. In the roofing industry, there are two basic bitumens: asphalt and coal-tar pitch. Before application, they are either heated to a liquid state, dissolved in a solvent or emulsified. See also *Modified Bitumens*.

Bituminous Coating   A water emulsion or solvent cutback of asphalt or coal-tar pitch used as a low-cost waterproofing agent in corrosive environments.

Blast Cleaning   Removal of surface imperfections by means of the high-velocity impact of substances such as sand, ice chips, pellets or other abrasive particles, usually propelled by compressed air.

BOCA Code   A code of building and construction standards published by the Building Officials and Code Administrators International Inc.

BOMA   Building Owners and Managers Association.

Borrowed Light   A framed glass opening (sidelight) in an interior wall that is not attached to a door. In facilities that have enclosed offices along the perimeter, borrowed light brings daylight from the exterior of a building into interior work areas.

Brady Unit   A self-contained workstation incorporating a hood, *HEPA* filter and connections for suction and supply lines. The unit can be moved into place and connected in a modular fashion to create a localized clean or sterile work place for cleanroom or wet-process component assembly. Named after Matthew B. Brady, a 19th-century photographer who traveled the American frontier carrying his complete wet laboratory in his wagon.

Bridge   An electronic device used to mix the signals from three or more locations for audio or audiographic teleconferencing.

Bridging Services   Telecommunications companies that sell bridge time to customers to link multiple locations for teleconferences.

Brightness   As applied to lighting applications, brightness is the intensity of the sensation which results from viewing a surface or space which directs light into the eyes.

British Thermal Unit (Btu)   The quantity of heat required to raise the temperature of one pound of water by one degree Fahrenheit.

Broadband   A communications channel with a bandwidth of more than 300 kHz. An example is a television signal modulated at 4.5 mHz. When broadband conductors are used to transmit data, the density of information can be increased by dividing a single channel into a number of smaller, frequency-independent channels, a process known as frequency-division multiplexing. See *Baseband* and *Multiplexing.*

BSL1-BSL4   See *Biosafety Levels.*

Build   Referring to built-up roofs, the thickness of a single application of coating materials.

Building Cooling Load   The amount of heat that must be removed hourly from a building to maintain comfort (measured in Btu).

Building Footprint   The ground mass and shape of the area under a building.

Building-Related Illness   An identifiable disease or illness that can be traced to a specific pollutant or source in a building. See also *Sick Building Syndrome.*

Built-Up Roof   A roof surfacing that employs a covering membrane that is "built up" with layers of asphalt or tar-coated sheets (felts) that are overcoated (mopped) with asphalt or coal tar. Stone aggregate is commonly used as a protective top surface. The number of felts, or plies, varies with the climate: two-ply roofs are prevalent in mild climates; three- and four-ply roofs are used in colder climates.

Bulletin Board System   Or BBS. On a computer network, a system for entering and retrieving public-interest messages, organized by topic. Readers log-in and have the option of reading only those messages that interest them. Readers can post findings, statements and queries for other BBS users.

BUR Membranes   Built-Up Roofing, used in roofing systems that employ asphalt or coal-tar-coated sheets (felts) that are layered on the roof over coats (moppings) of asphalt or coal tar. Usually surfaced with aggregate. Number of felts, or piles, is variable. On an uninsulated roof, heat loss keeps the membrane flexible during winter. In warm weather, radiant heat softens and "heals" any minor cracks or splits that develop.

Burp Tank   A tank located in the discharge piping from a reactor's rupture disk or relief valve that provides a reservoir for materials released due to an excessive reaction. Material collected in the burp tank can be disposed of appropriately.

Bus Network   A network in which each computer system is attached, in sequence, along a data communications line. A bus network does not form a closed loop, which differentiates it from a ring network. See also *Local Area Networks.*

Bypass   The attempt by large corporations or users with multiple locations to erect their own telecommunications networks so they can bypass the local telephone operating companies. The companies thus become their own carriers for local access, local transport and communications. Bypassing is under considerable scrutiny by Congress, the FCC and others concerning how much bypass is permissible and the regulation of access fees.

C

Cable Management   Most planners know the experience of having miles of cable running through ceilings that is of no use because they don't know were it is going. One method of avoiding this problem is to have all cable originating in a dedicated room. Cables terminate on plastic boards with their origination and destination rooms. Then each of the major bays in the building would have small dedicated closets where the cables terminate.

CAD   See Computer-Aided Design.

CADD   See Computer-Aided Design and Drafting.

CAFM   See Computer-Aided Facilities Management.

CAM   See Computer-Aided Manufacturing.

Capital Lease   A lease transaction that is financially reported by the lessee in the same manner as if the asset acquisition had been purchased and paid for with borrowed funds. In a capital lease the liability and the asset are both recognized on the lessee's balance sheet and reported expenses consist of interest and depreciation.

Carbon Absorber   An add-on control device that uses activated carbon to absorb *volatile organic compounds* from a gas stream. (The VOCs are later recovered from the carbon.)

Carbon Adsorption   A treatment system that removes contaminants from ground water or surface water by forcing it through tanks containing activated carbon treated to attract the contaminants.

Carbon Fines   Very small particles of carbon that may wash out of an activated carbon filter in a water purification system.

Cartridge   A container that is prepackaged with filtering components for a water purification system. The module design of filter cartridges makes it easier to change used filters.

Cast In-Place Concrete   Concrete which is poured and left to harden in its permanent location, also called cast-in-situ concrete and in situ concrete. See also *Pre-Cast Concrete.*

CBER   See Center for Biologic Evaluation and Research.

CBX   A telecommunication switchboard that switches or exchanges data and voice signals. (PBX refers to phone or voice switches only.)

CDRH   See Center for Devices and Radiological Health.

Cellular Raceway   A single-level in floor distribution system for power, lighting, electronic and communications systems that is either embedded in the concrete or included as part of the structural load-carrying floor member of the building. Two- or three-celled metal ducts spaced at regular intervals (usually 5 feet) form channels for distributing cables to workstations. This system often uses an open header trench that is covered after the wiring is in place. Header or trenchducts connect distribution runs, which are typically on 5- or 6-foot centers. Preset inserts are on 2- to 2 1/2-foot centers to allow for activations under desks. Activations are accomplished in recessed, flush or pedestal configurations at preset locations. See also *Underfloor Raceway* and *Metal Raceway.*

Cementitious Core   A lightweight fill material used to improve the impact load resistance, rolling load capacity and acoustical properties of access floor panels.

Center for Biologic Evaluation and Research (CBER)   The branch of the FDA that regulates drugs and biological products.

Center for Devices and Radiological Health (CDRH)   The branch of the FDA that regulates public health and safety aspects of medical devices and radiation emissions from electronic products.

Centrex   A service offered by local telephone companies in which computerized telephone switching equipment is owned, operated and maintained by the phone company and is located on its premises.

Centrifugal Chiller   A machine which produces chiller water typically for facility air conditioning. A centrifugal chiller utilizes a rotating turbine to generate the compression within the refrigeration cycle.

Centrifugal Fan   A fan contained in a scroll-shaped housing. Air flows radially into and out of the fan through the impeller (the rotating element of the fan). Centrifugal fans are used for both general and fume hood exhaust.

CERCLA   See Comprehensive Environmental Response, Compensation and Liability Act.

CERCLIS See Comprehensive Environmental Response, Compensation and Liability Act Information System.

Certificate of Occupancy A document issued by a governmental authority certifying that all or a designated portion of a building complies with the provisions of applicable statutes and regulations, permitting occupancy for its designated use. When renovation of a facility—or part of a facility—begins, the structure or the part being renovated loses its certificate of occupancy.

Chalking A form of paint degradation in weather resulting in loose, powdery pigment on the painted surface.

Change Order Written authorization given by a building owner or the owner's agent to a contractor to change the scope of work, design or materials used or equipment to be installed. One way to reduce change orders in a new construction project is to delay interior design until the last possible moment. This allows all the user changes to accumulate during structural construction resulting in the final programming data.

Changes in the Work In construction contract terminology, these are changes ordered by the owner consisting of additions, deletions or other revisions within the general scope of the contract. The contract sum and the contract time are adjusted accordingly. All changes in the work, except those of a minor nature not involving an adjustment to the contract sum or the contract time, should be authorized by change order.

Channel A three-sided, U-shaped member in a sash or frame to receive a glass or panel insert.

Charette An intensive group work session or meeting for a group task. After char (work) and -ette (small), the term reportedly comes from French schools of architecture where student teams are required to produce architectural models as a major school project. The models are called charettes (small works); the same term applies to the all-night work sessions that are a customary part of their production.

Chargebacks Refers to the practice of the FM function charging other divisions for services provided.

Checking Breaks or cracks in the film of a coating that may or may not penetrate to the underlying surface.

Checkpoints Facilities planners should set up checkpoints during the life of a project. It is impossible for planners to know ahead of time what the business environment will be when the project is finished. Built-in milestones help planners peg progress and prevent irreversible obsolescence.

Chemical Sensitization A health problem characterized by symptoms such as dizziness, chest tightness, eye and throat irritation and nasal congestion when an individual is exposed to even trace amounts of certain chemicals they are sensitized to.

Chromatography   The analysis of a solution or mixture by using an adsorptive substance. As the mixture or solution flows over this substance (for example a strip of paper) the parts of the substance are separated out and can be identified. They often have a color that helps identify them.

Churn Rate   The amount of change in a given facility or organization due to personnel relocation. Churn rate can either be calculated as the amount of floor space changed per year expressed as a percentage of the total amount of floor space, or the number of personnel relocations per year as a percentage of the number of personnel in the facility. Even if the same worker moves several times in a year, those moves count in determining the churn rate. It is the costs associated with moving furniture and materials and the cost of reconfiguring the vacated space for a new user that are important to the facilities manager.

CICEP   See Construction Industry Cost Effectiveness Program.

Cladding   The exterior skin of a building. Examples are glass curtain walls, metal panels or precast cladding of various types.

Claims-Made Policy   An insurance policy that covers only those claims that occur and are reported during the policy's stated period and subsequent renewal periods.

Class 1-100,000   Measures of air purity for cleanrooms. See *Cleanrooms*.

Clean/Dirty Corridor Systems   A system of using two different sets of corridors to separate contaminated staff and supplies from clean staff and supplies. Used in both hospital operating suites and animal facilities.

Cleanrooms   Specially constructed, mechanically intensive areas or structures with strict environmental controls for airborne particles, temperature, humidity, air motion, etc. Although initially used in the aerospace industry, cleanrooms are now used in many fields, including pharmaceuticals, food processing, manufacturing and microelectronics. Most cleanrooms in use are vertical downflow rooms: air enters through a high efficiency filter in the ceiling and exits low on the peripheral walls or through perforations in the floor.

Cleanrooms are rated for purity according to guidelines established in Federal Standard 209D. Each rating class (1, 10, 100, 1,000, 10,000 and 100,000) is a logarithmic curve relating different combinations of particle size and particle count. Air cleanliness is specified in terms of the number of foreign particles per cubic foot (or cubic liter) of air. Lower numbers represent cleaner rooms. How particles are counted depends on particle size: air with smaller particles can have higher particle counts and still meet the class designation.

Class 1: The most stringent standard, allowing only one particle per cubic foot, where particles measure 0.5 micron or less in diameter.

Class 10: 10 particles per cubic feet of space where the particles measure 0.5 micron or less in diameter.

Class 100: Class 100 means 100 particles per cubic foot where the particle size is 0.5 micron or less.

Class 1,000: 1,000 particles per cubic foot, etc.

Class 10,000: 10,000 particles per cubic foot, etc.

Class 100,000: The minimum least stringent standard for cleanrooms.

Raytheon's $35 million, 115,000-square-foot microelectronics center, opened in 1985, features several design innovations that have improved cleanroom operations. One is an anteroom built next to the cleanroom used for vacuuming all incoming lab equipment. The anteroom is located next to the service elevator in the chase that runs between the northern building perimeter and the cleanroom. This vacuum procedure allows the continuous operation of the cleanroom without downtime to get operations back up to the specified class after equipment changes.

The facility also uses a chemical pass-through between the service chase and cleanroom. Every day a one-day supply of chemicals is brought up from the basement and placed in a sliding tray in the service chase outside a given bay. The tray slides inside the lab where researchers take the chemicals a short distance to the work area. The pass-throughs control the flow of chemicals by limiting the distance that individual bottles of chemicals travel inside the lab. The pass-through also serves as an air lock so the cleanroom is not contaminated when chemicals are delivered.

Prefabricated cleanrooms have a number of potential advantages, one of which is a shorter construction schedule. They can be designed and manufactured off-site while other construction continues, then raised into place. Lower energy consumption and operating costs are also possible. The extensive ductwork associated with conventional cleanrooms create resistance to air flow, or static pressure. which requires additional power to achieve proper airflow. As modular system have almost no ductwork, they use considerably less power.

Renovations. In retrofitting space for reuse as a cleanroom laboratory, determine the dynamic loading of the equipment to be placed around the cleanroom—fans, pumps, motors, transformers—to predict the nature and magnitude of vibration of the structure when the cleanroom becomes operational. Vibration data must be accumulated from an existing cleanroom in operation in the facility. If no such cleanroom exists, then the dynamic loading data must be estimated based on data for similar cleanrooms in other locations. These data are then used in analyzing the dynamic response of the existing structure.

Clerestory   A high window in an exterior or interior wall of a building located at or near the eaves or ceiling.

Clinical Trials   In the pharmaceutical industry, product testing using human subjects to demonstrate product efficacy. Informed consent and protection of human rights are prerequisites.

Closed Loop System   A heating or cooling system where the refrigerant is enclosed in a piping system that is not vented to the atmosphere. (Uniform Solar Energy Code)

CMOS   See Complementary-Metal-Oxide-Semiconductor Devices.

Coating   A material that is applied in a liquid or gel state and allowed to cure to a solid protective finish. All paints are coatings, but not all coatings are paints.

Codec   An electronic device which converts analog signals to digital form and vice versa. "Codec" stands for COder/DECoder. A codec is usually made up of a central processing unit (CPU) and memory. Codecs also compress and decompress data to allow real time transmission over digital link with 56 Kbps to 45 Mbps of bandwidth.

Codec Bandwidth   Video codecs are generally broken into two categories: low *bandwidth* codecs that operate at 56 Kbps to 384 Kbps and high bandwidth codecs that operate at 384 Kbps to 1.544 Kbps (or higher). Economic low bandwidth codecs are generally used for individual or small group applications. Large group situations generally require a higher bandwidth codec to insure good picture quality.

Coefficient of Utilization (CU)   A measure commonly applied to indicate the efficiency of a *luminaire*. CU comprises a ratio of the light delivered to the area to be illuminated compared to the total light output of the lamp or lamps alone.

Cohesive Failure   Rupturing or tearing of a sealant in which the sealant material itself ruptures without loss of bond to substrate. See *Adhesive Failure.*

Collector Sewers   Pipes used to collect and carry wastewater from individual sources to an interceptor sewer that will carry it to a treatment facility.

Colloid   A stable dispersion of molecular aggregates in water that have a size ranging between one hundred and two hundred millimicrons. Colloidal iron, aluminum and silica are commonly found in water.

Color Rendering Index (CRI)   An international reference system for comparing the color rendering properties of lamps. To determine CRI, a light source is compared to a reference source of similar color temperature and assigned a number. A source with a CRI number approaching 100 renders colors equivalent to the reference source. When comparing lamps of a similar type, CRI numbers provide guidance in selecting the lamp with better color-rendering properties.

Common Carrier   An organization (such as a telephone operating company) that provides communication services to the general public at nondiscriminatory rates, without control of message content. See also *Bypass.*

Community Relations   Community relations at Motorola has found it very useful to appoint a senior facility manager to act on behalf of all facility operations in dealing with the local communities, local utility companies and so forth. This person's job is to go out during "peacetime" and establish a rapport with these folks. When problems arise, the people in the community know this person and are more likely to go the extra mile to help solve problems.

Community Relations Plan (CRP)   Required by the 1980 Comprehensive Environmental Response, Compensation and Liability Act (CERCLA) in the event of a hazardous materials release or threat of release. The plan specifies the communication activities to be undertaken and provides for public comment on the remedial alternatives being considered. See also *CERCLA*.

Complementary-Metal-Oxide-Semiconductor Devices (CMOS)   CMOS produces an electrical circuit with a current of mixed positive and negative charges.

Componentry   Elements of office or laboratory furniture such as storage cabinets and work surfaces that are hung from walls, partial-height partitions or frames. Componentry excludes seating.

Comprehensive Environmental Response, Compensation and Liability Act (CERCLA)   Passed in 1980, this is the original Superfund law, that committed $1.6 billion to the long-term, permanent cleanup of the United States' worst hazardous waste sites. CERCLA, which was amended and reauthorized in 1986 by the Superfund Amendments and Reauthorizations Act (*SARA*), has spawned further acronyms to indicate the stages of a cleanup. These include PA (preliminary assessment), SI (site investigation), *RI* (remedial investigation), FS (feasibility study), *RAP* (remedial action plan), *RD* (remedial design), *RA* (remedial action) and *CRP* (community relations plan).

Comprehensive Environmental Response, Compensation and Liability Act Information System (CERCLIS)   The Environmental Protection Agency's computerized database that tracks the status of suspected hazardous waste sites.

Compression   In audio visual terminology, the action taken by a video *codec* in reducing the data rate required for the transmission of television signals between sites.

Computer-Aided Design (CAD) The production of engineering or architectural plans, drawings, visual displays, specifications, bills of materials, etc., using an interactive computer system and operator-provided numerical input.

Computer-Aided Design and Drafting (CADD)   With regards to CADD training, it has been said that the cost in CADD isn't in the hardware or software. It's in the training—keeping people trained and keeping trained people.

Computer-Aided Facilities Management (CAFM)   The combination of *CADD*, database management and specialized software for space planning and optimization, forecasting and other functions performed by facility planning and management professionals.

Computer-Aided Manufacturing (CAM)   The discipline of programming and using computers to control production machinery such as robots, service machines and numerically controlled machine tools, and to perform related production planning and control functions such as cost estimating, job costing, inventory control and scheduling. Related to *CAD* (CAD/CAM) when computer-generated and stored design data is directly used as the basis for this planning and control of automated production procedures.

Computer Terminals   Companies building new R&D facilities have to provide ample space for functions that are growing faster than the R&D organization as a whole. One function often allotted insufficient square footage in most organizations is technical computing. Computer terminals in R&D are no longer merely equipment: they have become building occupants. Many corporations now plan for a density of 1.2 to 1.3 terminals per office. This density raises the HVAC heat load criteria from less than one watt per square foot to 2.5 watts per square foot. See also *Cable Management*.

Conductive Coating   A coating specially formulated to conduct static electricity.

Constant Pressure Control   A control system for maintaining proper room pressurization. The system causes dampers or fans to react when the pressure in a room changes (for example, when a door opens).

Constant Volume Bypass   An "opening" in a wall that allows the airflow between rooms to remain constant whether doors are opened or closed.

Constant-Volume Reheat System   An air-conditioning system that maintains space temperature conditions based on a fixed flow of air to each space or zone, but with a variable temperature supplied to each zone. Temperature variations are provided by a reheat device—for example hot water or an electric coil—which collects thermal energy to raise the temperature of the air, thereby reducing its cooling capacity. If reheated above the space temperature, supply air can be used to heat the zone. This type of system is accurate for temperature control, but it is energy-intensive.

Construction Cost   The cost of all of the construction portions of a project, generally based upon the sum of the construction contract or contracts and other direct construction costs. The construction cost does not include the compensation paid to the architect and consultants, the cost of the land, rights-of-way or other costs that are defined in the contract documents as being the responsibility of the owner.

Construction Industry Cost Effectiveness Program (CICEP)   A collection of published guidelines developed by the Business Roundtable to improve the quality of U.S. construction and reduce construction costs.

Construction Management (CM)   Various forms of contracting for new construction in which the owner contracts for and entrusts to a third party various management functions that are intended to control or reduce project costs and time and to assure construction quality.

Contained Drain System   A segregated, closed drain system for the removal and subsequent collection of biological waste that will eventually either be chemically and/or physically decontaminated before it is introduced into the sewer system.

Container   A term used by designers to refer to a set of physical boundaries that encloses three-dimensional space. A container can be an entire building or the space on a single floor or in a room.

Containment Housing   Housing for research animals that protects the environment from contaminants within; accomplished through procedure and facility design. In contrast, *barrier housing* protects the animals from outside contamination.

Contract Research   Scientific and engineering research services performed by or for others under the terms of a contract. Utilizes the skills, knowledge and capital assets of others without long-term obligations on the part of the purchaser.

Contrast   In lighting, the relationship between the brightness of an object and its immediate background. An example of this would be the relationship between the letters printed on this page and the paper itself. An example of poor contrast would be a third or fourth carbon copy of a purchase order or computer printout.

Control Point Adjustment   In information systems, the procedure for changing the operating point of a local loop controller from a remote station through the use of a pneumatic or electronic control-setting device.

Control Point   The basic remote signal generator for environmental control in a computer-controlled building system.

Conversion Rate   In water systems, a quantification of the relationship between the volume of feed and product water of a reverse-osmosis membrane.

Cooling Electricity Use   Amount of electricity used to meet the building cooling load.

Core Drill   A process for drilling through concrete. A solid cylindrical "core" is removed in the process of cutting the hole, similar to an apple core. Core drilling is used to bore holes ranging from two-to-six inches in diameter for wiring poke-throughs or other utility access routes. Core drilling is also used in older buildings to extract concrete samples for strength tests. Core drills can cut through steel decking and reinforcing bars in addition to concrete.

Coverage Ratio   A term applied in financial analysis to measure the debt capacity of an organization or institution. Defined as net available cash flow per year divided by annual debt service requirements (principal and interest).

Cracking   Breaks in a coating that penetrate to the substrate. See also *Crazing, Checking* and *Alligatoring*.

Crazing   The development of a maze or random pattern of fine cracks in a material's surface caused by extreme cold, internal stresses or lack of elasticity under external forces of weathering.

Creep   Especially in roofing, the property of a substance that allows it in time to become permanently deformed when subjected to a stress. Creep is greater at higher temperatures; creep at room temperature is sometimes called cold flow.

CRI   See Color Rendering Index.

Crowbar   An electronic circuit that can rapidly sense an overvoltage condition and provide a solid-state low-impedance electrical path to eliminate the transient condition.

CRP   See Community Relations Plan.

Cryogenic Welding   A method of joining pipes and tubing (three-inch diameter or less) without heat, flame or the use of contaminating fluxes. This welding method employs special Raychem nickel alloy fittings that are packed in a cryogenic (cold) storage container; they shrink to a high-pressure fit when exposed to any ambient temperature in the range of -65° to 575°F. The benefits of the process are cleanliness, ease of installation and reliability.

Cultures and Stocks   Infectious agents and biologicals including: cultures from medical labs, waste from the production of biologicals, discarded live and attenuated vaccines and devices used to transfer, inoculate and mix cultures.

Curie   A measure of the rate at which energy is released by a radioactive material.

Curtain Wall   A wall that is part of the exterior envelope of a building, but isn't a structural component. Usually made of glass, metal or composite panels. The curtain wall provides building aesthetics and the basic weather seal for the building.

D

Dalton   A unit of molecular mass, 1.66×10^{-24} grams. One Dalton is equivalent to the mass of one hydrogen atom.

Daylight Control   A lighting-control strategy in which a photocell is used with a dimming system to provide a fixed light level at the workplace by increasing the amount of electric light with decreasing daylight levels and vice-versa. See also *Daylighting*.

Daylighting   To be effective, daylighting does not simply provide daylight. Daylight must be properly directed into interior spaces, and the intensity and quantity must be controlled. What is true of artificial light is also true of daylighting: a unit of light coming from the side, providing good contrast, is worth three units of light overhead. Properly daylit buildings will save owners money by reducing energy costs at peak demand, but even greater benefits may result from the aesthetic effects of daylit spaces. Productivity may be enhanced by the improved working environment.

DDC   See Direct Digital Control.

Dead Loads   Non-moving loads, such as mechanical equipment, air conditioning units and the deck or floor itself.

Debt Financing   In university environments, the use of bond issues, mortgages or other loan arrangements to fund capital projects. Most facility-related debt results from bond issues. From the university's standpoint, the main justification for debt financing a research facility is the institution's scientific and engineering potential relative to the outlook for funding research in the field for which the facility will be used.

Debug   Used in the computer field, the term means to eliminate errors and malfunctions from a computer program. The term was coined when an early room-size IBM computer malfunctioned because a moth had gotten inside the unit.

Decibels   From Deci- (10), and bel (after Alexander Graham Bell). A measure of power gain or loss in a sound wave relative to an arbitrarily chosen power level. Equal to ten times the logarithm of the ratio between output power and baselevel power. A difference in one decibel in the power supply to a telephone receiver produces approximately the smallest change in volume of sound which a normal human ear can detect. As applied to speech and sound levels in buildings and factories, dB is a measurement of sound energy ratios on the A-scale (440 Hertz). At 130 dB, sound is painful and deafening. The sound level on a busy city street is 100 dB. The average sound level in a large office is 60 dB.

Deck   The structural surface to which the roofing or waterproofing system (including insulation) is applied.

Declination   The angle of a heavenly body north or south of the celestial equator. Declination of the sun varies 23° from summer to winter.

Decontamination   Removal of harmful substances such as noxious chemicals, harmful bacteria or other organisms, or radioactive material from exposed individuals, rooms and furnishings in buildings or the exterior environment.

Dedicated Lines   Leased telecommunications circuits that are devoted to a specific application such as a teleconference network connecting fixed locations.

Deep-Well Injection   Disposal of liquid wastes by pumping it into deep wells where it is contained in the surrounding geologic formation.

Deionization   The process of removing the charged constituents or ionizable salts from solution. A water purification process that uses synthetic resins to accomplish the selective exchange of hydrogen or hydroxyl ions for the ionized impurities in the water.

Delta   An increment, usually very small, that is symbolized by the Greek letter for D: Δ. From calculus where the sum of a function, $f(x)$, over an interval can be approximated by dividing the interval into very small pieces (Δx), solving the function for each interval and then adding the increments ($\Delta f(x)$).

Deluge Fire Sprinklers   Open heads attached to a dry pipe sprinkler system. When activated by smoke or heat sensor devices, a valve opens to provide a dense, uniform coverage of water over the protected area.

Design Creep   The cumulative budget effect of changes and upgrades to a project.

Design/Build   Construction collaboration by the designer with the contractor where the design and construction processes overlap.

Dial-In/Dial-Out Bridge   A device that interconnects multiple telephone lines. Participants dial the bridge number (dial-in) or the bridge operator dials them (dial-out) to bring them on-line.

Diffuser   In lighting, a device commonly put on the bottom or sides of a luminary to redirect or spread the light from a source. In HVAC, a device used to disperse air flow as it enters a room. Especially important in animal-holding rooms.

Digital   In the context of smart buildings, pulses of electricity or light that can be transmitted as binary code at very high speed over wire or optical fiber.

Direct Digital Control (DDC)   An energy management system using the digital output signals of a control computer to directly adjust the position of HVAC valves and dampers without the use of intermediate pneumatic or electromechanical devices such as a receiver-controller.

Directional Transmitting   In lighting, a property of certain glazing materials that changes the direction of transmitted light via refraction. For example, light-directing glass block employs prisms on the two faces for directional control. Directional transmitting is used to reflect daylight onto a room's ceiling to increase light levels deep in the interior. In the case of skylights, light is transmitted in such a way as to maintain a reasonably low surface brightness.

Disconfiguration   The breaking up of efficient groupings of workers or work areas as the result of building constraints such as floor plan, column spacing, service areas and fixed utility systems.

Discount Rate   Following the principle that the value of money received (or money paid) is dependent on when it is received (or paid), the discount rate is the annual interest rate, compounded annually, used to determine the present value of money to be received (or paid) at a future date.

Discretionary Productivity   The extra performance that workers give when they are motivated to do their best work. Motivating factors include a clear relationship between one's task and the recognition received for it, meaningful work, money, the right tools and work environment design. Discretionary productivity can be thought of as the difference between the output employees could produce if they really wanted to and what they do produce in order to keep from being fired.

Disintermediation   In capital markets, disintermediation refers to the practice by investors of shifting their investments away from intermediate financial institutions, such as banks and savings institutions, to direct investments at a higher rate of interest in the securities and obligations of primary borrowers. This structural change in the financial services industry raises interest rate expectations of investors and, hence, raises the cost of the supply of funds to intermediate credit sources such as banks and savings institutions. Since intermediate financial institutions are the prime source of construction financing, disintermediation has the effect of raising construction costs.

Dissolved Inorganics   A water contaminant that includes calcium and magnesium ions dissolved from rock formations, gases that ionize in water, silicates leached from sandy river beds or glass containers, ferric and ferrous ions from rusty iron pipes, chloride and fluoride ions from water treatment plants, phosphates from detergents and nitrates from fertilizers.

Dissolved Organics   A water contaminant that may include pesticides, herbicides, gasoline and decayed plant and animal tissues. Dissolved organics also include the plasticizers leached out of plumbing lines, styrene monomers from fiberglass-reinforced storage tanks, deionization resin materials and carbon from activated carbon filters.

Distillation   The act of purifying liquids through boiling, so that the steam condenses to a pure liquid and the pollutants remain in a concentrated residue. See also *Reverse Osmosis*.

Distillation Hood   A type of laboratory *fume hood* that provides a work surface approximately 18 inches above the room floor to accommodate tall apparatus.

Distribution List   A file on an electronic mail system that contains a list of names. The file is often accessible to many users, and addressing a message to the distribution list will generate a copy for every person on the list.

Diurnal   Refers to day/night. Frequently used in reference to day/night control of lighting in animal rooms.

Downstream Processing   The stages of a biotechnology process that take place after the fermentation or bioconversion stage. Downstream processing includes separation, purification and packaging of the product.

DTS   Digital Transmission Services.

Dual Duct   An HVAC system in which both heated and cooled air are simultaneously supplied to the work area in separate ducts, and temperature control of the area is achieved by varying the mix of hot and cold air at a constant air volume. The system provides constant air circulation and localized temperature control. Two-duct installation means higher first costs, and energy inefficiencies occur when both hot and cold air are used to reach a room temperature that is equal to, or nearly equal to, the outside ambient temperature.

Duct   A passageway or conduit made of sheet metal or other suitable material used for conveying air or gas at low pressures.

Dump Cabinet   A specially designed hood used for the dumping of contaminated materials such as bedding or feces. It allows control and collection of particulate released during dumping.

Duplex Audio   An audio teleconferencing system which allows all sites to be heard simultaneously rather than only one party.

Dynamic Joint   A joint intended to accommodate expansion and contraction movements of the structure. Also called an expansion joint.

E

Echo Canceller   A device that blocks echo reflections during a conference while one person is speaking.

Echo Suppressor   An echo-control device that switches off the transmission path from the listening party to the talking party, thus blocking echo reflections.

Effluent   A liquid waste discharge from a manufacturing or treatment process. The waste may be untreated, partially treated or completely treated before discharge into the environment.

Effluent Limitations   Restrictions set by a regulating agency on concentrations, quantities and rates of wastewater discharges.

EIR   See Environmental Impact Report.

EISA   See Extended Industry Standard Architecture.

Elastomer   A material that cures to a synthetic rubber material capable of returning to its original dimensions after tensile or compressive forces are applied, within limits of the material's yield strength. Also called Elastomeric, Elastic Sealant.

Electronic Blackboard   A communications device that has the appearance of a normal chalkboard but in fact is an electronic transponder that converts handwriting on the board's surface into digital signals. The signals can be transmitted over a normal telephone line and reconverted at a remote location to a TV monitor display. Electronic blackboards are useful in teleconferencing, and the data link required for their use is less expensive than video transmission requiring satellite or broadband cable transmission. AT&T manufactures and markets the blackboard under the name Gemini.

Electronic Mail   The lack of face-to face contact and the permanency of electronic mail or e-mail requires a different communication style than telephone or face-to-face interactions. The Rand Corporation recommends the following to help e-mail users communicate more effectively:

- A message on a single subject, as opposed to multiple subjects, is easier to scan by subject header, answer and file electronically.

- Address the minimum number of recipients, and, when responding address only the sender. Unnecessary messages tend to proliferate when a message goes to a large group and each recipient then responds to the whole group.

- Forward missent messages to intended recipients.

- Label personal opinions explicitly because readers, especially those unknown to the sender, may not be able to distinguish opinion from fact. Respond to an opinionated message with facts or evidence.

- Avoid sending emotional messages, or label them as such. E-mail cannot be softened by tone of voice, backtracking or facial expressions. The subject header "flame" announces that the message contents may be negative and possibly mean-spirited. It is also a good idea to delay responding to an inflammatory message until the emotion provoked by it has passed.

- Attempts at humor and irony often create ambiguity and should be avoided or labeled explicitly. Jokes and ironic comments are natural in conversation but easily misunderstood on the computer screen, especially by readers who don't know the sender personally.

- When sending messages to networks or electronic bulletin boards, identify yourself and your affiliations and be careful to distinguish personal opinion from company policy. If you send a message criticizing a third party, send a copy of the message to them.

- Thank someone who provides information. This lets them know you received the information and makes them more likely to help again.

Electrowriter   A communication system for sending handwritten information over a telephone line. The sender writes on a special pad, and the receiver then sees the writing appear on a piece of paper or on a projection screen.

ELF   See Equivalent Lineal Feet.

Encryption   The coding or scrambling of a signal for secure transmission. The information must be decoded at the receiving site. Can be used for voice, video, and other communication signals.

Energy Recovery   Obtaining energy from waste through a variety of processes (e.g., combustion).

Energy Units   Energy is the capability to do work (i.e., water stored at high elevation, a moving flywheel, a combustible liquid). Energy units are the same as work units: *Btu*, joules, kilowatt-hours, foot-pounds. 3,400 Btu = 1 kilowatt-hour. A gallon of gasoline contains roughly 127,000 Btu.

Enthalpy   Actual heat content. In HVAC systems, often refers to heat recovery from exhaust air or heat-generating equipment.

Environmental Audit   An independent assessment of the current status of a part's compliance with applicable environmental requirements or of a party's environmental compliance policies, practices and controls.

Environmental Impact Report (EIR)   The report based on intensive study of the implications of a building project on the environment: air, wildlife, erosion, soil, noise, etc.

EPDM Membranes   Ethylene Propylene Diene Monomer membranes. This single-ply roofing material is formed by mixing EPDM polymer (a sticky black substance) with oils and carbon black, as well as a number of other materials. EPDM membranes have good weatherability, elasticity, ultraviolet resistance and flexibility at low temperatures. One disadvantage of EPDM is that the field-fabricated seams formed by applying contact cement to lapped sheets are vulnerable to poor workmanship and are not as strong as the membrane. Lapped seam failures are the most common type of EPDM membrane failure.

Epidemiology   The field of science that deals with the cause, study and control of epidemics and outbreaks of communicable diseases as well as diseases caused by chemicals and other environmental factors.

Epistitial Space   Utility distribution on the outside of a building, rather than in between floors or in the ceiling. See also *Interstitial Space.*

Equivalent Lineal Feet (ELF)   The length of floor space occupied by permanent apparatus (such as hoods and lab benches) and movable items used on a regular basis (such as carts and refrigerators). ELF is a measure of usable work area used as an architectural programming guide or method of facility evaluation in facilities where personnel access to multiple work surfaces is an important operating criteria.

Ergonomics   Human factors in a work situation (erg = work, nomics = study of). The science of human manipulative use of equipment and machinery. As applied to the office environment, it is the study of how people use seating, work space, communication devices, lighting, office equipment and tools to perform specific tasks.

Ethernet   The most widely used *local area network* technology.

Etiological Research Facility   A facility dedicated to research and study relative to the cause or causes of disease.

Excess Insurance   Provides a higher limit of coverage than that provided by a primary insurance policy. Excess insurance goes into effect when the loss exceeds the limit of the primary insurance.

Exoskeleton   Regarding building shells, a building type in which all vertical structural members, utilities and drains are located within the outside double walls of the building envelope. The advantage of this plan is that it affords great flexibility in the use of the interior space and provides easy access to utilities.

Explosive Limit   The amounts of vapor in the air that form explosive mixtures—the limits give the range of vapor concentrations that will explode if an ignition source is present.

Extended Industry Standard Architecture (EISA)   An internal connection scheme for communication within a computer. Also referred to as a communication bus.

Extended Services Construction Management   An organization and contractual approach to construction management in which the construction manager is cast in a dual role as either AE/CM or CM/contractor or constructor when initial services are expanded to include additional responsibilities. See also *Construction Management*.

F

Fan Coil Unit   Also called fan convector unit. A fan and a heat exchanger for heating and for cooling that is assembled within a common casing.

Feasibility Study (FS)   The phase of a hazardous waste investigation undertaken under the Comprehensive Environmental Response, Compensation and Liability Act (CERCLA) cleanup in which remedial action alternatives are developed, evaluated and selected. See also *CERCLA*.

Fee for Service   Healthcare term also known as indemnity. The traditional system in the U.S. in which patients or insurers are billed by physicians or insurers and hospitals for each service rendered. Also known as Cost-Based Reimbursement.

Feedwater   Water entering a purification system.

Fermentation   The process of growing microorganisms for the production of chemical or pharmaceutical compounds. Large tanks, called fermenters, contain the microorganisms along with the nutrients that microorganisms require to multiply.

FF&E   See Fixtures, Furniture and Equipment.

Fiber Optics   A means of transmitting data and communications in which light transmitted through thin glass fibers is intensity modulated by data signals. The use of fiber optics significantly reduces the large volume of wire or conductors (coaxial and twisted pair) normally used. The fiber optics method of transmitting information significantly increases transmission capacity and, correspondingly, reduces the size of communications conductors. Fiber optics requires the use of special source drivers and modems. Terminations and connections tend to be costly because fiber ends require special polishing.

Fiber-Reinforced Concrete (FRC)   Concrete-based construction material used in applications such as slabs and overlays, precast products, structural beams and girders and shotcrete applications. Glass, polyethylene or steel fibers are added to the other concrete ingredients. Addition of the fibers results in an improvement in strength, shock resistance and ductility.

Filter Efficiency   The efficiency of various filters. Collection efficiency is established on the basis of particles that are entrapped in a filter, and penetration efficiency is established on the basis of particles passed through a filter.

Fingerwall   A vertical maintenance access area incorporating a service rack for the distribution and connection of utilities. In *cleanrooms* and laboratories, repetitive fingerwalls can serve the additional function of air return *plenums*.

Fit-Up   Commonly used to refer to all building construction and improvements other than the basic shell components of the building, consisting of foundation, structure, external walls and roof. There are basically two classes of fit-up work. Building fit-up includes air conditioning, lighting, mechanical and all interior construction (wall, wall coverings, carpeting) pertaining to the function of the space (offices, production, research). User-group fit-up includes furniture, fixtures and all moveable improvements. See also *FF&E*.

Fixed Position Concept   A plant layout method that allows the product or assembly to remain stationary while tools, machinery, workers and supplies are brought to the product.

Fixed Visual Relief   Open areas adjacent to window areas that provide workers in internal spaces visual access to the outside. These areas can double as break areas, but they must be located or sized so that they cannot be converted to additional offices.

Fixtures, Furniture and Equipment (FF&E)   The moveable components of a facility. In labs and special high-tech facilities, FF&E is typically equal 1 to 1.2 times the total construction budget.

FLAA   See Flame Atomic Absorption.

Flame Atomic Absorption (FLAA)   A laboratory technique used for trace element analysis.

Flanking   Sound that travels from one point to another by other than a direct path. Sound may be reflected, transmitted by structural means or leaked. Like ripples in a still pond, sound waves proceed from the original source to the nearest hard surface and then reflect in a different direction. When considered in this light, the "overlap" problem of flanking provides insight into the fluid, three-dimensional nature of acoustics.

Flat Cable   A mix of flat and round flexible copper conductors laminated in an insulating material laid under carpet to distribute power and communication services from transition boxes in columns or walls to pedestal outlets at individual workstations. Cables are approximately .03 of an inch thick, placed side by side and encased by insulating material. This system requires special connectors and the use of carpet tile for better access.

Flexible   A term that is loosely applied in describing facilities capable of responding or conforming to changing or new situations. The range of specific meanings include: (a) used differently without modification, (b) easily modified to suit a different use or (c) easily replaced.

Flicker   The perception of variation in the brightness of a VDT display or fluorescent light. VDT flicker is not believed to cause any permanent visual damage; however, the perception of flicker is annoying and may cause visual fatigue. Flicker in fluorescent lights can be avoided by using high-frequency ballasts. See also *Ballast*.

Flood Plain   The lowland and relatively flat areas adjoining inland and coastal areas subject to a one percent or greater chance of flooding in any given year.

Floor Area Ratio   The gross square footage of a building divided by the square footage of the building site. A general planning specification used principally in urban situations to limit the density of building in a particular zone. If the FAR equals 1.0 for a 100,000-square-foot site, the maximum square footage in a building that can be built on that site is 100,000 square feet. If the FAR equals 2.0 for the same site, then the maximum amount of building space is 200,000 square feet.

Floor Boxes   Conduit termination points cast into concrete that house wiring devices and modular jacks. Activations can be with pedestal, flush or recessed fittings. The most appropriate use of floor boxes is for service requirements at precise locations that will not change.

Flue Gas   The air coming out of a chimney after combustion of a product.

Foot Candle   The basic measure used to indicate illuminance (level of illumination). One foot candle is equal to one unit of light flux (one *lumen*) distributed evenly over a one-square-foot surface area.

Foot Candle (or Uniformity) Ratio   The relationship between average foot candles and minimum foot candles (such as 3:1) or maximum foot candles and minimum foot candles (such as 6:1). The maximum:minimum ratio generally is preferred because average foot candles cannot be seen.

Foot Candles, Average   The theoretical average amount of light falling on a surface, as derived by averaging the illumination falling on all points of the surface. Two systems may produce identical average foot candles while providing highly dissimilar illumination.

- **Horizontal**   Foot candles perpendicular to a horizontal surface, such as a street. All horizontal foot candles are in the same plane for the same surface. They can be added together arithmetically when more than one source provides light to the same surface.

- **Initial**   Foot candles (minimum, maximum or average) produced when lamps and luminaries are new.

- **Maintained** Foot candles (minimum, maximum or average) calculated through application of a light loss factor.

- **Minimum** The amount of light falling on the point of a surface with the least illumination.

Force Majeure French for superior or irresistible force. A clause commonly added to construction contracts to protect the parties in the event that a portion of the contract cannot be performed because of intervening causes outside the control of the contracting parties, i.e., natural disasters.

Formaldehyde CH_2O. A colorless, pungent and irritating toxic chemical that is present in building materials, furniture, textiles, resins and tobacco smoke. It is used in the production of synthetic urea and phenol-formaldehyde resins, which are used in manufacturing plywood, fiberboard, laminates and particleboard. Urea formaldehyde was used in building insulation foams.

Formulation and Fill The last sterile process in a pharmaceutical manufacturing process producing a finished product. Formulation is the combination of active pharmaceutical ingredients with excipients (inactive ingredients) such as gelatin, sodium chloride or water. Fill is the process of pumping of the formulation into ampules, bottles or vials and can include stoppering, capping and sealing.

Four-Wire Circuit Refers to a telephone network with four-wire cabling instead of the conventional two-wire cables typically used in phone systems. A four-wire circuit allows users at two locations to talk and be heard simultaneously. The four-wire circuit usually avoids problems of echo and leakage associated with two-wire telephone circuits.

FRC See Fiber-Reinforced Concrete.

Free Address Offices A non-territorial office plan. A Japanese corporation, Shimizu Corp., found that the maximum occupancy rate in their R&D offices at any one time was 75 percent, with an average occupancy of 51 percent. This space was replanned so that only secretaries have designated desks, because they occupy them full-time. Each research worker is given a personal radio phone, a mobile lockable three-drawer pedestal and a personal laptop computer. Enough chairs and tables are provided to accommodate a 75 percent occupancy rate and are all located on a "first come, first served" basis. All archival and reference materials are stored centrally. The extra 25 percent space is used for group meeting areas.

Free Cooling System As applied to computer room air conditioning units, when the outside air temperature falls below a certain level, the units turn off the mechanical refrigeration system and reject computer-generated heat to the atmosphere using an antifreeze solution, pumps and coils. The system is "free" because it does not use fan energy for the fluid coolers of the compressor in the units.

Freeze-Frame Video   A relatively inexpensive way to add pictorial information to an audio teleconference by transmitting and/or receiving still video pictures over a telecommunications channel, usually a voice-grade telephone line or a lower-speed data channel. In a typical system, the graphic material is placed in front of a standard closed-circuit TV camera. The camera is connected to a scan converter that transforms the picture into a still image that can be transmitted over a telephone line or other communication link. The time required for transmitting a single frame ranges from 8 to 70 seconds depending on the bandwidth available and whether the image is black-and-white or color. The term "freeze-frame video" may also refer specifically to a still-frame video unit that "grabs" the image from the camera or other video source and "freezes" it. See *Slow-Scan Video.*

Freezer Farm   A consolidated frozen-materials storage area.

Frequency   A measure of pitch that distinguishes a "high" sound or note from a "low" one, measured in *Hertz.* Most sounds are complex—they contain a mixture of many frequencies. A few sources, such as tuning forks or oscillators, can generate single-frequency "pure tones."

Friable Asbestos   A material that contains more than one percent asbestos and can be crumbled or pulverized by hand.

FS   See Feasibility Study.

Fugitive Emissions   Air contaminant emissions from sources other than stacks, ducts or vents or from nonpoint emission sources.

Full Duplex   Two-way communication in tele- or video conferencing. In a two-site duplex video conferencing, both parties can send and receive video, audio and data simultaneously. See also *Duplex Audio.*

Full-Motion Video   A term that distinguishes between high-quality video employed in teleconferences and a lower quality video that is more like "freeze frame." The lower quality video can be transmitted at slower speeds over less expensive and more readily available transmission media (i.e., phone lines). Full-motion video generally requires coaxial cable.

Full-Spectrum Lighting   Fluorescent lighting that very closely matches the spectral energy distribution of sunlight. Full-spectrum lighting is important in animal research facilities because the lack of it in animal housing can affect animal maturation and sex habits. Research indicates that animals bred under non-full-spectrum lighting have undersized sexual organs.

Fume Hood   A self-contained work area inside a laboratory room from which potentially dangerous fumes are exhausted from the enclosed work surface by means of a separate air exhaust system. Fume hoods can be bench-type, in which the researcher reaches into the hood to work, or walk-in types in which the researcher enters a chamber to do experiments. The velocity of exhaust air typically needed for fume hood operation ranges from 80 to 110 fpm. Accommodating researchers' individual preferences, ensuring safety, solving the HVAC problems caused by researchers leaving fume hood doors open, responding to the trends toward larger hoods and bearing associated expenses are important planning issues for R&D labs.

Functional Silos   A method of corporate structuring that divides the company into groups by function—e.g. accounting, research, manufacturing, marketing, engineering—in contrast to cross-departmental teams focused on specific projects.

Fungi   A group of plantlike organisms that lack chlorophyll, including molds and mildews.

Fungible   Interchangeable. Serving equally well in the fulfillment of an obligation. Commonly applied to commodities, energy and currency. In facilities planning, it describes general purpose office space suitable to any kind of office work or department use (fungible space), or furniture that can be used throughout an office (fungible furniture).

Fungistat   A chemical that keeps fungi from growing.

G

Ganged Exhaust Systems   Multiple exhaust points connected together. Frequently used in reference to multiple hoods connected to a common exhaust duct which in turn is connected to a single exhaust system.

Gas Chromatography/Mass Spectrometry (GC/MS) A laboratory technique used for trace organic analysis.

Gateway   A connector that interfaces two or more dissimilar communications networks and provides a common protocol, thus permitting accurate communications between networks.

Gauss Moat   A protective design solution to contain fringe magnetic fields around MRI equipment.

GC/MS   See Gas Chromatography/Mass Spectrometry.

Gene   The smallest portion of a chromosome that contains the hereditary information for the production of a protein.

Gene Machine   A computerized device for synthesizing *genes* by combining nucleotides in the proper order.

Gene Mapping   Determination of the relative locations of genes on a chromosome.

Gene Splicing   The technique of inserting new genetic information in a plasmid. The same as recombinant DNA.

Genetic Engineering   A process of inserting new genetic information into existing cells in order to modify any organism for the purpose of changing one of its characteristics.

Gentrification   Middle- and upper-class restoration of deteriorating urban property, especially in working-class neighborhoods.

Geographic Information System (GIS)   A computer system designed for storing, manipulating, analyzing and displaying data in a geographic context.

GFAA   See Graphite Furnace Atomic Absorption.

Gflops   A unit of measure of the speed of a computer expressed as billions (giga) of floating-point operations per second.

GFRC   See Glass Fiber Reinforced Concrete.

Ghost Corridor   Circulation space within a lab, i.e. an open walkway that is not separated from the labs by a wall, but is defined by the arrangement of the benches or by colored tile.

GIS   See Geographic Information System.

Glare   A discomforting or disabling condition which occurs when a high-brightness source contrasts with a low-brightness background, making it difficult for eyes to adjust. High brightness alone does not cause glare.

Glass Fiber Reinforced Concrete (GFRC)   Concrete-based structural materials used in applications such as curtain walls that are manufactured in a modeling process where fiberglass is blown in as the concrete is poured. A labor-intensive process, the material is considerably more expensive than conventional concrete panels, but lighter in weight. Using GFRC reduces the overall weight of the structure and facilitates materials handling during construction.

Glove Box   A sealed enclosure in which all handling of items inside the box is carried out through long rubber or neoprene gloves sealed to the ports of walls in the enclosure. The operator places his hands and forearms in the gloves from the room side of the box so that he is physically separated from the glove box environment but is able to manipulate items inside the box with relative freedom while viewing the operation through a window.

GMPs   Good Manufacturing Practices (as opposed to guaranteed maximum price).

GMPC   See Guaranteed Maximum Price Construction.

Golden Parachute   A contractual clause in an employment agreement giving a large severance bonus to a top corporate manager should he or she be fired. Fears of hostile corporate takeovers have seen an increase in these agreements.

Gown Room   An anteroom contiguous to a biological research suite. It is used by research personnel for donning protective clothing prior to entering an area where pathological substances are present. Gowning typically includes the use of headcovers, gowns, foot booties and, in some cases, face protection.

Gowning   In precision processing environments, refers to the procedures for entering and exiting clean or sterile areas. These procedures typically involve disrobing, "gowning-up" with protective and sterile clothing—masks, cloaks, gloves, hoods and foot coverings—then "gowning-down" for garment removal and disposal.

Graphite Furnace Atomic Absorption (GFAA)   The most sensitive laboratory technique used for trace element analysis.

Gravel Stop   A flanged device, frequently metallic, designed to prevent loose aggregate from washing off the roof and to provide a continuous finished edge for the roofing.

Greenfield Site   An undeveloped site with no previous construction. The term was originally used to describe rural sites.

Greenhouse Effect   Heat buildup caused by a glazing material's transmission of solar radiation (shortwave) into an enclosure where the long-wave radiation becomes trapped.

Greenmail   Payment by a company to buy back its own common stock at a premium price from a select group of shareholders (such as a "raider") to fight off a hostile takeover attempt. Such payments reduce shareholder equity and may result in increased debt for the company.

Gross Square Feet   All of the floor space inside a building measured from the outside surfaces of exterior walls. See also *Net Square Feet.*

Grossing Factor   A number that is used to estimate the gross square footage of a building once the program space or assignable space is known. The number ranges from 1.3 for office buildings to as high as 2.0 to 2.5 for cleanrooms and research buildings.

Groundwater   Water in an underground saturated zone.

Group Relamping   A process of replacing all lamps in a lighting installation after a period of time equal to 50 to 80 percent of the rated lamp life. Individual lamps that burn out prior to their lamping time are either ignored or replaced with lamps saved from the previous group.

Group Technology   An organizational scheme for manufacturing and processing operations in which purchased items and fabricated parts are classified and numerically coded to reflect similar attributes such as geometric shapes, dimensions, tolerances and raw material composition. Group technology management maximizes production efficiencies by:
1. Simultaneously performing similar activities to avoid wasteful change-over time;
2. Avoiding unnecessary duplication of efforts by standardizing closely related activities;
3. Reducing the search time for information related to recurring problems.

Guaranteed Maximum Price Construction (GMPC) Sometimes referred to as Contractor "CM" because the CM at some point during the design modifies his agreement with the owner to specify a guaranteed maximum price for the cost of construction. Under GMPC, the CM is postured in a dual role of construction manager and contractor once the arrangement is made.

H-6   The Uniform Building Code embodiment of the Semiconductor Industry Association's 1981 "Green Book." Adopted January 1, 1985, H-6 sets the design standards for electronics and R&D facilities using any of the "no exemption" highly toxic chemicals or gases found in Table 9A of the Uniform Building Code.

Hand-Operated Positive Energy Control (HOPEC)   A fume hood accessory used as a means of cutting total energy demands by 50 percent. In both vertical and horizontal hoods, HOPEC locks the sash in a half-raised position during use to avoid the energy expense of researchers working with the hoods wide open. The equation for measuring the energy efficiency of HOPEC is total exhaust capacity of fume hood in cfm = rate of flow x areas of full sash opening. For example, a four-foot hood that has a face opening of 8.6 square feet with face velocity air at 100 fpm uses 860 cfm; with HOPEC, the door opens only to 4.3 square feet, reducing the exhaust capacity by 430 cfm.

Hardness   Referring to water, the scale-forming and lather-inhibiting qualities that water possesses when it has high concentrations of calcium and magnesium ions. Temporary hardness, caused by the presence of magnesium or calcium bicarbonate, can be removed by boiling the water to convert the bicarbonates to insoluble carbonates. Calcium sulfate, magnesium sulfate and the chlorides of these two elements cause permanent hardness.

Hardwire Systems   A method of providing electricity in which conduit and junction boxes serve as the distribution system over a specific grid layout. Activation is accomplished at workstations by poke-through outlets, partition raceways or service poles and at lighting fixtures by flexible conduits. Data and communications cables can also be run through hardwiring.

Harvest Room   In biotechnology facilities, a room for purification of products produced or fermented by biohazardous microorganisms in a bioreactor. Operations conducted in a harvest room include centrifugation, filtration concentration, dialysis and chromatography. The space is designed to prevent the unplanned release of biohazardous materials outside secondary containment. Workers must normally use protective equipment in the harvest room during operations that involve process materials. The area is designed so that the room and associated equipment can be rapidly decontaminated. Workers must sometimes wear ventilated suits while inside the room, which requires them to take a disinfectant shower upon exiting to decontaminate the exterior of the suit.

Harvesting   In animal research facilities, the collecting of animal organs for use in research. In biotechnology facilities, harvesting refers to the processing of product. After the product is produced by microorganisms in a bioreactor, it is transferred to a harvest room for purification ("harvesting").

Hawthorne Effect   A term generally used to describe an improvement in worker productivity that arises when the worker's environment is changed experimentally, even if the change is for the worse. The idea behind the Hawthorne effect is that experimentation, per se, conveys a message that management is vitally interested in its employees and that this message alone can stimulate improved performance. From 1927 to 1932, Mayo and Roethlisberger experimented with lighting levels at Western Electric's Hawthorne plant in Chicago. They found that worker performance increased with every change in the lighting level, even when the change was to reduce illumination. This unexpected result has been attributed to the change in worker attitudes resulting from simple human attention. The significant implication of the Hawthorne experiment is that one should not rely on early productivity and worker satisfaction measurements when trying to assess the true impact of changes to a given work environment.

Hazardous Processing Materials (HPM)   A solid, liquid or gas that has a degree of hazard rating in health, flammability or reactivity of 3 or 4 as ranked by Uniform Fire Code Standard number 79-3. HPM are used directly in research, laboratory or production processes that have as their end product materials that are not hazardous.

Hazardous Waste   Solid wastes which, because of their quantity, concentration, or physical, chemical or infectious characteristics, may (1) cause or contribute to an increase in mortality and serious, irreversible or incapacitating illness, or (2) pose a present or potential health hazard when improperly treated, stored, transported, disposed of or otherwise managed. See also *Autoclave*.

HAZMATS   Hazardous materials.

Headhouse   Area adjacent to a greenhouse which contains racks, drying equipment and other important research tools.

Health Plan Purchasing Cooperative (HPPC)   Under a managed-care system, an organization that would purchase healthcare for its members. Generally would be used by groups that are not large enough to effectively bargain for competitive pricing.

Health Maintenance Organization (HMO)   Prepaid health plans that provide a range of services in return for fixed monthly premiums. Virtually any organization can sponsor an HMO, including the government, medical schools, hospitals, employers, labor unions and insurance companies.

Heat Wheel   An energy-saving device that exchanges heat between exhaust (tempered) air and supply (untempered) air. This device transfers both sensible and latent energy. While this device is effective in transferring energy between the two air-streams, caution must be used in its application since this device requires the two air streams to join in close proximity, risking potential reintrainment of exhaust air.

Heavy Metals   Metallic elements with high molecular weights. Even in low concentrations, heavy metals are generally toxic to plant and animal life. Such metals are often residual in the environment and exhibit biological accumulation. Examples include mercury, chromium, cadmium, arsenic and lead.

HEPA Filter   See Highly Efficient Particulate Air Filter.

Hertz   A unit of measure of frequency (cycles per second) abbreviated Hz.

HID Luminaries   See High-Intensity Discharge Luminaries.

HID   See High-Intensity Discharge.

High-Intensity Discharge (HID)   A type of lighting, including mercury vapor, metal halide and high-pressure sodium light sources, where a small arc tube generating heat and pressure much higher than that of a fluorescent tube is enclosed in an outer bulb. Atoms of metallic elements vaporized within the arc tube emit high levels of electro-magnetic energy in the visible range, producing light. HID sources are the most efficient light sources in terms of lumens of light produced per watt. Although low-pressure sodium lamps are sometimes included in the HID category, they are not HID sources.

High-Intensity Discharge (HID) Luminaries   These lamps have a very high light output and a relatively long life. Types of HID luminaries include the mercury vapor (bluish) and sodium vapor (yellow-orangish) lamps found in street lights.

Highly Efficient Particulate Air (HEPA) Filter   Used in cleanroom laboratories to filter out contaminating particles as small as 0.5 micron in diameter. HEPA filters were first used in hospital operating rooms for heart transplant surgery. See also *ULPA Filter*.

HMO   See Health Maintenance Organization.

Hood Capture Efficiency   Ratio of the emissions captured by a fume hood and directed into a control or disposal device, expressed as a percent of all emissions.

Hood Certification   Certification made by a qualified person signifying that required air flow tests have been performed and that a *fume hood*'s performance is in accordance with the manufacturer's data. In the case of biosafety cabinets, certification signifies that performance is in accord with the requirements of the National Sanitation Foundation's (NSF) Standard.

HOPEC   See Hand-Operated Positive Energy Control.

Hot Spots   In a sound masking system, those areas in a room where the hissing of white noise is louder than elsewhere. Technically, called poor spatial uniformity. The problem derives from plenum speakers located too far apart, right next to a reflecting element such as a big duct, or from openings in the ceiling for air return or light fixture cooling. Ceiling products with low transmission loss or low STC ratings are prone to hot spots.

Hot Wire Anemometry   Thermal Anemometry. A technique of measuring air movement in an exhaust duct or at the face of a fume hood. Air is moved across a heated wire, cooling the wire. The measure of the wire's change in resistance is directly correlative to the speed of the air.

Hoteling   A generic approach to the office where desks are not assigned to any particular employee. Employees do the bulk of their work outside the office. When they do come into the central facility to work, they are assigned a desk equipped with basic office supplies, a phone and perhaps a computer terminal. See also *Virtual Office, Alternative Office* and *Telecommuting*.

HPM   See Hazardous Processing Materials.

HPPC   See Health Plan Purchasing Cooperative.

HRS   Hazard Ranking System. The principal screening tool used by the EPA to evaluate risks to public health and the environment associated with abandoned or uncontrolled hazardous waste sites. The HRS calculates a score based on the potential of hazardous substances spreading from the site through the air, surface water, or ground water and on other factors such as the density and proximity of human population. This score is the primary factor in deciding if the site should be on the National priorities List.

Huddle Space   Another term for interaction space.

Humidifier Fever   A respiratory illness caused by exposure to toxins from microorganisms that flourish in humidifiers and air conditioners. Characterized by tightness of the chest, cough, muscle aches, fever and chills, it has been reported among office workers since 1970. Also called air conditioner or ventilation fever. See also *Sick Building Syndrome*.

Hybridization   Production of offspring, or hybrids, from genetically dissimilar parents. The process can be used to produce a hybrid plant (by cross-breeding two varieties) or hybridomas (hybrid cells formed by fusing two unlike cells, used in producing monoclonal antibodies). Industrial Biotechnology Association

Hybridoma   The cell produced by fusing two cells of different origin. In monoclonal antibody technology, hybridomas are formed by fusing a cancer cell and an antibody-producing cell.

Hypermedia   A term that refers to a variety of electronic technologies that support cognitive tasks. Includes desktop publishing, windowing computer environments, video disc-based and digital map systems, enhanced graphics, animation and database and query systems.

Hypersensitivity Pneumonitis   A group of respiratory diseases that cause inflammation of the lung. Most forms of hypersensitivity pneumonitis are caused by the inhalation of organic dusts, including molds.

I

I-Point   Inspection or Identification point. The place in a manufacturing operation where a product is checked for quantity, weight, height, dimension or fit.

IAQ   Indoor Air Quality

ICAM   See Integrated Computer Aided Manufacturing.

ICP-AES   See Inductively Coupled Plasma-Atomic Emission Spectrophotometry.

Illuminance   Lighting level, expressed in lux (metric unit) or footcandles (English unit).

Immuno-Compromised Animals   Animals that have a defect or abnormality in their immunologic systems. The defect can be inherited, as in nude mice, or may be induced by radiation or by some other method. These animals are valuable for immunology research, but require special environmental conditions because of their susceptibility to disease.

Impoundment   A body of water or sludge confined by a dam, dike, floodgate or other barrier.

Incompatible Waste   A waste unsuitable for commingling with another waste or material because commingling could result in one or more of the following: (1) the generation of extreme heat or pressure, (2) explosion or violent reaction, (3) fire, (4) formation of substances that are shock sensitive, friction sensitive or otherwise have the potential of reacting violently, (5) formation of toxic dusts, mists, fumes, gases or other chemicals, (6) volatilization of ignitable or toxic chemicals, (7) escape of the substances into the environment and (8) any other reactions contrary to the Air Human Health & Environmental Standard.

IND   See Investigational New Drug.

Indoor Air Pollution   Chemical, physical or biological contaminants in indoor air.

Indemnity   Payment by an insurer covering the claimant's entire loss.

Indirect-Cost Reimbursement   A financing method that allows universities to be reimbursed for their expenses in building research facilities. Institutions determine the reimbursement amount by either levying a "use charge" or by depreciating the facility. Interest on debt incurred in financing a facility can also be reimbursed. It is estimated that universities recover through indirect-cost reimbursement only about 40 percent of the full value of the capital initially used to fund facilities.

Inductively Coupled Plasma-Atomic Emission Spectrophotometry (ICP-AES)   A laboratory technique used for trace element analysis.

Infectious Waste   Hazardous waste with infectious characteristics, including: contaminated animal waste; human blood and blood products; isolation waste, pathological waste; and discarded sharps (needles, scalpels or broken medical instruments).

Infiltration   Leakage of air into a building. Infiltration rates vary depending upon factors such as wind pressure and the difference between indoor and outdoor temperatures.

Infrared Sensor   A heat-sensing device. These sensors are used in lighting control and intrusion alarms.

Infrastructure   Pertains to site developments such as utilities, roads and storm water management that are in place and accessible for use.

Inorganic Chemicals   Chemicals of mineral origin, not of basically carbon structure.

Inpatient Acuity   The degree of illness suffered by a patient in a hospital.

Inside/Outside Wiring   Typically used in a three-lamp fluorescent parabolic fixture to provide three levels of light. The center tube of the fixture is connected to a single lamp ballast with the two outside tubes connected to a two-lamp ballast. The fixture is wired to allow the center and outside tubes to be switched independently so that three levels of lighting can be achieved by having one, two or three lamps operating.

Integrated System   A *CADD* system that has an integrated database management and retrieval system. The key features of such a system are the ability to independently address graphic files and an associated database and to update or change graphics from the database and database attributes from graphics.

Injection Well   A well into which fluids are injected for purposes such as waste disposal.

Integrated Computer Aided Manufacturing (ICAM)   Conceptually, the computer-controlled linkage of a series of CAM systems or "cells" to form an automated manufacturing line with a broad range of capabilities.

Interaction Areas   Areas in a building that are largely used by employees for talking and meeting with each other. Cafeterias and dining halls are an example. Seating configuration in dining facilities influences whether the area will enhance or inhibit conversation and relaxation. The most inefficient seating configuration is for six; preferred seating arrangements are for two and four. Approximately 60 percent of the technical information in an organization is exchanged informally: workers talk over coffee, in chance meetings by the photocopy machine or in the corridors. One way to enhance interaction is to create common nonterritorial workspace, or "group space," that is shared by a group or unit. In some facilities, companies have reduced the size of individual offices to a single work surface with storage cabinets and have contributed the remainder of the traditional office space allotment to the group area. Corridors provide an excellent opportunity for employees to interact. Because shorter corridors encourage more group contact, managers prefer to limit corridor lengths to 100 to 125 feet in work areas and 40 feet in sub-work areas. Activity nodes strategically placed along the corridors increase interaction. Intersections, vending areas with seating, office supply storage and lavatories are the most effective activity nodes. The physical distance between workers bears a direct correlation to the probability of communication among those workers. There is a 25 percent probability that researchers situated within 5 meters will talk to each other daily. There is a 10 percent probability that workers located between 10 and 45 meters will talk.

Interconnectivity   Making the communication systems and protocol of machinery manufactured by a variety of companies compatible with other equipment used in the same plant.

Internal Rate of Return   The annual discount rate which makes the present value of future cash flow equal to the actual initial investment outlay for a particular project. Projects with high internal rates of return make better use of capital than projects with low internal rates of return. Also called "Equalizing Rate of Discount" or "Return on Investment" (ROI).

Interstitial Skip Floor   An alternative approach to providing the advantages of interstitial space for mechanical systems without committing one separate service floor to each program floor. This is achieved by creating an interstitial service floor above and below each pair of dedicated program floors. This idea is helpful in renovation projects where the distribution of services is critical but where giving up 50 percent of the floors to mechanical is not practical or economical.

Interstitial Space   A building design concept whereby open work space and flexibility in space usage and utility reconfigurations for a given building shell is maximized by locating utilities between floors, i.e., "interstitially." Vertical clearances for interstitial space vary typically from 6 to 10 feet depending on the quality, sophistication and access requirements of building utilities. Fast-track construction is possible with interstitial space because different trades can work simultaneously in the same space, reducing total labor hours. Interstitial space minimizes lab downtime because time-consuming modifications and repairs do not take place in the laboratory. There is a tendency in interstitial design to think that utilities can be run any place and the design will somehow work out right. This is a false premise. The truth is that utilities must be carefully zoned. Furthermore, the construction manager or contractor has to serve duty as a drill sergeant to indoctrinate the trades and make sure that utilities are installed in the proper zones.

Investigational New Drug (IND)   Refers to a "test" drug produced by a drug discovery program from which data is collected and evaluated to demonstrate that the drug is safe and effective. Prior to commencing clinical trials (which must be performed on human subjects), an Investigational New Drug Application must be filed with the FDA. The IND application must contain information that will demonstrate the safety of testing in human subjects, including: drug composition, manufacturing and control data, results of testing on animals, training and experience of investigators and a plan for clinical investigation. In addition, assurance of informed consent and protection of the rights and safety of human subjects is required.

ISO 9000   Referred to generically as ISO 9000, this is actually a series of five standards (ISO 9000 - 9004) that provide a model for documenting an organization's quality-management system. Developed in 1987 by the International Organization for Standardization in Geneva, Switzerland, the standards assure that an ISO 9000-registered supplier (a product or service provider) is capable of controlling the processes that determine the acceptability of its product or service. Note: The standards apply to the quality of the process and *not* the quality of the product or service.

   •   ISO 9000 and ISO 9004 introduce the standards, define terminology and guide a company in selecting to which of the standards — 9001, 9002 or 9003 — it should register. Additionally, they describe the 20 quality-systems elements against which the company will be audited.

   •   ISO 9001, the most stringent and broadest standard, confirms process conformance for the entire product cycle, from design and development to production, installation and service. A company registering to this standard must meet all 20 quality-system elements.

   •   ISO 9002 applies only to production and installation. Eighteen of the 20 quality-system elements apply to this level. It is normally used by a product manufacturer.

   •   ISO 9003 applies only to final inspection and test. It is not widely used and then primarily by service providers such as distribution companies. Twelve of the 20 quality-system elements apply to this level.

To receive ISO 9000 registration, a company must pass an audit conducted by a third-party organization — the registrar. The registrar sends auditors (sometimes called assessors) to the company to verify that it complies with the standards. If it does, the registrar issues the company a registration certificate. Many customers require that the registrar itself be accredited by a nationally recognized accreditation body. The Registrar Accreditation Board (RAB) provides that function in the United States.

Increasingly, customers (purchasers) — especially European customers — require that their suppliers be ISO 9000 registered. In the case of products sold in Europe that have a health, safety or environmental impact, this requirement comes from the European Union itself, which demands that those products be manufactured under ISO 9000 standards.

ISO 9000 can have a direct impact on facilities planners, particularly if the planner is responsible for specifying capital equipment used in the manufacture of the product. Special facilities considerations such as clean rooms, air or water filtration systems, and secure installations could also be subject to ISO 9000 if those items impact product or process quality.

For more information or to order copies of the standards, contact the American Society for Quality Control: Telephone (414) 272-8575 or fax (414) 272-1734.

J

K

J-Box   A term for an electrical junction box.

Kb/s (or Kbps)   Kilobits per second, or one thousand bits per second.

Kill Tank   A biological piping system for collecting and decontaminating infectious and hazardous organisms from laboratory effluent. The tank is connected to a contained drain system. The operational objective of a kill tank is to either achieve a logarithmic reduction of the producing organism, such as can be achieved by pasteurization, or to sterilize the entire contents of the vessel.

Kleenedge Laminar Flow   A trade name for a patented laminar flow system manufactured by VECO International. The filter module in the system features an adjustable high-velocity air curtain, thereby eliminating the need for vinyl or acrylic curtains. The filter module can be self-contained (that is, containing its own blower units) or connected to a central supply system.

Knowledge Workers   The class of employees regarded as "professionals": executives, managers, planners, engineers, programmers and researchers, as distinguished from clerical or production workers.

L

Lab Neighborhoods   Groupings of labs that share common equipment and interaction spaces between disciplines.

Laboratory Analytical Protocol (LAP)   Defines the set of laboratory procedures to be used for analyzing a set of samples collected from a Superfund protocol site.

Laminar Air Flow   Uniform direction movement of air. Laminar air flow is generally associated with fume hoods or biological safety enclosures that utilize this characteristic to capture and carry away airborne particles.

LAN   See Local Area Network.

LAP   See Laboratory Analytical Protocol.

Laws of Thermodynamics   First Law: energy can be converted from one form to another, but it can neither be created nor destroyed. Second Law: any system that converts energy from one form to another is less than 100 percent efficient; with each conversion, some amount of energy is lost to the system.

LC50/ Lethal Concentration   A standard measure of toxicity or "median-level concentration" that tells how much of a substance is needed to kill half of a group of experimental organisms in a given time.

LCUR   Local Computer User Room.

LEL   See Lower Explosive Limit.

Lens   A glass or plastic shield that covers the bottom, and sometimes sides, of a luminary. Lenses can also be designed to control the direction and brightness of the light as it comes out of the *luminary*.

Leveraged Buyout   A method for purchasing control of a company through loans based on the company's own assets, rather than on some other collateral. This new debt, when combined with normal levels of business debt, can create cash flow problems that may force companies to sell off divisions or certain assets after such a transaction has occurred.

Life Cycle Costing   The comparison of alternative projects or design solutions on the basis of total costs over a comparable time period. In this analysis, total costs are the sum of initial costs, operating, maintenance and replacement costs, less salvage value.

Life Safety Speakers   Fire-rated speakers that are a part of a building's emergency system and that are used to make announcements to evacuate the building in the event of an emergency.

Light Loss Factor   A multiplier which is applied to account for the conditions which reduce light output over time. These include temperature and voltage variations, lamp aging and dirt build-up on lamp, luminary and room surfaces. In common practice, light loss factors are applied to initial foot candles to determine the light level that will be maintained in a given area.

Light Pen   Light Wand. A device used on microcomputers and terminals that locates a point on the CRT screen. The computer senses the position of the pen whenever it touches the screen. The light pen is often used for "drawing" on the screen or for selecting a displayed item.

Light Pipe   A tube with a prism inside that conveys light from exterior locations to remote interior or subterranean locations in a building where workers may be psychologically deprived of the relief and comfort of natural light.

Light Shelf   A horizontal reflection surface located either on the outside or the inside of an exterior window of a building. A light shelf reflects daylight deep into a building as a source of ambient lighting for interior work places. Designs for daylit interior areas use interior daylight shelves to reflect light toward the ceiling and to reflect light down toward work areas. See page 173 in the Facilities Planning Concepts section for more information.

Limited Motion Codec   A picture processor or codec which takes full motion video information and reduces it to a series of video snapshots to be transmitted at a low data rate between sites. Does not include codecs which convey full motion video. See also *Codec*.

Link   A communications channel which ties together only two sites. A network is made up of many links.

Liquidated Damages   When late completion of a project will result in financial losses to the owner that would be difficult to determine exactly, an agreement is reached between the owner and the contractor to have the contractor pay the owner a pre-agreed amount as liquidated damages. This is usually on the basis of a set dollar amount for each day the work exceeds the contract time. Courts generally hold that, to be enforceable, the amount specified as liquidated damages must be reasonably related to probable actual financial damages.

Literium (Li'trium)   A skylighted central court or atrium designed to provide daylight to interior offices. The word was coined by Lockheed Missiles & Space Company to emphasize the utilitarian aspects of a Sunnyvale, Calif., office building built around a 60' x 300' five-story glass-covered courtyard.

Load Shedding   A lighting control strategy for selectively reducing the output of lighting fixtures on temporary basis as a means to reduce peak demand charges.

Loadbearing Wall   Wall supports itself and floor structure.

Local Area Network (LAN)   The connection of communication and data devices within an office, building or plant site. There are three basic network configurations: (1) the *bus network*—a central cable with spur connections to each piece of equipment, (2) the *ring network*—a loop of cable connecting equipment pieces and (3) the star network—each piece of equipment connected to a central controller, like the old phone systems.

Local Control Unit   A microprocessor that receives data from sensors and responds to instructions contained in a software program run by the applications processor. Architecture

Local Exhaust Ventilation   A form of containment control where contaminants are "captured" at the source of generation. Examples of "capture hoods" are canopy hoods, slot hoods and laboratory chemical *fume hoods*, which completely enclose the source of the contaminant.

Long-Span Construction   Refers to the structural design of buildings in which the unsupported length of horizontal beams (between columns) is greater than 50 feet. The unsupported span may be up to 200 feet long, but typical long-span structures feature unsupported beam lengths from 50 to 70 feet. Long-span structures typically use steel trusses instead of beams. The principal benefit of long-span construction is more column-free open space for flexibility. The cost of this flexibility lies in the use of more expensive trusses and the loss of vertical space.

Loss Ratio   An insurance term for net losses divided by net premiums.

Louver   In lighting applications, a series of baffles arranged in a geometric pattern used to shield a lamp from view at certain angles, to avoid glare from the bare lamp.

Low-E Coating   Low Emissivity Coating. One of the new generation of high-performance glazing coatings for windows designed to improve thermal performance.

Lower Explosive Limit (LEL)   The concentration of a compound in air below which the mixture will not catch on fire.

Lumen   Basic unit of luminous flux, or total visible energy emitted by a source per unit time through a unit-solid angle (steradian).

Luminaire   A complete lighting unit consisting of a lamp (or lamps), together with a housing, the optical components to distribute the light from the lamps, and the electrical components (ballasts, starters, etc.) necessary to operate the lamps.

Luminary   A complete lighting fixture including one or more lamps and a means for connection to a power source. Many luminaries also include one or more *ballasts* and elements to position and protect lamps and distribute their light.

LUST   Leaking Underground Storage Tank. Also referred to as LUFT (Leaking Underground Fuel Tank).

Lyophilization   A process that involves that rapid freezing of a preparation to a very low temperature, followed by rapid dehydration—without thawing—under a high vacuum. The water sublimes, i.e., passes directly from liquid to vapor from the preparation. Also referred to as "freeze drying."

Lyophilization Chamber   The space in which the lyophilization process occurs. It is designed to withstand the extremes in both temperature and pressure that lyophilization requires. For pharmaceutical preparations, chambers are typically fabricated of stainless steel and are made to endure conditions required for sterilization of the chamber, i.e., chemicals or high-pressure steam.

MAD   Mass Air Displacement.

MADC   See Mass Air Displacement Cleanroom.

Main Street   The main public thoroughfare in a building, designed to give workers from various parts of a facility the chance to meet and interact. It is also the primary access to offices, labs and other work areas or to branch streets.

Maintenance   Including a representative from maintenance or operations on a design team assures that what is built and installed can be serviced economically. Serviceability is not a priority item with most design teams, but if it isn't built in, future service can be very expensive.

Maintenance Factor   A factor used in lighting calculations to account for the natural decrease in light output that results from lamp aging and dirt accumulation on the lamp, fixture and room surfaces.

Man Trap   An entry chamber or passageway that is constructed to accommodate one person at a time. The trap has an entry-only door that allows entrance into the chamber and an exit door that must be opened either by a guard or by satisfying the security system—pass card or key code. Man traps are used extensively in the banking industry and often in high-security computer facilities. The drawbacks of man traps are the expense of installation and the slowdown of foot traffic.

Managed Care   Prepaid care provided by health maintenance organizations and other groups that hold down costs by requiring pre-admission approval for hospital stays and closely monitoring other medical services. The program is designed around channeling patients to general practitioners, "family doctors," first with a concentration on promoting healthy life-styles.

Managed Competition   A fundamental restructuring of the US healthcare system to make consumers more cost-conscious. Most Americans would get health insurance though *Health Plan Purchasing Cooperatives*, which would drive hard bargains with a variety of insurers and providers. Some plans would be health maintenance organizations that limit choice of doctors and hospitals but other might still offer traditional fee-for-service coverage. The cooperative would determine what the best price for a comprehensive benefits package defined by a National Health Board. Consumers would bear the extra cost of added benefits and might be taxed on the value of benefits above the minimum.

Manufactured Wiring Systems   Power, lighting, electronics and communications distribution systems designed for use in ceiling or raised-floor plenums. They consist of flexible metal clad cables with built-in connectors and adaptors for power and lighting requirements. Floor and wall outlets, service poles, partitions and pre-wired office furniture can be fed with these systems.

Manufacturing Trains   In pharmaceutical facilities, the technologies, equipment and unit operations that make up the process environment through which a product is manufactured, separated and purified. A facility may contain more than one manufacturing train operating simultaneously, but segregation of materials, product and personnel must be maintained through design and procedure to prevent the cross-contamination of product and materials.

Masonry Veneer   A masonry facing applied to or laid against a wall but not integral to the building structure.

Mass Air Displacement Cleanroom (MADC)   A *cleanroom* used in conjunction with animal housing in research facilities to keep the environment free of hair, dandruff and other airborne contaminants. The level of cleanliness is determined by the number of air changes per hour and the numbers and types of animals held in the cleanroom.

Massing   The segment of the design process for a new building in which various options for the overall shape of the building (tall, lean, square, stacked) and the scale of the building are considered in light of the surrounding environment and other buildings (existing or planned) in immediate proximity.

Material Representation   A statement made on an application for insurance coverage that affects the underwriter's decision in issuing a policy. A material representation that is proved false may negate policy coverage.

Material Safety Data Sheets (MSDS)   A compilation of information on the identity of hazardous chemicals, exposure limits, health and physical hazards and precautions. Originated by the Occupational Safety and Health Act of 1970. The 1986 Superfund Amendments and Reauthorization Act (SARA) requires facilities using or storing any of 402 "extremely hazardous substances" to make MSDS available to local authorities. They are also required under the OSHA Communication Standard

Maximum Upset Price   An amount agreed upon, by contract, at the beginning of a project that guarantees a maximum price. If the set price is exceeded, the contractor is responsible for producing the extra amount. If the contractor stays below the guaranteed price, the contractor and client split the profit.

Mb/s (or Mbps)   Megabits per second, or one million bits per second.

MDL   See Method Detection Limit.

Meet-Me Bridge   A type of telephone bridge that can be accessed directly by calling a certain telephone number. It allows "dial-in" teleconferences.

Metal Panels Sandwich   Dense foam core, aluminum (hexel) core; Plate-steel, aluminum.

Metal Raceway   A two-level underfloor raceway system consisting of a two- to three-inch deep upper-level header duct (or trench) that feeds cable to lower-level distribution cells (structural steel metal decks) that run at right angles to this header. Distribution cells are created by covering the voids in the underside of the structural metal deck with a metal plate. Wire can then be distributed through the header trench and out to workstations through the distribution cells. See also *Cellular Raceway* and *Underfloor Raceway*.

Method Detection Limit (MDL)   The minimum concentration of a substance that can be measured and reported with a 99 percent confidence that the concentration of the substance is greater than zero.

Mflops   A unit of measure of the speed of a computer expressed as millions of floating-point operations per second. Mflops has replaced Mips as the rating for new supercomputers. Unlike Mips, Mflops counts the number of straight calculations a CPU carries out per second. A 14-Mips general-purpose system is basically the same processor speed as a 7-Mflop supercomputer.

Micro Einstein   A measure of light energy square foot. (200 micro Einsteins = approximately 800 *footcandles* per sf.)

Micro-Inch   One one-millionth of an inch. It is the predominant unit of measurement in the United States for line widths and vibration tolerances in the manufacture of semiconductor circuits. See *Micron*.

Microenvironment   The particular environments: temperature, humidity, lighting, level, noise and air changes at a particular place in room. Frequently this term refers to the particular microenvironment within an animal cage. These conditions generally differ between different cages and in turn differ from the macroenvironment or general room conditions.

Micron   One one-millionth (10^{-6}) of a meter; approximately 40 microinches. Used predominantly in Europe as a measure for line widths and vibration tolerances in the semiconductor field. (Note: the terms "micron" and "microinch" are commonly confused. A vibration standard of 20 microinch displacement is the same as a half micron.)

Microorganisms   Small, unicellular life forms, such as bacteria. In reference to facilities, they are a source of contamination for high-precision processes, or a potential health hazard to people in indoor environments. Microorganisms such as bacteria can be chemically killed; algae, which are unicellular forms that link together, need to be mechanically removed. Legionnaires' Disease is one example of microorganism contamination of an *HVAC* system.

Microprocessor   A single computer chip that contains all the logic and arithmetic circuits of the computer. It is, in effect, the "brain" of the entire machine.

Minicomputer   Minicomputers fall between microcomputers and mainframes in terms of size, price and performance. Typically, a mini consists of a central processor, one to two hard disks, a tape drive, at least one line printer and up to 20 terminals.

Mips   Millions of Instructions Per Second. A measure of the information processing capacity of a computer in terms of hardware processing speed. See *Mflops* and *Gflops*.

Mist   Liquid particles measuring 40 to 500 microns formed by condensation of vapor. By comparison, fog particles are smaller than 40 microns.

Modem   Modulator-Demodulator. Electronic equipment that modulates digital signals and demodulates analog signals so that digital signals can be transported over an analog telephone line.

Modified Bitumens   Formed with *bitumens*, a chemical additive to enhance the plastic and elastic properties of bitumen, and a reinforcement fabric, such as scrim, for added tensile strength. Chemical additives in the membrane composition include fillers and polymers intended to alter and improve the performance of bitumen. The fillers enable the bitumens to maintain their manufactured shape; the polymers give the bitumen greater elasticity, ultraviolet resistance and improved weathering.

Modified Bitumen Membrane   A single-ply roofing membrane developed in Europe. Modified bituminous roofing membranes are made up of *bitumen*, reinforced fabric—such as scrim—for added tensile strength and a chemical additive to enhance the plastic and elastic properties of bitumen. The great advantage of modified bituminous membranes are their compatibility with asphalt. Chemical fillers used in the membrane enable the bitumens to maintain their manufactured shape; polymers give the bitumen greater elasticity, ultra violet resistance and improved weathering. Modified bitumens, however, sometimes develop the same problems that plague built-up roofs: brittleness at low temperatures and degradation from ultra violet light. Some manufacturers coat their modified bituminous membranes with fabric, foil or aggregate to improve weatherability and screen out ultraviolet light.

Modified Open Plan   An office layout that mixes open-plan office space with private offices and ceiling-high partitions.

Modular Wiring   A branch circuit wiring method that uses in-line connectors for easy reconfiguration.

Monitoring Well   A well used to measure groundwater levels and to obtain samples for water quality analysis.

Monumenting   Refers to the establishment of floor-mounted electrical and communication outlets wired through the floor from an under-floor cable network. Floor-mounted receptacles resemble small monuments in that they are fixed, visible and they can be stumbled over.

Mouse Condos   Ventilated, filtered plexiglass containers that can house one or more rodents. Also called filter-top cages.

MSDS   See Material Safety Data Sheet.

Muffle Furnace   A furnace that heats materials to high temperatures for ashing.

Multiplex   To combine several different signals (video, audio, data) and transmit them on a single communication channel. In time-division multiplexing, different messages are sent over the carrier at staggered times. With frequency-division multiplexing, messages are transmitted simultaneously, but at different frequencies.

Multipoint Videoconference   A videoconference of three or more sites.

Multizone Unit   An air conditioning unit capable of handling variable loads from different sections of a building simultaneously.

N

National Priorities List   A list of the United States' worst hazardous waste sites, established by the EPA. Placement on the list qualifies a site for the use of federal funds, which the government tries to recover from the responsible parties later.

N-Channel-Metal-Oxide Semiconductor (NMOS)   NMOS produces an electrical circuit consisting of purely negative charges. NMOS is the predecessor to CMOS circuitry.

NDA   See New Drug Application.

Nebulizer   An apparatus for producing a fine spray or mist by rapidly passing air through a liquid or by vibrating a liquid at a high frequency so that the particles produced are extremely small.

Necropsy Room   An autopsy or postmortem room for research animals. Design requirements depend on the size and type of animal being researched. If the animal has been held in containment housing, the necropsy room must be immediately adjacent to an autoclave and other types of hazardous waste disposal facilities.

Net Square Feet   The net floor space in a building measured from the inside surfaces of exterior walls and excluding interior walls and partitions, mechanical equipment rooms, lavatories, janitorial closets, elevators, stairways, major circulation corridors, aisles and elevator lobbies.

Network   An interconnected and coordinated system of devices (computer or communication terminals) so that information transmission to or among any of the devices is practical and reliable.

Networking   The connection of office communication terminals through various cabling and switching schemes so that terminal users can communicate with each other. According to David Liddle of Xerox, "Hooking electronic office machines together so they don't 'smoke' and so they can exchange information without annoying each other."

New Drug Application   This application is required before a new drug can be approved for commercial use. The NDA must contain: full reports of clinical investigations demonstrating that the drug is safe and effective, a list of components, a statement of the drug's quantitative composition, a description of the methods used for the manufacturing, processing and packaging of the drug, samples and the proposed label.

New Technology   RAND's research shows that user acceptance of new systems is correlated with the amount of effort that goes into user training. If you are introducing a system that changes the way workers do their jobs, showing a video or distributing a manual will not be adequate. It is also wise to think of implementing new technologies as an ongoing process, rather than as a discrete phase. Successful companies in the future will be those that learn to manage continual change. Companies that can organize around task oriented work groups instead of conventional departments may gain an advantage in this area.

NIMBY   Not In My Backyard.

Nine Yards   As in "the whole nine yards." Refers to the bygone practice of delivering concrete to job sites in trucks which carried nine cubic yards. The driver would then ask if you wanted "a partial, or the whole nine yards."

NMOS   See N-Channel-Metal-Oxide Semiconductor.

Node   In a topological description of a communications network, a node is a point of junction of the communication link.

Noise   A serious environmental impediment to health in the workplace is a high ambient noise level. Distractibility, slight increases in blood pressure, slight arrhythmias and a change in the electrical activity of the brain begin when the sound level is at 75 decibels. This level of ambient noise is found in various common work environments: in facilities built near freeways, typing pools, data processing areas and telephone banks. There is also evidence that workers directly in the takeoff zones of airports experience a 10 to 12 times higher incidence of major and minor cardiovascular disease, including hypertension and heart failure.

Noise Criterion Curves   A set of curves used to rate the relative acceptability or intrusiveness of sounds in buildings. Values below 25 are very quiet, 25 to 40 are normal and above 40 are generally too noisy for office criteria. For adequate speech privacy, an NC value near 40 is maintained usually with an electronic masking system. Current criteria are called Room Criterion (RC) Curves, but NC is still widely accepted.

Noise in R&D Buildings   The large and noisy central heating and cooling facilities for R&D labs must be adequately sound isolated with sufficient construction to block the noise. Designers should allow enough space for the installation and maintenance of noise and vibration devices. For cleanrooms, the required large air handling systems are usually located close to the labs to minimize costs. Because the systems continually operate at high horsepower, the sound attenuating treatments must also have low-flow resistance to avoid excessive energy consumption.

Noise in Renovated Buildings   There is a tendency to underestimate the detrimental effect that renovation work in occupied buildings has on the people who are working in those buildings. If you have to renovate, it's important to go to great lengths to control noise, dust and the intrusion of outside workers. These three factors can bring your entire workforce down to about 20 percent output and cost you many times the cost of the project in lost production. Construction noise gives people headaches. Dust will clog your filters and ruin office equipment and computers. Make sure tradespeople have separate access and parking.

Noise Reduction Coefficient (NRC)   NRC refers to the absorption capability of sound absorption material used in the work environment. A 0.80 to 0.85 rating is average. NRC readings miss sounds below 250 Hertz and above 2,000 Hertz. Because of conflicting noise sources in open office plans, it is difficult to get a reliable NRC reading for materials used in open offices. Speech Privacy Noise Isolation Class (NIC') is the more accurate measure for open office absorption elements. See page 139 in the Facilities Planning Concepts section for more information.

Non-Aspirating Diffuser   An air diffusing device that delivers air into a space in such a manner that room air is not aspirated or mixed due to high-velocity jets. These diffusers generally distribute air perpendicular to the face of the diffuser. Frequent applications include: animal rooms where drafts can be troublesome or in laboratories where aspirating or standard diffusers would cause drafts (i.e., near *fume hoods* or high air quantity locations). See also *Aspirating Diffuser.*

Nonblocking Systems   A communications switching system that allows continuous access to a dial tone regardless of the amount of user traffic. Nonblocking systems are particularly important in facilities that must support a large number of data users who log onto the mainframe computer for extended periods of time.

NPL   See National Priorities List.

NRC   See Noise Reduction Coefficient.

Nucleic Acids   The chemical bases that make up DNA and RNA. DNA stores information about the organism that is transmitted to progeny. RNA represents transcriptional information stored in the DNA which is translated into proteins. See also *Gene.*

Nude Mice   Mice with a genetic mutation that results in a lack of body hair as well as a deficiency of T-lymphocytes and a lack of a thymus. These mice are valuable for immunology research, but are susceptible to disease and thus need special environmental conditions.

Nurse Server   A cart containing basic supplies that can be stored in or easily accessed from a patient room. These are sometimes kept in pass-through cabinets with hall access for easy servicing.

Occupancy Sensors   A lighting conservation feature that uses motion or sound to switch lights on or off. See also *Ultrasonic Sensors*.

Occurrence   In insurance, an accident of exposure to injurious conditions during the policy period that results in bodily injury or property damage.

OCM   See Owner Construction Management.

OCR   See Optical Character Recognition.

Octave   Two different frequencies with a 1:2 ratio are one octave apart. 500 *Hertz* to 1,000 Hertz is one octave; so is 23 Hertz to 46 Hertz.

Off-Gassing   Also known as outgassing. The release of volatile, often noxious fumes and chemicals from new carpeting and other finishes.

Open Loop System   A heating or cooling system where the refrigerant fluid is enclosed in a piping system that is vented to the atmosphere.

Open Offices   Offices that are defined by partitions or other furniture arrangements rather than by full height walls.

Adequate secondary circulation is needed in open space plans to maintain an acceptable level of privacy and comfort. Workers feel that they have more space in their own work areas if they can look up and see some open space outside their workstations.

There is good evidence to show that the environment in open-plan offices often fails to satisfy personal work privacy requirements and often is a highly distracting setting in which to work. These problems create stress for some employees. Typically, the problems of poor privacy and frequent distractions are worse for those who are performing complex work that demands concentrated effort, such as professionals and managers. Those performing less demanding or even boring work typically show a more favorable reaction to open plans because of the increased opportunity of informal social contact.

Open-Path Monitoring Environmental Technology   An optical technique by which you can measure, on a real time basis, trace levels of pollutants in the air.

Open Systems Interconnect An internationally standardized model for defining protocols for *local area networks*.

Operating Lease A lease accounted for by the lessee without showing the asset for the lease right or the liability for the lease payment obligation on the lessee's balance sheet. Rental payments made by the lessee are merely shown as expense in the period paid.

Opportunity to Cure In construction contracts, a seller of goods who has made a nonconforming tender of goods (i.e., steel, flooring materials, furnishings and equipment that does not meet contract specifications) can avoid a major breach of contract by curing the defect within the contract time. Under the Uniform Commercial Code, to cure, the seller must notify the buyer of his intention to supply the conforming goods, and he must deliver the goods before the contract expires.

Optical Character Recognition (OCR) OCR readers are devices that scan printed material and then use software to recognize the text in the image and then store the information as text. The text may then be accessed and used as any other data that is input.

Organic Compounds Chemicals containing carbon. *Volatile organic compounds* vaporize at room temperature and pressure. Found in many common building materials.

Orphan Drugs Drugs with limited markets because of their small patient populations.

OSI See Open Systems Interconnect.

Outsourcing The practice of turning over one or more service functions to outside contractors.

Owner Construction Management (OCM) OCM places the CM function in the hands of the owner either fully or partially. The owner determines a CM format that meets his needs, matching the capabilities of in-house staff.

Oxbridge Room A type of interaction area that has features such as tables, writing surfaces, free coffee, periodicals and comfortable chairs. The idea is that researchers who come to the room to get coffee or use scientific journals will stay to interact with their colleagues. The term "oxbridge" comes from tea rooms at Oxford and Cambridge where research fellows meet to talk.

P

P&ID   See Piping and Instrumentation Diagram.

PA   See Preliminary Assessment.

Panel Roof Systems   A roof framing system using panels—two sheets of $4' \times 8'$ plywood—that are preframed on the ground. The panels are lifted up and placed between purlins, typically eight feet on center, that span between steel or wood glue laminated beam girders supported by columns or walls. Panel roof systems are preferred for many types of one- and two-story buildings because of the structural strength and low cost.

Parabolic Lighting   Fluorescent light fixtures with an "egg-crate" louver instead of a flat plastic diffuser. The parabolic louver directs light downward, eliminating the glare on VDTs associated with nondiffused light.

Paraformaldehyde Generator   An electrically operated portable gas generator that utilizes a prescribed quantity of liquid paraformaldehyde that is converted to a gaseous vapor and released directly into the atmosphere of a contaminated area. As the vapor permeates the area, all surfaces are effectively decontaminated. After the required time of exposure, the surfaces are wiped dry and free of any residual condensate.

Pareto's Law   Law of distribution for general application. As applied to facilities budgets: a small number of elements (20 percent) accounts for the greatest percentage of costs (80 percent).

Partial Containment   An enclosure which is constructed so that contamination between its interior and the surroundings is minimized by the controlled movement of air. Class I and Class II safety cabinets are examples. With partial containment a small percentage of the aerosol in the cabinet (usually less than 0.01 to 0.0001 percent) can escape into the laboratory. In many cases it takes a significant number of organisms—1,000 or more—to cause an infection. Therefore, the escape of a very small number is allowable.

Particulate   Fine liquid or solid particles such as dust, smoke, mist or fumes found in air. Airborne particulate matter is typically in the size range of 0.01 to 100 micrometers.

Partnering   A cooperative management structure focusing on common goals and benefits—focuses management effort on conflict resolution.

Parts Per Billion (ppb)/Parts per Million (ppm):   Units commonly used to express contamination ratios, as in establishing the maximum permissible amount of a contaminant in water or soil. In soil: ppm = milligrams of contaminant to one kilogram of soil, ppb = micrograms of contaminant per kilogram of soil. In water: ppm = for water is milligrams of contaminant per liter of water, ppb = micrograms of contaminant per liter of water.

Pass Box   A chamber where researchers can pass parts, tools, animal carcasses and other work items in and out of a containment lab without entering the lab itself. The concept is to create an air lock housing that minimizes the air that enters or leaves the lab. Pass boxes are used to eliminate personnel traffic into containment laboratories.

Pathological Destructor   A specially designed gas-fired incinerator that usually has a capacity of 100 pounds per hour. It is used to reduce solid wastes and animal carcasses to a state of totally decontaminated ash. The effluent gases produced in the process are then passed into *HEPA*-filtered exhaust systems.

Patient-Focused Care   See page 152 in the Facilities Planning Concepts section for information. See also *Planetree*.

Payback Period   A measurement used in financial analysis to evaluate and choose between alternative investment opportunities. Specifically, the period of time it takes for projected savings or revenues from an initial outlay of funds to equal the amount of the outlay. Routinely applied to small investment decisions without regard to interest costs, differences in the expected lives of equipment or costs and savings beyond the payback period. For large projects, the payback period is a useful measure of risk: a project with a long payback period is more vulnerable to unforeseen events before the project has paid for itself.

PBX   See Private Branch Exchange.

Perforated Bench Tops   Lab tables that have small holes in them in order to allow for more uniform vertical air flow.

Perinatal   Pertaining to an infant both shortly before and after birth.

Permeability   The rate at which liquids pass through soil or other materials in a specified direction.

PET   Positron Emission Tomography.

pH   A measure of acidity or alkalinity. The negative logarithm of the hydrogen ion concentration per liter. The level pH 1 is very acidic; pH 7 is neutral and the theoretical pH of pure water; pH 14 is very alkaline or basic.

Phasing Plan   In renovation projects, refers to the plan for evacuating, rebuilding and reoccupying small areas of a building sequentially until the entire facility has been renovated. The purpose of a phasing plan is to accomplish a renovation with a minimum of disruption to ongoing operations and loss of productivity.

Photopic Spectrum   The visual efficiency curve of the cone pigments of the retina of the eye, primarily in the central vision. This is what is measured by a standard light meter. New findings suggest that good lighting design should involve not only the photopic spectrum but also the scotopic spectrum. See also *Scotopic Spectrum*.

Phototropism   The tendency to turn toward or fixate on a light source. The human eye is phototropic and is naturally attracted to bright light. Applies to interior lighting design in that bright light sources (windows, light fixtures, reflecting surfaces) can be undesirable distractions and can cause eye fatigue and headaches.

Photovoltaic Cells   A form of silicon solar cell that converts solar energy into electricity.

Physical Containment   Procedures or structures designed to restrict the release of viable organisms.

Picocurie   A unit for measuring radioactivity, often expressed as picocuries per liter of air. 1×10^{-12} *Curies*.

Piezometer   A well that is used to determine water table elevation so that the direction of groundwater flow, or gradient can be determined.

PID   See Proportional-Integral-Derivative Controller.

Pigtail   A type of "extension cord" that provides good flexibility. For example, in lighting a pigtail provides several feet of extra cord from the receptacle for the electrical source to the light.

Piping and Instrumentation Diagram (P&ID)   Schematic single-line diagram of a process or piping system, showing the relative location and identification of tanks, vessels, piping, valves and instrumentation (such as controllers, transmitters and gauges).

PLA   See Product License Application.

Planetree   Extension of the "patient-centered care" concept—a model for healthcare delivery that includes self-medication, open charts, libraries for patient education, open nursing stations and increased patient control. See page 166 in the Facilities Planning Concepts section for more information.

Plasmid   A small circular piece of DNA found outside the chromosome in bacteria. It carries certain genes and is capable of replicating independently in a host cell. Plasmids are the principal tool for inserting new genetic information into organisms.

PLC   See Programmable Logic Controller.

PLEC   See Power, Lighting, Electronics and Communications.

Plenum   An air compartment or chamber to which one or more air ducts are connected. It is the part of an air handling system that supplies conditioned air, circulates air or exhausts air.

Plume   A visible or measurable discharge of a contaminant from a given point, e.g. a plume of smoke. A plume can be thermal as well as visible, such as a discharge of hot water into a river.

Plume Discharge Velocity   The velocity of an exhaust gas from a vertical stack measured at the point of discharge. The higher the velocity of the exhaust gas, the higher the plume and the greater the dispersion of exhaust gas into the atmosphere.

Pneumatic Control   A mechanism activated by an analog or digital signal that regulates the escape of compressed air to move mechanical controls such as valves and levers.

Pocketwall Distribution   A plan for the distribution of mechanical and electrical services in laboratories and other equipment-intensive space above the finished floor level by providing a walled-in chase between back-to-back laboratory casework installations or equipment stations.

Point-to-Multipoint   A teleconference configuration which allows information to be communicated from one source to many different locations or points. In some point-to-multipoint teleconferencing systems the receive sites can transmit back to the point of origination, but not to other locations receiving the signal.

Point-to-Point   A teleconference configuration where only two sites can communicate with each other. In most cases, the sites can send as well as receive.

Poison Pill   Actions taken by management during a takeover attempt to make their corporation less attractive to the party staging the takeover. Examples are selling off a highly desirable division or a onetime cash distribution to all shareholders, which can use up available cash and increase the company's debt.

Poke-Through System   A wire power, lighting, electronics and communications distribution plan in which cables are distributed in the ceiling space of the floor below. Cable access to the work area (floor above) is achieved by a preset or cut-in hole in the floor through which wire is connected to a floor-mounted junction box. Poke-through units can be fed with manufacturing wiring systems or conduit for power; data and telephone cables are encased in conduit or coated. A flame and heat-spread retardant placed in the hole protects the integrity of the floor. The principal disadvantages of this system are the high cost of changing outlet locations and the limitations on the number of holes that can be cut under fire code restrictions. The system can be used in either steel or concrete structures.

Polish   In water purification, the process of removing the remaining contaminants from preprocessed feedwater.

Post-Occupancy Training   Introducing workers to a new space by teaching them how to use new furniture, lighting, acoustics, HVAC, office automation and phone systems. For example, workers might accidentally ruin the effectiveness of new acoustic panels by covering them with paper, which reflects sound instead of absorbing it. But if the purpose of the panels is explained, workers will understand that they will be giving up acoustical privacy if they cover them.

Potentially Responsible Party (PRP)   Any entity that can be held responsible for contamination. These can include past or present owners or operators of facilities that generate, use, treat, store or dispose of hazardous wastes; contractors hired to transport wastes and owners or operators of sites bordering a contaminated site that might have contributed to the problem. These parties, once identified, are notified of their responsibility for cleanup. If Superfund money must be used for the cleanup, the law provides for recovery of the money from PRPs; triple damages can be assessed.

Power   Power is the rate at which work is done and so is measured as work per unit of time. Examples of units include watts, joules per second and horsepower (one horsepower equals 746 watts).

Power Columns™   A column manufactured by Hill-Rom used in hospital rooms containing monitors and gases normally contained in a headwall unit. All four sides of the column can be used, and the patient bed can be placed on either side of the column.

Power, Lighting, Electronics and Communications (PLEC)   The physical wiring and wiring distribution scheme or plan for all electrical equipment in a building.

Power Pole   A rectangular, floor-to-ceiling metal tube two to three inches wide used as a vertical cableway to get power, telephone and computer wires from a horizontal wire distribution grid in the ceiling to individual workstations or clusters of workstations on the work floor. The tube can be fitted to the ceiling and floor at any location; services (power, telephone, computer) are partitioned within the tube to prevent crosstalk.

PQL   See Practical Quantitation Limit.

Practical Quantitation Limit   The concentration of a substance that can be measured and reported within specified limits of precision and accuracy.

Pre-Fee Negotiations   A pre-fee negotiating meeting is a meeting conducted by the owner with the architect and the engineer to clearly spell out owner expectations on the scope of the work, the type of detail required, the quality of work, design standards and any special studies required.

Precast Concrete   Refers to concrete panels usually made in factories and delivered to the construction site where they are hoisted onto the structure. Sometimes concrete panels are poured at the site and then hoisted on the structure.

Preliminary Assessment (PA)   The first step required by the 1980 Comprehensive Environmental Response, Compensation and Liability Act (CERCLA) when a hazardous substance has reportedly been released. The preliminary assessment involves collecting available information to determine the size of the site, the types and quantities of wastes that may have been disposed of, the potentially responsible parties, local hydrological and meteorological conditions and the potential impact of contamination if it has indeed taken place. See also *CERCLA*.

Present Value Analysis   The comparison of alternative projects or design solutions on the basis of the sum total of all initial and future costs and revenues for each project. Future dollar amounts are discounted to the present at a given annual discount rate reflecting the time-value of money. The project or solution with the highest present value is the most favorable at the assumed discount rate.

Pressed Wood Products   Materials used in building and furniture that are made from wood veneers, particles or fibers bonded with an adhesive under heat and pressure.

Pressure Differentials   Laboratories and vivariums are generally designed with varying pressure differentials. These differentials cause airflow between areas, therefore containing odors, particles and microbial matter.

Primary Containment   The first point of containment in which an inner surface of a containment structure comes into immediate contact with the hazardous material to be contained.

Private Branch Exchange (PBX)   A computerized switchboard that routes voice and data traffic throughout an office building.

Procedure Room   In animal-related research, refers to a room where procedures can be performed, other than the holding room or the researcher's laboratory.

Product License Application   An application for any product applicable to the prevention, treatment or cure of human diseases and injury that is submitted to the Director of the Office of Biologics Research and Review. Included in the application is data derived from clinical and nonclinical studies that demonstrate that the manufactured product meets prescribed standards of safety, purity and potency. Additional information includes: the name and address of the manufacturer and each location at which the product is manufactured; the license number of the establishment; and the proper name of the product with any additional specification that may be required for additional labeling purposes. A product license is granted after it has been demonstrated that the establishment and the product for which the license is issued have met all applicable regulating standards published in Title 21, Code of Federal Regulations.

Product-Tight   Quality of being impervious to a hazardous material that is to be contained, thus preventing the seepage of the hazardous material from the primary containment. To be product-tight, the container must be made of a material that is not subject to physical or chemical deterioration for a given hazardous material.

Programmable Logic Controller (PLC)   A programmable computer that enables the automatic monitoring and control of process and manufacturing functions (such as fluid temperatures, tank pressures and levels, robotic device movements and *AGV* pathways) within an industrial facility. Today's PLCs are capable of handling thousands of inputs and outputs and can also be networked to other PLCs throughout a facility.

Programming   That portion of the planning process for a new building, group of buildings or area within a building which, through the collection and analysis of data on occupants, work patterns and required equipment, leads to the statement of the design problem and the *specifications* for its solution.

Project Finance   The securing of funds from a financial institution for construction and equipment in which revenue generated by the project and the project's assets are the only sources of repayment and credit worthiness. In this form of financing, the project owner's balance sheets either do not or cannot support the credit. The lending institution looks to the surety of future project revenue, performance and completion guarantees and other forms of assurance that the project will generate revenue that is sufficient to repay the debts.

Project Management   The planning, organizing, directing and controlling of the activities of one or more groups of people for a limited period of time to produce a single, specified product or result on a specified date in the future. What differentiates project management from management in general is the finite period of time in which groups or individuals work together and the importance that is placed on achieving the planned result on or before a predetermined date.

Project Manual   A book containing all written contract documents except the drawings. This may include the bidding documents, sample forms, general and supplemental conditions, Division 1 documents (which spell out particular conditions of a specific project) and technical specification. Often referred to as the "Specifications." See also *Specifications*.

Project Planning   When planning any facility changes that will affect people, announce the changes well in advance of the design start date to give the people who will be affected by the change time to think about the proposed project and give you feedback before you start.

Proportional-Integral-Derivative Controller (PIDC)   An electronic adjustable controller for HVAC systems in R&D facilities that prevents a system from "hunting" under changing air flow conditions. PID is an outgrowth of proportional-derivative systems originally designed for electronics facilities. The PID system measures the amount and rate of change and deviation from points. Components are adjustable for maximum stability in a system based on operating characteristics.

Proprietary Purchasing   When an owner and architect specify a particular brand in the construction documents.

Protocol   A set of rules for communicating format, timing, hierarchy and error control between computers.

Prototype Construction   An approach to interior design and construction that involves building out and furnishing a typical office module or section of a floor before finalizing the design. Prototype construction can establish uncertain construction and material costs, prove innovative plans to management and help allay employees' fears about unknown changes.

PRP   See Potentially Responsible Party.

Pulse-Code Modulation   A translation method for converting an analog signal into a digital signal.

Punchlist   The list of tasks not completed or the list of owner complaints requiring attention before a construction job is considered finished. The term comes from the early practice of using a conductor's ticket punch to indicate when individual tasks had been completed.

Purge Rate   Refers to the process in which gaseous formaldehyde is used to decontaminate a laboratory facility of microorganisms. The building is evacuated (after-hours or on weekends) and sealed up; formaldehyde is then pumped through the facility's ventilation system to decontaminate it. The facility is "purged" by slowly introducing outside air to dilute the formaldehyde, which is then slowly exhausted through the exhaust system. The purge rate is the rate at which the formaldehyde can be exhausted safely to the outdoors and the predetermined time that must elapse before workers can reenter the facility without needing respiratory protection.

Put Bond   A long-term bond that offers the buyer the option of putting the bond back to the issuer prior to maturity. The yield rates for put bonds are calculated on the basis of the put period, not the maturity period, resulting in lower interest costs during the early period of the bond.

Putrescible   Able to rot quickly enough to cause odors and attract flies. Kitchen waste, offal and dead animals are examples.

PVC Membrane   A single-ply roofing membrane made of polyvinyl chloride and plasticizers that turn semi-rigid PVC into a flexible roofing membrane. PVC is resistant to water and many chemicals and can be formed into strong field seams and patches through the use of solvent or heat welding. It can also be bonded to PVC-coated metal, simplifying connections to flashings, roof curbs and other building materials.

Pyrogens   The name given to the cellular fragments of bacterial cell walls, and literally meaning "fever causing." Pyrogens cause a fever in mammals when injected or infused.

Q

QAPP   See Quality Assurance Project Plan.

Quad   In the United States, one quadrillion (1015) Btu. A measure for large-scale energy use such as a national level of use or use by sectors of the economy. In Great Britain and Germany one quadrillion equals 1024 Btu.

Quality Assurance Project Plan (QAPP)   Required by Comprehensive Environmental Response, Compensation and Liability Act (CERCLA). This plan sets forth policies, procedures and activities for ensuring that the data collected meet quality standards. See also *CERCLA*.

Quality of Life   Term for the local constellation of community, climate, culture, recreation, transportation, schools and affordable housing. It is an important element in site selection for rapidly growing firms that need to recruit large numbers of skilled workers.

Quench Tank   A water filled tank used to cool hot materials during industrial processes.

R&D Budgets: Equipment　During the very first week of planning for a new R&D facility, people on the project should go out look for special systems, special equipment and anything that is unusual in the existing building. This includes the isolated cleanroom, the researcher who needs a biolevel-3 fume hood, the piece of equipment that has high point loads on the floor, the guy that forgot to mention the radio frequency isolation he wants, the EMI projection and special skunk works. The costs of these additional items can run between $2 a square foot and $1,000 a square foot. They blow whole budgets apart; they ruin project schedules and entire projects.

R&D Standards　As early as possible in the conceptual design phase, seek to reaffirm or fix project standards for these design issues: labs, offices, aesthetics, codes and regulations, energy conservation, operating costs, automation, hood air velocities (R&D), emergency power, lighting levels, standard floor plans, furniture and security.

R&D Buildings　One method of upgrading an old R&D facility is to add a vertical service corridor to the outside of the existing facility. AT&T Bell Laboratories in Murray Hill, N.J., renovated a 40-year-old building by attaching 120-foot wide vertical mechanical and electrical service corridors to the exterior of the four- and five-story-structure. The service corridor is an independent structure with isolation joints between it and the lab buildings. One advantage of the outer service corridor is increased vibration control for the labs. The corridor also improves the facility's overall energy efficiency, creating an additional buffer against outside temperatures. Service elevators in the corridor allow delivery of equipment and materials directly to the service corridor without transport through personnel areas.

If sufficient headroom is available in an R&D retrofit project, an open plenum system between the ceiling framework and the service deck may be preferable to installing a ducted air distribution system. In 1985, AT&T renovated an existing manufacturing plant that included building in 108,000 square feet of cleanroom lab space to the facility originally built in the 1960s. The advantage of the plenum was that it did not require balancing to achieve an acceptable velocity profile, and it required less duct work. The system operated at a lower pressure drop and cost less to install than a ducted air distribution system.

RA   See Remedial Action.

Racetrack   An arrangement of corridors and rooms where the corridor runs around the outside of a big block of rooms clustered in the center of the building.

Raceway   An enclosed channel designed expressly for holding wires, cable or bus bars, with additional functions as permitted by the National Electric Code.

Radon   A colorless radioactive gas formed by radioactive decay of radium atoms in soil or rock.

Raider   A name used to describe the individual leading an unfriendly takeover of a publicly held corporation. In many of the takeovers in the early 1980s, assets such as oversubscribed pension funds were quickly drained, contributing to the concept of a raider.

RAP   See Remedial Action Plan.

Rate of Rise Heat Sensors   A fire detection device that will indicate any unusual increase in heat, particularly in areas where combustible liquids or gases are employed or stored.

RCRA   See Resource Conservation and Recovery Act.

RD   See Remedial Design.

Recombinant DNA (rDNA)   The new DNA formed by combining segments of DNA from different organisms. The technique involves isolating DNA pieces and inserting them into the DNA of a cell thus "recombining" DNA.

Record of Decision (ROD)   The official document, approved and signed by the EPA, of the remedial action selected for hazardous waste cleanup under the 1980 Comprehensive Environmental Resource, Compensation and Liability Act (CERCLA). See also *CERCLA*.

Recycled Furniture   Office furniture that has been refurbished and is being used again. The idea of recycling used furniture is appealing to many cost-conscious companies. Instead of getting rid of old furniture and purchasing new, the company can maintain it if it's reusable and give it a second go-round. Systems components, especially fabric panels, are ideal for reusing or refurbishing because they have no moving parts that wear out or need replacement.

Red Tag   The little piece of cardboard, often red, which the fire marshal attaches to an item that needs to be changed to meet fire-code requirements. Also used as a verb, e.g. "The inspector red-tagged the whole stairwell."

Reflection   The "bounce" or return of an energy (such as sound or light) wave from a surface. The fraction of energy not reflected is absorbed by or transmitted through the surface.

Reinsurer   A party that accepts all or part of liability for risk from a professional liability insurance company. For example, an insurance company that provides $3 million coverage may pass to a reinsurer all risk above $1.5 million.

Reject Water   The water which carries the contaminants filtered out by a reverse osmosis membrane. It contains a higher concentration of contaminants than the feedwater.

Remedial Action (RA)   A term from the 1980 Comprehensive Environmental Response, Compensation and Liability Act (CERCLA) that describes the implementation of the remedial design at the hazardous waste site. Remedial actions include encapsulation, incineration, neutralization and collection and removal of hazardous wastes as well as non-engineering solutions such as institutional controls and relocation. See also *CERCLA*.

Remedial Action Plan (RAP)   Required by the Comprehensive Environmental Response, Compensation and Liability Act (CERCLA), the Remedial Action Plan and the methods to be used in implementation of this action for cleaning up hazardous wastes. The RAP is selected from a feasibility study. See also *CERCLA*.

Remedial Design (RD)   The phase of cleanup under the 1980 Comprehensive Response, Compensation and Liability Act (CERCLA) in which the remedy selected for cleaning up hazardous wastes is developed into engineering plans and specifications for implementation. See also *CERCLA*.

Remedial Investigation (RI) The phase of hazardous waste assessment under the 1980 Comprehensive Environmental Resource, Compensation and Liability Act (CERCLA) during which data is collected and analyzed and the site is characterized. The RI involves both existing data on the site and data collected through new field studies. See also *CERCLA*.

Remedial Investigation/Feasibility Study (RI/FS)   An in-depth study to gather data needed to determine the nature and extent of contamination at a site, establish cleanup criteria, identify preliminary alternatives for remediation and analysis of alternatives.

Repetitive Stress Injuries (RSI)   Also called repetitive motion injuries or RMI. In 1990, RMIs were 43% of all occupational injuries according to the Department of Labor's Bureau of Labor Statistics.

Resource Conservation and Recovery Act (RCRA)   Passed in 1976, this act set up a comprehensive federal program for monitoring and controlling the generation, treatment, storage, transportation and disposal of hazardous materials.

Retainage   A portion of the money earned by the contractor, withheld from periodic payments and held by the owner as assurance that the contractor will complete the project.

Reverse Osmosis   A water-purification method where water is forced under pressure through a semipermeable membrane under pressure, leaving behind a percentage of dissolved organic, dissolved ionic and suspended impurities.

Reversible Space   Adaptable space that can function as either open-plan or cellular, or a mixture of these in any proportion.

RI/FS   See Remedial Investigation/Feasibility Study.

RI   See Remedial Investigation.

Ring Network   A data communications network composed of a number of computer systems linked together in series by a data communications line.

Risk Assessment   Quantitative and qualitative evaluation of the risk posed to health and/or the environment by the presence and or use of specific pollutants.

Robotics   Methods by which a process or operation can be performed by a remote-controlled device.

ROD   See Record of Decision.

Roller Bottle Process   A process used in biotechnology in which living cells are put inside "roller bottles" along with the nutrients that support them. The cells grow on the inside surface of the bottle, which are gently turned from time to time so that all the cells receive nourishment. As they mature, the cells begin to produce the substance that is the crude product, which is then removed and purified.

Romeo and Juliet Space   An interior area in a multistory building that connects two or more floors and allows people to interact with workers on the floor above or below. Examples include staircases or balconies that jut out into atriums.

RSI   See Repetitive Stress Injuries.

S

Safe Carts   Conveyance vehicles designed for moving hazardous chemicals in R&D facilities. The use of safe carts helps prevent and contain potentially harmful spills.

Safety Laboratory   An alternative term for a high-containment lab.

Sag   Flow of an uncured sealant within a joint that results in the loss of the sealant's original shape.

Sanitary Landfill   A land disposal site employing an engineered method of disposing of solid wastes. The process minimizes environmental hazards by spreading the solid wastes in thin layers, compacting the solid wastes to the smallest practical volume and applying and compacting cover materials at the end of each operating day.

SARA   The Superfund Amendments and Reauthorization Act. Passed in 1986, SARA strengthened the Superfund legislation and authorized $8.5 billion in new funds for hazardous waste cleanup. See also *Superfund*.

Scale-Up   Transition from small-scale pilot manufacturing to large-scale production of industrial quantities.

Scheduling Lighting   An energy-saving lighting control strategy where lights are dimmed during hours when a building space is unoccupied.

SCID Mice   See Severe Combined Immunodeficiency Mice.

SCIF   See Sensitive Compartmented Information Facility.

Scotopic Spectrum   The visual efficiency curve for the pigment of the "rods" of the retina. It determines the size of the pupil; a small pupil will increase depth of field, increase visual acuity and decrease the amount of accommodation needed for near tasks. Thus, small pupils reduce "eyestrain." Many indoor lights such as incandescent, warm light fluorescent and especially sodium lamps are deficient in the scotopic part of the spectrum and thus may promote eyestrain. A good lighting system in the work environment bathes the area surrounding the task with scotopically rich light. (Note that color is not always a good indicator of the lighting spectrum. See the manufacturer's specification.)

Screen   In open plans, any element—file bank, workstation, freestanding divider, partition—that acts as a barrier to direct propagation of speech from one point to another. It usually refers to elements that do not extend to the ceiling.

Scrubbing   The washing of impurities from any process gas stream.

Sealant   An elastomeric material with adhesive qualities that joins components of a similar or dissimilar nature to provide an effective barrier against the passage of the elements. See also *Cohesive Failure* and *Adhesive Failure*.

Secondary Containment   Enclosures that surround primary containment for hazardous materials. Outer bottles, piping, tank vaults and even chemical storage buildings are forms of secondary containment. See also *Primary Containment*.

Semi-Works Space   Sometimes referred to as low-bay process areas. Areas in research facilities that have all of the lab services provided but lack research benches or hoods. This type of space is useful for trial manufacturing operations, special projects, or prototype jobs because required machinery can be easily moved into the area without the restriction of fixed walls or benches. Floor-to-ceiling heights for this type of space vary from 14 to 18 feet. Can also be used as space for future lab expansion.

Semiconductors   Semiconductor materials that are made from compounds of two or more elements in the Group III and Group V columns of the periodic table. Examples of semiconductor materials are gallium arsenide, indium phosphide and aluminum indium phosphide.

Sensitive Compartmented Information Facility (SCIF)   A secure facility that meets the requirements of government specification DIAM 50-3 to protect activities occurring in the facility from espionage. The specification dictates requirements for STC ratings, acoustical control in duct work, man bars, construction and other facility features to maintain security.

Server   A shared device such as a printer, file storage or modem connected to a *local area network*.

Service Corridor   A corridor in a facility that is used as a distribution pathway for building services such as cable, compressed air, deionized water, etc.
    A dedicated service corridor can sometimes be a functional block because people will rarely cross it to go into another lab. With a modified concept, where the service corridor is also the circulation corridor with offices, the block is not there either physically or psychologically. Central service corridors in labs can provide low-cost space to put necessary, but unsightly, equipment that does not need to go into expen-

sive office or laboratory space.

Severe Combined Immunodeficiency (SCID) Mice   These rodents, used in research, have no immune systems. See also *Nude Mice*.

Shared Tenant Services   Services shared by tenants of a building. Telephone is usually the primary shared service. Advances in telephone systems permit building owners to offer a host of other services, including integrated data and teleconferencing, security, energy management and fire-safety systems.

Shear   The strain in or failure of a structural member at a point where the lines of force and resistance are perpendicular to the member.

Shop Drawings   Detailed drawings prepared by the contractor or subcontractor to show the exact configuration of an item or assembly proposed for use on the project and how it fits into the surrounding construction. Shop drawings are reviewed by the architect (and consulting engineer, where appropriate) for overall conformance to the specifications and design intent of the contract documents. It is the contractor's duty to verify all critical dimensions at the site and to confirm that the item or assembly can be installed as shown in the shop drawings.

Shoutdown System   A single circuit intercom that can be used to broadcast messages. A person speaks into the phone and connects with all parties on the line, whether they are within the building or even across the country. The person receiving the message need not pick up the receiver if the phone is equipped with a speaker, because the message is "shouted" into the room.

SI   See Site Investigation.

Sick Building Syndrome   A malaise that affects occupants of a contaminated building during the time they spend in the building and then diminishes during periods when they are away from the building. Cannot be traced to specific pollutants or sources within the building. The occupants complain of irritation in the eyes, nose and throat. Manifestations also include a general feeling of mental tiredness and a sense that there is a persistent odor in the space. See also *Building-Related Illness*.

Indoor air pollution, despite rumors to the contrary, is a source-dominated problem. Traditionally, planners think that correcting the air quality in a building means changing, adjusting, increasing or decreasing ventilation. Although ventilation is often used as the panacea for the sick building, facility users cannot cure the problem until the sources of indoor air pollution are controlled.

Planners should do a "walk-through" analysis of their HVAC system, including HVAC control strategies, if inadequate indoor air quality is reported. The initial investigation should also include available documentation of potential pollution sources and building occupant concerns. Planners should also account for the impact of lighting, acoustics, ergonomics and interpersonal relationships on sick building syndrome complaints.

Ventilation systems can cause their own potential problems in a sick building environment. It is important that outdoor air used to dilute pollutants actually gets down to the occupant of a workspace. A common ventilation design problem is that locating supply and return air in the ceiling can prevent the ventilation air from mixing throughout the space. The better design puts the inlet and outlet systems at different levels in the room. The design requires more expensive construction but provides better ventilation to remove pollutants.

During the first six months of operation, a building should provide excess ventilation. Increased ventilation rates help overcome the problems associated with emission from construction materials (off-gassing), a major cause of sick building syndrome.

SIG   see Special Interest Group.

Simplex (Half Duplex)   A single-direction signal, as opposed to full duplex or two-way communication. In reference to videoconferencing, simplex means that one location is sending video, audio, and data. See also *Full Duplex.*

Single-Ply Roof   A roof surfacing that employs a single sheet of membrane manufactured under factory control. Manufacturers of single-sheet roofing membrane materials claim that roofs can be waterproofed at a lower cost and have a longer life than conventional built-up roofs.

Site Investigation   The step following preliminary assessment in a hazardous waste cleanup under the Comprehensive Environmental Resource, Compensation and Liability Act (CERCLA). The SI involves visiting the site to collect all data required for ranking the hazard potential. See *CERCLA.*

Skin   Exterior walls of a building. Also the exterior building materials attached to the structural system to enclose the building—precast concrete, brick, glass, etc.

Skunk Works   An informal area much like a workshop or garage where scientists can experiment with instruments and processes or manufacture prototypes without interrupting production lines. The idea originated in the polymer processing and chemicals fields, from which it spread to the biotechnology, oil exploration and food industries.

Slippage   The relative lateral movement of adjacent components of a built-up membrane. It occurs mainly in roofing membranes on a slope, sometimes exposing the lower piles or even the base sheet to the weather.

Slit Sampler   An impinger-type sampling device used to determine the concentration of a known, viable spore that has been placed in an aerosol at a specific location. Fluid from the slit sampler is placed aseptically on an appropriate media and incubated to ascertain if test spores are present and to quantify the concentration.

Slow-Scan Video   Same as freeze-frame video, but in teleconferencing, refers to a scan converter that accepts graphic materials only one line at a time, requiring that the object in front of the camera remain stationary for several seconds. The converter operates differently than a freeze-frame scan converter that "grabs" the entire graphic all at one time. See also *Freeze-Frame Video*.

Sniff Ducts   Flexible hoses at the benchtop which provide localized exhaust.

Snorkels   Used for the spot exhaust of fumes from sensitive laboratory experiments or tests. Snorkels are flexible units that resemble an inverted funnel or elephant trunk; they can be positioned above a particular benchtop experiment. Snorkels are HVAC efficient, using exhaust air for up to a 150 fpm face velocity but at a low overall volume.

Soft Space   Interaction areas such as circulation lounges and breakout areas that bind together the heavily programmed areas of a facility. This type of space can be thought of as a facility's "connective tissue."

Solid Waste   Non-liquid, non-soluble materials ranging from municipal garbage to industrial wastes that contain complex and sometimes hazardous substances. Waste treatment plants, water supply treatment plants, air pollution control facilities and industrial, mining and agricultural operations produce solid waste. Solid waste does not include solid or dissolved material in domestic sewage, irrigation return flows or industrial discharges subject to the Federal Water Pollution Control Act. Special nuclear and by-product material as defined by the Atomic Energy Act of 1954 are also excluded from the definition.

Solid Waste Management Unit (SWMU)   A unit for disposal of solid hazardous wastes, as defined by the 1976 *Resource and Conservation Recovery Act* (RCRA). Units may include waste piles, landfills, ponds, landfarms and incinerators.

Sound Attenuation   Describes the drop-off of sound between two locations out-doors or between two workstations in an open-plan office. The amount of sound attenuation that occurs between open-plan workstations depends on (1) the distance between the workstations, (2) the shielding provided by carrier screens and (3) the effectiveness of sound-absorbing finish materials—acoustical tile or carpet—used on the ceiling, floor and surrounding wall surfaces.

Sound Power Level   The power level of a noise source is the total energy emitted in 1 second, expressed in watts. Sound power level is this figure expressed in decibels. The formula is:

$$SWL = 10 \log (W/W_0) \text{ dB}$$

where W (watts) is the sound power of the source and W_0 is the standard reference sound power 10^{-12}W. Sound power level can either be abbreviated SWL or PWL.

Sound Pressure Level   The magnitude of a sound wave. The human ear, which detects sound waves logarithmically, reacts to the average value of pressure in a sound wave. Sound pressure is expressed in decibels. The formula for sound pressure level (SPL) is:

$$SPL = 20 \log (P/P_0) \text{ dB}$$

where P is the sound pressure of the source and P_0 is $2 \times 10\text{-}5 N/m^2$ (the smallest pressure the ear can detect).

Spatial Uniformity   A measure of the evenness of sound loudness (decibels) over a given area. With a spatial variation of ±2 dB, the sound variance would not likely be perceived as someone moves through the space.

Special Interest Group (SIG)   In electronic mail, a distribution list of people who share a common interest in a particular topic.

Specific-Pathogen-Free (SPF) Mice   Mice that are free of specific diseases such as salmonella.

Specifications   Customarily taken to refer to the book of written material that, along with the drawings, constitutes the contract documents describing in full the requirements and terms of the agreement between owner and contractor. More properly called the Technical Specifications.

Specimen Room   A receiving area in a laboratory where specimens are held before they are distributed.

Spectrum   With respect to acoustics, spectrum is the range of frequencies that make up a sound. It can also be referred to as the distribution of noise with frequency.

Speech Privacy Noise Isolation Class (NIC')   A rating schedule for elements—i.e., partitions, ceilings—in the contemporary open-plan office. A Class-A, or excellent, rating for vertical elements is NIC' 25; a minimum of NIC' 21 is required for Class-B. See also *Noise Reduction Coefficient.*

SPF Mice   See Specific-Pathogen-Free Mice.

Spill Light   *Lumens* distributed by a luminary which are outside the beam spread.

Spill Tanks   Holding tanks used to collect chemicals discharged from a chemical storage facility. Usually located away from a facility on a tank farm, individual spill tanks are connected to different waste-line systems to prevent the mixing of incompatible chemicals.

Spread Rate   The theoretical area that will be covered by a gallon of coating at the manufacturer's recommended wet film thickness.

Square   A term used by roofers to indicate an amount of roof area equal to 100 square feet (92.2 square meters). It refers to roofing material sufficient to cover 100 square feet of roof area.

Squeeze-Downs   Contract clauses and provisions that reduce the equity share of joint venture partners when other partners or outside parties invest more money in the project to cover unanticipated capital needs.

Stack Effect   The tendency of buildings to be hotter on the upper floors.

Stack Velocity   The minimum gas velocity in a laboratory facility's air exhaust stack that is required to effectively dilute a given gas into the environment.

Static Pressure   The pressure of a fluid exerted in all directions that is equal and opposite to the pressure tending to compress the fluid. In ventilation applications, static pressure is usually the difference between the pressure in an exhaust system and atmospheric pressure. Static pressure less than atmospheric pressure is termed "negative static pressure" and static pressure above is termed "positive static pressure." Positive and negative static pressure can be thought of as the tendency to burst or collapse the pipe.

Sterile Fluids   Fluids which may be demonstrated to be free of viable contaminating microorganisms. Such liquids may be obtained by sterilization of the preparation in a suitable container or by filtration through a filter that is 0.45 micron or smaller.

Strategic Facilities Planning   The process of incorporating corporate long-range goals and philosophies into a responsive facilities building plan. See also *Strategy*.

Strategic Information Mapping   A programming method that establishes optimum facilities design parameters for a given organization on the basis of the identification, grouping and graphical representation of the information flow between people and groups that is crucial to the strategic purpose of the organization. The methodology involves top management participation and decision-making to determine and express the organization's strategy, purpose and critical information needs.

Strategy   From the Greek *strategia*—meaning generalship, maneuvers. A set of decisions and policies made in the context of present conditions to achieve a planned advantage. A strategy specifies an organization's long-range objectives and prescribes well-defined management actions concerning the acquisition, use and disposition of resources to attain those objectives.

Example of a facility strategy: to improve profitability and attract higher caliber personnel for its national field sales organization: Corporation A reduces its office rental expense by 20 percent over the next five years and offers an improved work environment for employees by (1) downsizing the standard sales office plan and changing interior standards to achieve a more flexible space plan, (2) relocating offices from urban centers to suburban locations, (3) negotiating long-term leases to obtain the lowest possible lease rates and (4) using rent subsidy incentives offered by landlords to defray short-term relocation and leasehold costs.

In relation to facilities planning, strategy refers to the corporate decisions and policies on facility locations, building types, designs, amenities, costs and financing that contribute to attaining expressed long-range organizational objectives. Facility strategies explicitly detail management actions governing the use of funds, capital equipment, land and personnel in the acquisition, use and disposal of facilities.

Structural Concrete   Conventionally reinforced pan-joist, skip joist, post tensioned flat slab, post tensioned beams and/or joist, precast, composite concrete and steel.

Substantial Completion   That point in a project when the owner may occupy the premises for the purpose intended (beneficial occupancy), even though not all items of work may be 100 percent complete. Under standard A.I.A. forms of agreement, most monies withheld are released to the contractor upon certification of substantial completion. Use of the term may not be appropriate in repair and renovation contracts where the owner occupies the premises throughout, because disputes frequently arise as to what constitutes "substantial" completion.

Superfund   The program operated under the legislative authority of CERCLA and SARA that funds and carries out EPA solid waste emergency and long-term removal and remedial activities. See also *CERCLA* and *SARA*.

Surface Impoundment   A natural topographic depression, artificial excavation or dike arrangement with the following characteristics: used primarily for the holding, treatment or disposal of waste; constructed above, below or partially in the ground or in navigable waters; with or without a permeable bottom and sides. Examples include holding ponds and aeration ponds.

Surge Space   The area outside training or conference rooms that is needed to accommodate the increased people traffic occurring when classes or conference sessions all end at the same time. Also shell space that can be quickly fitted and occupied when needed.

Suspended Particles   Small particles in water, including silt, plumbing pipe debris and colloids. Suspended particles can clog valves, lab tubing, reverse osmosis membranes and conductivity meters. A 10- to 20-micron prefilter is often placed as the first component in a water purification system to filter out the larger particles; small particles are removed by reverse osmosis, submicron filters and ultrafiltration membranes.

S-VHSA   A half-inch videotape format that has better audio and video quality than VHS.

Swing Space   Space in a building that is used to house workers who must be moved out of their permanent space during a renovation program. Swing space can be a separate facility or a fixed area within a building, or it may be "floating" space that is freed up in different locations as a phased renovation program progresses.

Switch   A device that opens or closes a circuit. In telecommunications, switches route telephone calls properly through the maze of equipment found in a typical system.

Switchable Glazing   Also called optical shutters. A glazing system used to change reflectivity in response to heat, light or electricity. By using glazing panel sandwiches filled with thermochromic material that turns nearly opaque and highly reflective at given preset temperatures, it is possible to control light transmittance by blocking 90 to 95 percent of the solar gain. Most research in this area has been for consumer products—sunglasses, camera lenses and liquid crystal watch displays.

SWMU   See Solid Waste Management Unit.

Synergism   An interaction between two chemicals such that their combined effect is greater than the effect of either acting alone.

System Balancing   The final stage in the installation of HVAC systems in which sensors, power controls, dampers, fan speeds and other system variables are adjusted to meet the air flow, pressurization, humidity, temperature, cleanliness and stability specifications for the overall facility. System balancing is especially complex in pharmaceutical applications and laboratory facilities that contain rooms with separate pressurization and air flow requirements and independent exhaust units (hoods) that interact with local HVAC environments. This is a source of contractor dispute when it is found that a system cannot be balanced. It can become a source of unforeseen costs and start-up delays.

T

T-Channel   A high-speed digital data channel. A T1 channel has a data rate of 1.544 Mb/s and is often used for compressed video teleconference networks.

T1   A transmission system that provides high-speed digital communication (1.544 million bits per second) of voice and data signals simultaneously by combining (multiplexing) 24 channels together into a continuous stream. AT&T term for a digital carrier facility used to transmit a DS-1 formatted digital signal at 1.544.

TAP   See Terminal Access Point.

Tank Farm   A location where many storage tanks are kept for holding liquids, usually chemicals or waste.

TCP/IP   See Transmission Control Protocol/Internet Protocol.

TDDs   Telecommunication Devices for the Deaf.

TDS   See Total Dissolved Solids.

Tear Strength   In roofing terminology, the maximum force required to tear a material. The force acts substantially parallel to the major axis of the test specimen. Values are reported in stress (e.g., pounds) or stress per unit of thickness (e.g., pounds per inch).

Technical Specifications   Those portions of the project manual that describe the scope of work, materials and procedures required of the various trades whose work makes up the construction of a project. See also *Specifications*.

Tegular   A grid-type acoustical ceiling tile in which the edges of the tile drop below the grid.

Telecommuting   A working style where employees work at home or in satellite offices but are linked to their companies by telephone, modem, personal computer and scheduled company interaction. See also *Virtual Office*.

Teleconferencing   A conference held between people in two or more remote locations through the use of electronic communications technology. Includes videoconferencing, audioconferencing, audiographic conferencing and business television. Videoconferencing provides image-to-image meetings; audioconferencing is limited to voice communication between locations. Specially designed full-motion video teleconference rooms are equipped with television cameras, sound systems, television screens, studio lighting and slide projectors that allow participants to see each other and view documents pertinent to a conference meeting.

Telephone Conference Bridge   A device to link three or more telephone channels for a teleconference. The term usually refers to a bridge from which the operator "dials up" each participant.

Telephone Dictation   Refers to the use of a standard touch-tone telephone to dictate messages to an administrative center for document creation and electronic revision. Typically, the dictation receiver is a central tape recording device controlled (cue, review, stop, play and record) by phone buttons.

Teleport   A managed satellite ground station site consisting of a large number of clustered satellite ground stations linked by cable and switchgear to large-scale tele-communications users, such as banks, insurance companies, brokerage firms and news organizations. Teleports may, like airports, become attractive office locations for major corporate operations centers.

Tempest Facility   A facility protected from electromagnetic emanations by tempest shielding, which generally consists of copper or steel sheets and electronic filters.

Tensile Strength   Resistance of a material to a force that tends to pull it apart, usually expressed as the measure of the largest force that can be applied in this way before the material breaks apart.

Terminal Access Point (TAP)   The point on a broadband network where network devices such as computers are connected.

Thermal Chimney   Also called Solar Chimney. A passive, double-chambered device that draws warm air out of a facility. The inside chamber is open to a high point in a facility. The outside surface is painted a dark color; when the sun beats on this surface the air inside the chamber is superheated, causing an updraft that draws warm air out of the building.

Thermal Energy Storage   The temporary storage of energy for later use. Examples of thermal storage are the storage of solar energy for night heating, the storage of summer heat for winter use, the storage of winter ice for space cooling in the summer and the storage of heat or coolness generated electrically during time when electricity is cheaper (off-peak hours) for later use when electricity rates are higher.

Thermal Envelope   Also called Building Envelope. The outer shell or the elements of a building through which thermal energy may be transferred to or from the outdoors.

Thermal Resistance   An index of a material's resistance to heat flow (R). It is the reciprocal of thermal conductivity (k) or thermal conductance (C). The formula for thermal resistance is:

R = 1/C or R = 1/k or R = thickness in inches/k.

Thermal Shock   The stress-producing phenomenon resulting from sudden temperature drops in a roof membrane when, for example, a rain shower follows brilliant sunshine.

Thief   In manufacturing, a long tube that is lowered into a bin or vat of material to take a sample.

Threshold Limit Value (TLV)   The concentration of an airborne substance that indoor workers may be exposed to repeatedly without adverse effects.

Threshold Theory   A measurement concept suggesting that problems have minimum and maximum thresholds of solutions. Once the requirements of a problem are defined and a set of alternatives is laid out, there is a minimum threshold (for example a minimum amount of dollars) that will solve the problem. Anything over the maximum threshold will not necessarily yield better solutions or more results. In other words, after a certain point, throwing money at a problem will not always help.

Throughput   The number of tasks accomplished per hour. Used to define the productivity of a system.

Tilt-Up Buildings   Buildings utilizing a tilt-up wall construction with concrete walls cast on the floor and then lifted into place. This type of construction is economical for one- and two-story buildings with more than 8,000 square feet of first-floor area.

Title III   Part of the 1986 Superfund and Amendments and Reauthorization Act (SARA). Title III establishes new requirements for emergency planning and preparedness, community right-to-know reporting and toxic chemical inventory and release reporting. See also *SARA*.

TLV   See Threshold Limit Value.

Token Ring   A circulating electronic token in *local area networks* for determining which computer can transmit.

Token   A sequence of binary code (bits) passed from one device to another along a network.

Topology   The physical arrangement of wires and hardware to form a network. In centralized networks or star networks each node is connected to a central node. Alternative topology is distributed—within limits, every node is connected to every other node (called a mesh network). Topology types include bus, ring and star networks.

Total Dissolved Solids (TDS)   All material that passes the standard glass river filter. Also called total filtrable residue. The term is used to reflect salinity.

Toxicity   A material's ability to produce injury or disease from exposure, ingestion, inhalation or assimilation by a living organism.

Transaction Surface   A secretarial station, surrounded by a modular wall approximately 40 inches high and topped by a horizontal desktop surface about 16 inches wide, upon which people can put papers instead of putting them directly on the worker's desk. The idea is to provide a common area that protects privacy and individual workspace.

Transceiver   A device that connects a network device such as a terminal or a computer and the transmission medium of the network—the physical cable, whether twisted-pair or coaxial. Also called an NIU (Network Interface Unit).

Transgenic Animals   Animals that are genetically manipulated so that their offspring will produce certain proteins in their milk, making them valuable models for scientific research. They can sometimes be used in place of bioreactors in biotechnology procedures. Because of their value and because they may have immunodeficiencies, these animals need special environmental conditions to protect them from disease.

Transition Space   An area that is a combination of open- and closed-plan offices. It is partially surrounded by enclosed offices with full-height walls, and within it are small areas of open-plan offices.

Translucent   Glazing materials that transmit light without permitting a view through the material, such as opaque and surface-treated glasses, diffusing and patterned plastics and glasses, corrugated plastics and glasses and diffusing glass block. The amount of light diffusion varies from slight diffusion spread over a small angle, to complete diffusion spread over a wide angle. Generally, transmittance decreases as diffusion increases.

Transmission Control Protocol/Internet Protocol (TCP/IP)   Refers to a popular set of local area network protocols originated by the Department of Defense.

Transmission Loss   Refers to the diminution in sound level that occurs as sound is transmitted through a barrier. If the sound energy is reduced by 20 dB when the sound passes through a plywood panel, the transmission loss of the panel is 20 dB. Transmission loss is not synonymous with noise reduction, which refers to the difference in sound level between two fully enclosed spaces. Noise reduction depends, in part, on the size of the wall carrier and the acoustical character of the listener's rom.

Transponder   The electronic repeater on board a communication satellite that receives the uplink signal and retransmits it to the downlink. See also *Uplink*.

Treatment, Storage and Disposal Facility (TSDF)   A site where hazardous wastes (liquid, solid or gas) are treated, stored or disposed of. TSDFs are regulated by the EPA and by *RCRA*.

Trombe Wall   A passive heating concept. Solar radiation is absorbed by a glass-covered masonry wall, converted into heat and conducted into a building.

TSDF   See Treatment, Storage and Disposal Facility.

Tunnel Washer   A large fixed, double-doored piece of equipment used in research and animal facilities that washes, rinses and dries cages, trays, lids, glassware and other small items. It differs from a rack washer in that it contains a conveyor belt that transports equipment from one side of the washer to the other.

Turbidity   Refers to the degree of cloudiness of water caused by the presence of suspended silt or organic matter.

Turnkey Construction   Public sector construction method in which the builder buys a site, builds a structure privately and sells it back.

Two-Wire Circuit   A typical telephone transmission circuit. In some applications, a two-wire system requires voice switching to avoid electrical echo and leakage and, thus, a four-wire system is preferable. See *Four-Wire Circuit*.

U

U Value   Heat transfer coefficient. A measure of the heat transmissivity of a particular insulation medium or combination of media. More specifically, the heat that is lost (or gained) through a unit area of the insulation medium per degree of temperature difference between the inside and outside surfaces. Units: Btu/hr/ft^2°F, or W/ m^2°C. Heat loss or gain of an entire wall system can be determined by multiplying the U-value times the total wall area, times the difference between the inside and outside temperatures.

U-Lamp   U-shaped fluorescent lamps with leg spacings of three or six inches to permit two or three lamps per 2″ x 2″ fixture. The characteristics of these lamps (lumen output, efficiency and CRI) are in general the same as the characteristics of their four rapid-start counterparts, but are two to three times more expensive.

U-matic   A 3/4-inch videotape format for recording and playing back video information.

UBC   See Uniform Building Code.

ULPA Filter   See Ultra-Low Particulate Air Filter.

Ultra-Low Particulate Air (ULPA) Filter   An air filter medium used in cleanroom applications to filter out particles as small as 0.125 micron at 99.9995 percent efficiency. See also *HEPA Filter*.

Ultrafiltration   A water purification process in which water flows tangentially across a semipermeable membrane having a highly asymmetric pore structure. The membrane is tight enough to filter contaminants and macromolecules while allowing water to pass through.

Ultrasonic Motion Detectors   Electronic motion sensing devices that are either wall- or post-mounted on the exterior of the building and around maximum-containment areas within the building. Unauthorized motion will initiate an alarm signal at the facility's guard station that indicates the location of the disturbance.

Ultrasonic Sensors   Sensors that use sound triggers to turn on the lights when someone walks into the room.

Ultraviolet Oxidation   Photochemical oxidation. A water purification process using extremely short wavelength light that can kill microorganisms (disinfection) or cleave organic molecules (photo oxidation), rendering them polarized or ionized and, therefore, more easily filtered from the water.

Ultraviolet Rays   Radiation from the sun that can be useful or potentially harmful. UV rays from one part of the spectrum (UV-A) enhance plant life and are useful in some medical and dental procedures; UV rays from other parts of the spectrum (UV-B) can cause skin cancer or other tissue damage. The ozone layer in the atmosphere partly shields us from ultraviolet rays reaching the earth's surface.

Umbilical   An enclosure for vertical electrical and utility drops from a ceiling to benchtops in labs. Umbilicals are removable shrouds, usually thin rectangular metal casings, used to dress up the vertical utility and electrical distribution links.

Underfloor Raceway   Floor ducts that are structurally part of the building and are used to separate and distribute wire and cabling to individual workstations throughout a floor area. See also *Cellular Raceway* and *Metal Raceway*.

Underwriter's Laboratories   A non-profit organization maintained in the interest of insurance companies to determine the fire resistance of various materials.

Uniform Building Code (UBC)   The model code of building and construction standards published by the International Conference of Building Officials. The UBC is generally adopted and enforced by municipalities in states west of the Mississippi.

Unitary Heat Pump   A small, self-contained air conditioner that has a reversing valve to change the direction of flow of the refrigerant and thereby heat or cool recirculated air.

Uninterrupted Power Supply (UPS)   An electrical power system for a building or an area within a building in which incoming AC power is converted to DC power, stored in batteries and then converted back to AC electrical power to supply building equipment. In the event of an external power failure, power is provided without interruption for a specified length of time from storage batteries. For computer installations, the UPS system performs the additional function of filtering incoming power through the battery packs.

Uplink   An earth station that transmits a signal to a communications satellite.

UPS   See Uninterrupted Power Supply.

Use Charge   An amount used in estimating indirect-cost reimbursements of university facilities. It is determined not only by the amount a university spends in nonfederal funds to build a new facility, but also by the cost of sustaining existing buildings. The current federally allowable use charge is two percent, based on the assumption that buildings have a 50-year life span.

Users   The people who occupy a building. At the earliest stages of planning a project, make sure who they are and what they want. There is nothing as unsettling and costly as getting new basic data from a previously unknown source during the advance stages of design.

Utilidor   A corridor used for utilities distribution and materials handling to labs and personnel circulation.

Utilization Efficiency   The ratio of net square feet to gross square feet of a facility (expressed as a percentage) is a measure of space utilization efficiency. In office buildings, the utilization efficiency is about 75 percent. In research and development facilities the ratio is lower, between 65 and 70 percent. See also *Net Square Feet* and *Gross Square Feet*.

V

Validation   A process used in industries that manufacture drugs, biologicals and medical devices that establishes documented evidence to provide a high degree of assurance that a specific facility and its supporting utilities will consistently meet predetermined specifications and quality attributes. These attributes and specifications encompass both regulatory and company requirements. Validation is regulated by the FDA, including *CBER* (Center for Biologic Evaluation and Research) and CDRH (Center for Devices and Radiological Health) as well as the Department of Agriculture.

Value Engineering   A process that identifies and assigns value to the various functions of a product (or facility) and then seeks a final design that maximizes functional value and reliability while minimizing cost.

Vapor Barrier   A layer of low-permeability material that prevents condensation within building sections.

Variable Air Volume (VAV)   An HVAC system in which a local thermostat controls room temperature by controlling the volume of fixed-temperature air (heated or cooled) delivered to the room. An advantage of VAV is its operating and first-cost economies. A disadvantage is that fresh air circulation is reduced when the required temperature setting has been reached.

VAV   See Variable Air Volume.

Variable Frequency Drive (VFD)   A system of controlling HVAC fan speed with motors and controls that change fan speed by varying the frequency of electrical power delivered to the fan motor.

VAX, VMS   See Virtual Access Memory, Virtual Memory Storage.

VDT   See Video Display Terminal.

Vector   In biotechnology, the agent used to carry new genes into cells. Plasmids are the current preferred vector.

Ventilation Rate   The rate that indoor air enters and leaves a building. Expressed either as the number of changes of outdoor air per unit of time (air changes per hour) or as the rate at which a volume of outside air enters per unit of time (cfm).

Venture Leasing   A real estate financing arrangement generally employed for high-growth companies that are beyond the venture capital first stages. In venture leasing, a lessor agrees to a low lease rate in exchange for warrants to purchase the growth company's stock at a fixed price at some future date.

VFD   See Variable Frequency Drive.

Vibration   Foot traffic vibration can be a serious problem in sensitive R&D environments. An above-grade floor acts somewhat like a trampoline: footfall impact sets the floor in motion, also setting into motion any floor-mounted equipment. Footfalls near the center of bays tend to cause the greatest vibration, with the resulting vibrations most severe at mid-bay and least severe near columns. Wherever possible, heavily-traveled areas should be confined to regions near column lines. Sensitive equipment should be placed near columns. Designers should avoid long straight corridors that invite rapid walking because fast-paced walking creates more severe footfall impacts. Structural solutions to footfall traffic are the most reliable.

In controlling vibration in sensitive R&D environments, designers should pay attention to the vibration transmission paths that can short-circuit machinery isolation systems or structural breaks. Transmission paths include piping, ducts and conduits that bridge the isolation systems. Transmission paths can be avoided by using flexible connectors and structurally isolating ducts, piping or conduits.

Video Codec   A bandwidth suppression device used to reduce the bandwidth of video signals transmitted via satellite. It requires two pieces of equipment, one to reduce the bandwidth and one on the downlink path to recondition the signal. Achieves significant cost reductions on the use of communication satellites with some degradation of signal quality. See also *Codec*.

Video Display Terminal (VDT)   A computer monitor.

People who don't wear glasses may need them for VDT work, and even workers with glasses or contact lenses may be unaware that they need a different pair in order to focus their eyes at the proper distance and height for the VDT screen. In addition, the screen should be examined for quality, image flickering, glare or reflection due to improper lighting and angle and distance from the operator. Also paperwork should be placed so that the user does not have to refocus when switching from paper to screen.

Adjustability appears to be a key factor in assuring comfort during VDT use. If the operator can move the screen, keyboard, reading material and an adjustable chair to the most comfortable positions, and can adjust the brightness and contrast of images on the screen, chances of eye or muscular discomfort are generally reduced. Expert groups suggest that the top of the VDT screen be at or slightly below eye level so the eyes gaze slightly downward.

To effectively accommodate VDT usage on a large scale in existing facilities: (1) use antiglare screens for all terminals, (2) treat exterior windows to reduce outside sun light, (3) use window blinds for windows so that operators can control their own exterior light, (4) replace all ceiling fixture light lenses with 1″ x 1″ grid deflectors to eliminate glare lines on screens caused by overhead fluorescents and (5) get rid of all double pedestal desks.

Video Wall   A collection of video monitors stacked on top of each other and grouped in rectangular clusters of 9 to 256 monitors. Video walls are usually used in sales, promotional and convention activities.

Videoconferencing   Communication via telecommunications channels between more than two groups or three individuals. Videoconferences can involve fully-interactive video and audio or one-way video and two-way audio. This includes full-motion video, limited motion video, and, in some definitions, freeze-frame video images.

Virtual Access Memory, Virtual Memory Storage (VAM/VMS)   A sophisticated software system that provides virtually unlimited memory to a given computer system. A VAX computer continually moves information into and out of the main memory so that the user has instant access to essentially unlimited equipment memory. VAX is the registered trademark of the Digital Equipment Corporation. VMS is IBM's virtual memory storage system.

Virtual Office   A briefcase approach to the office; where everything necessary to do work, from fax to phone to laptop computer, is portable. With the ultimate virtual office, employees would work at home and convene periodically to share ideas. This would mean that the only facility required would be a centralized conferencing area, or a facility with generic desks and shared administrative support that can be used occasionally by workers. See also *Hoteling* and *Telecommuting*.

Vivarium   A facility or part of a facility that is designed to hold animals for laboratory research.

VOC   See Volatile Organic Compound.

Voice Switching   An electrical technique for opening an audio circuit only to the person who is currently speaking. The system allows only one person to speak at a time, often without the capability to be interrupted. Voice switching is an effective technique for avoiding specific acoustical and electrical problems that are often associated with audio teleconferencing.

Volatile Organic Compound (VOC)   Any organic compound that contributes to atmospheric photochemical reactions.

Waffle Slab Construction   A building system using concrete "waffle slab" floors supported by columns. The waffle slab is a monolithic-poured concrete slab with a flat top surface and an under-surface made of a rectangular grid of deep concrete beams running at right angles. The floor area between the grid beams is a thin flooring section. From the underside, the slab resembles a waffle. The floor is supported by columns spaced typically 30 feet on center. The system is used in cleanrooms, areas that require isolation from low-frequency vibrations and areas that require low floor deflection.

Waste Lines   In laboratories, the plumbing that carries liquid waste from the lab areas to a centralized processing station. Usually kept separate from sewage lines in the building to allow special waste processing before the lab waste is injected into public sewer systems.

Water Heat Pump System   Heat pumps are refrigeration machines that use changes in pressure to enable a refrigerant to transfer heat by condensing and evaporating at different temperatures. The key to the system is the refrigerant, such as freon, which can evaporate or condense at convenient temperatures, depending on pressure. A heat pump produces approximately 14,000 Btu per hour of heat for one kilowatt of electricity, contrasted with resistance heating which produces about 3,400 Btu per hour for one kilowatt.

A water heat pump system uses the heat pump to draw heat from the water. The captured heat is used in the winter for heating. During the summer, the heat pump draws heat from the building to cool the structure. The heat is then absorbed by the water. In some situations, well water is used instead of a cooling tower reservoir. Annual overall heating and cooling costs are substantially lower with a heat-pump system as compared to oil or electric-resistance heating.

Water for Injection (WFI)   Denotes an absence of impurities such that the distilled water can be injected into the human body without causing a fever.

Watts per Square Foot   The power requirements of a building. The use of demand watts is preferable since the demand usage can be actually measured. Connected watts must be developed from a survey of the space. The area used in any calculation of watts per square foot may be rentable or usable, as long as everyone involved understands the terms.

Wayfinding   The design of visual cues including lighting, color, artwork and surface materials that help facilities occupants and visitors orient themselves and find their destination.

Weld Plate   In the pre-manufactured building industry, a weld plate attaches a modular building to a permanent foundation and provides seismic resistance. The weld plate is a 6″ x 9″ x 3/8″ steel plate with hooks that is placed in wet cement. When it hardens, it becomes a homogeneous part of the foundation. The steel frame of the building is then welded to it. The number of weld plates, their location and the number of welds depends on the seismic zone, occupancy rating, wind and snow load, soil-bearing pressure and size of the building.

Wet Floor   A floor used to routinely collect, contain or maintain standing liquids or to transmit standing liquids on a more or less continuous basis.

WFI   See Water for Injection.

What You See Is What You Get Interface (WYSIWYG)   Graphical interface on a computer that gives the user a display that fully represents how the output will appear.

Whip   Flexible conduit located in underflooring, in ceiling spaces or in a wall. It has a plug at one end and a duplex or fourplex outlet at the other and can be easily unplugged from a junction box and moved to another outlet. Whips allow flexibility at a low cost; theoretically, they reduce the need for electricians. They are often used in lighting systems.

White Noise   Noise that contains all sound frequencies. It is often used for sound masking in offices and work areas. In a uniform frequency distribution, there are more high frequencies than low frequencies, and high frequency noise tends to irritate people. "Pink noise" is white noise with the high frequencies cut out. Sound at frequencies above 5,000 Hz is not effective for sound masking and is an annoyance.

Window Investment   R&D expenditures into an emerging technology for the purpose of gaining access to a new field without a clearly defined product or technology development goal.

Wire Management   Refers to planning, directing and controlling the electrical and electronic hookups in a building in order to meet the various and changing requirements for office equipment, communications systems, security, lighting and power. Wire management is becoming an important facilities planning issue because of the trend toward flexible space for office reconfiguration and the increasing number and sophistication of communication devices in office buildings. Many structures built as recently as the late 1970s have little or no capacity for communications wiring, and many have cable raceways already full of wires that have unknown beginnings, endings and routes.

Work Work is the product of the force acting on an object and the distance the object is moved. The units are the same as for energy: Btu, erg, joule, kilowatt-hour, foot-pound, electron volt, calorie. See also *Power* and *Energy*.

Workgroups The organization of workers functionally and/or administratively as a unit with a unique and definable mission. The workgroup is coordinated by a single manager or supervisor. Although workgroups in an organization have a mission that makes them unique, in some cases there may be larger workgroups administratively subdivided to maintain an appropriate span of control for supervisors. Workgroups can be organized for sequential work flow (production lines, chain tasks), independent work (self-completion), or team interaction (group completion).

Workplace The entire office environment: floors, ceilings, walls, furnishings, wiring, lighting, heating, air conditioning and business machines of all kinds. Workplace is far more inclusive than "workstation."

Workstation Personal computer. Also the space allotted to one worker. Also computers with intensive processing capabilities, similar to those of a small mainframe computer. See also *Microcomputer*.

Wrinkling The formation of a wrinkled surface in the top coat of paint due to an excessively thick application of coating or to slow drying conditions.

WYSIWYG Interface See What You See Is What You Get Interface.

X.25 An international protocol for wide area networks.

XNS Xerox Network Services. Refers to a set of *LAN* protocols.

Zero Coupon Bonds A bond that carries no coupon or dividend rate, but is sold at a deep discount from its face value. Zero coupon bonds offer investors guaranteed yield and face discounts useful in tax planning for investment portfolios.

Z-list OSHA's tables of toxic and hazardous air contaminants.

Zone In HVAC systems, an area composed of a building, a portion of a building or a group of buildings affected by a single HVAC device or piece of equipment.

Zone Negative Draft Level A containment area in which the atmospheric air pressure is lower than an adjacent area. It indicates that air flow is directionally controlled.